Capitalism, Not Globalism

Michigan Studies in International Political Economy

Michael J. Gilligan
Empowering Exporters: Reciprocity, Delegation, and Collective Action in American Trade Policy

Barry Eichengreen and Jeffry Frieden, Editors
Forging an Integrated Europe

Thomas H. Oatley
Monetary Politics: Exchange Rate Cooperation in the European Union

Robert Pahre
Leading Questions: How Hegemony Affects the International Political Economy

Andrew C. Sobel
State Institutions, Private Incentives, Global Capital

Roland Stephen
Vehicle of Influence: Building a European Car Market

William Bernhard
Banking on Reform: Political Parties and Central Bank Independence in the Industrial Democracies

William Roberts Clark
Capitalism, Not Globalism: Capital Mobility, Central Bank Independence, and the Political Control of the Economy

Edward D. Mansfield and Brian M. Pollins, Editors
Economic Interdependence and International Conflict: New Perspectives on an Enduring Debate

Capitalism, Not Globalism

Capital Mobility, Central Bank Independence, and the Political Control of the Economy

WILLIAM ROBERTS CLARK

The University of Michigan Press
Ann Arbor

Copyright © by the University of Michigan 2003
All rights reserved
Published in the United States of America by
The University of Michigan Press
Printed and bound by CPI Group (UK) Ltd, Croydon, CR0 4YY

2006   2005   2004   2003   4   3   2   1

A CIP catalog record for this book is available from the British Library.

Library of Congress Cataloging-in-Publication Data

Clark, William Roberts.
    Capitalism, not globalism : capital mobility, central bank independence, and
the political control of the economy / William Roberts Clark.
        p.   cm. — (Michigan studies in international political economy)
    Includes bibliographical references and index.
    ISBN 978-0-472-11293-7 (cloth : alk. paper)
    1. Monetary policy.   2. Economic policy.   I. Title.   II. Series.

HG230.3.C55   2003
339.5—dc21   2003044773

    ISBN13 978-0-472-11293-7 (cloth)
    ISBN13 978-0-472-03116-0 (paper)
    ISBN13 978-0-472-02491-9 (electronic)

Dedicated to the memory of Thomas F. and Marjorie L. Clark

Contents

Acknowledgments   ix

Chapter 1   Introduction   1

Chapter 2   The Structural Context of Macroeconomic
            Policy Choice   13

Chapter 3   Partisanship and Fiscal and Monetary Policy   41

Chapter 4   Elections and Fiscal and Monetary Policy   85

Chapter 5   Partisan Differences and Macroeconomic Outcomes   105

Chapter 6   Elections and Macroeconomic Outcomes   141

Chapter 7   Conclusion   169

Appendix A Derivation of Proposition 1   177

   Notes   179

   References   193

   Index   205

Acknowledgments

This book is the product of three related prejudices, traceable in part to teachers and colleagues, who have thus contributed to the development of this book in profound, though indirect, ways. First and foremost is a belief in falsificationism. Science is important not because it leads to the correct answer, but because it provides us with the best chance of discarding wrong answers. I am grateful to Jack Levy and John Vasquez for introducing me to the work of Karl Popper and Imre Lakatos and for instilling in me a desire to think self-consciously about epistemological issues. I also thank Tom Walker and Mark Yellin for the many late-night discussions that provided sufficient heat to test the mettle of my views on this subject.

The second prejudice is a belief in the utility of comparing what some consider to be incomparable. The discipline of political science seems to be divided between scholars with an intuition that events are the unique product of circumstances that will never be replicated, and those who view the social world as inherently systematic and therefore amenable to comparison and generalization. In this crude form, both views are incorrect; but if forced to choose, I would classify myself in the latter camp. For it is only in looking for regularity that we may see conjunctural events clearly. It is only in lumping that we can produce both evidence for the need to split and an understanding of where and when to split. Robert Kaufman and Michael Shafer had a tremendous impact on my thinking on this subject, and I am immensely grateful to them.

The third prejudice underlying the following work is an assumption that political and economic actors are, for the most part, goal-oriented actors and that their behavior can best be understood if we begin by positing what their goals might be and reasoning backward toward the behaviors we therefore expect them to engage in. Jeff Frieden—a long-distance mentor, cheerleader, and, when needed, severe critic since my second semester in graduate school—had an early, deep, and sustained influence on my thinking.

While I referred to each of the above as prejudices, they are not *blind* prejudices. I believe that a commitment to falsificationism can be defended logically (although the best that one can show is that it will do no worse than alternative paths to knowledge, for it takes a leap of faith to assert that it will actually lead to knowledge); and I believe that a commitment to broad comparisons and an emphasis on goal-oriented behavior can both be shown to follow from a belief in falsificationism.

This project began in an undergraduate comparative political economy class at Georgia Tech, where Kevin Parker and Sandy Lomas—inspired by reading Alt and Chrystal's *Political Economics* (1982)—began some empirical tests on context-dependent political business cycles. I am grateful to them for their willingness to be the first to dip their feet in those waters. Not only would this book otherwise probably not have been written, but my research interests would likely have developed along entirely different lines. As usual, the students had a greater effect on the professor than vice versa. Many other students and colleagues (at Georgia Tech, Princeton, and New York University) contributed their time and energy in ways that proved helpful. I am particularly grateful to Rebecca Hagstrom, Will Hakes, Stephen Flanders, Courtney Kinney, Priti Lokre, and Tovah Simon for their research assistance.

This book leans heavily upon, and borrows liberally from, collaborative work; I thank my coauthors Mark Hallerberg, Usha Reichert, Kevin Parker, and Sandy Lomas both for their generosity and for their help in sharpening my thinking on these matters for years. Indeed, portions of the book may be familiar to some readers. Chapter 2 clarifies and extends theoretical arguments published in *International Organization* (Clark and Nair Reichert 1998) and the *American Political Science Review* (Clark and Hallerberg 2000). In particular, I emphasize the extent to which these previous articles are in tension with each other. Chapter 4 is a replication and extension of some of the empirical analysis in the *APSR* article. Chapter 6 is a fundamental reconsideration and critique of the *IO* article.

I thank Geoffrey Garrett, Jakob de Haan, Mark Hallerberg, and Beth Simmons for their generosity in sharing data. I am also grateful to participants in various seminars at Georgia Tech, Harvard University, Princeton University, Rutgers University, Washington University, St. Louis, University of California at Berkeley, University of Pittsburgh, and Yale University.

I thank Thaddeus Agar, David Andrews, Kirk Bowman, Peter Brecke, Lawrence Broz, Benjamin Cohen, David Denoon, Herbert Doering, Martin

Edwards, Jesus Felipe, Colin Flint, Jeffry Frieden, Fabio Ghironi, Joanne Gowa, Mark Hallerberg, Bill Keech, Peter Kenen, Jeffrey Lewis, Bill Mabe, Jonathan Moses, Louis Pauly, Shanker Satyanath, Alberta Sbragia, Radwan Shaban, Beth Simmons, Rolf Strauch, Richard Tucker, Michael Wallerstein, Katja Weber, and Tom Willett, who provided comments on sections of the text or related papers. I am also grateful to Adam Przeworski, Mike Gilligan, and David Leblang and his class at University of North Texas, who read and critiqued the penultimate draft of the entire manuscript; and to Matt Golder and Becky Morton for useful discussions regarding econometrics. Any remaining errors are my responsibility.

The first draft of the manuscript was completed while I was a visiting fellow at the Center for International Studies at Princeton. I am grateful to Kate Mc-Namara, Michael Doyle, and the MacArthur Foundation for making that visit both possible and extremely enjoyable. I am also indebted to Alan Blinder, Harold James, Peter Kenen, Paulo Pesenti, and Ken Rogoff for their help and hospitality during my year at Princeton. It is hard to imagine a better environment in which to write about the politics of macroeconomic policy. Subsequent drafts and revisions were written while I was a member of the Politics Department at NYU. I thank my colleagues and students there for a warm and stimulating environment.

Finally, on a more personal note, I am indebted to many friends and family for their support during the completion of this book. I am eternally thankful to Bob Cushman, Pat and Chloe Colgan, Paul and Pam Reilly, Bill and Tia Smallwood, my bandmates, and many others at Princeton Alliance Church for their support and encouragement over the last years of this project. The book might have been the same without you, but I would not be. Last but not least, I thank my wife, Laurie and our children, Meaghan, Brian, Liam, and Cameron, for putting up with me. Though I can never adequately repay you for sticking with me, I am going to try.

CHAPTER 1

Introduction

As soon as they decided to compete for votes, sometime between 1884 and 1892, socialist parties sought to gain the electoral support of people other than workers.

As socialists become parties like other parties, workers turn into voters like other voters.

—Adam Przeworski (1985)

On May 2, 1997, Tony Blair, an advocate of "Christian socialism" since his university days, became prime minister of the first Labour government in Britain in eighteen years. On May 6, his "New Labour" government moved to enhance the independence of the Bank of England by transferring day-to-day control over monetary policy from Whitehall to the "Grand Old Lady of Fleet Street." On September 27, 1998, Gerhard Schroeder was elected head of the first Social Democratic government in Germany in sixteen years, ending the record-setting tenure of conservative chancellor Helmut Kohl. Six months later, Schroeder parted ways with his finance minister amid concerns that Oskar Lafontaine's left-wing politics would no longer be tolerated by international markets—or, for that matter, by the Bundesbank. In both cases, left-wing governments were elected to replace long-lived conservative predecessors, only to take actions that appeared to hardwire policy outcomes that were strikingly similar to those favored by the conservatives. In the popular press, these and countless similar events have been interpreted as evidence of a growing convergence around market-friendly policies. National governments, it is widely argued, have been forced to accept this convergence because of the workings of an ongoing historical process known as globalization. The engine behind this globalization is believed to be the rapid increase in international financial integration that has taken place in the last few decades.

While this "convergence" view of the current international political economy is widely accepted, there is virtually no evidence to support its main dynamics. Empirical studies have been unable to demonstrate a convergence in either the macroeconomic policies or the macroeconomic outcomes produced by governments of the left and right as capital mobility has increased. This is surprising, because it is reasonable to expect that as it becomes easier to move financial assets to the place where they will bring the highest return, governments of every political stripe can ignore the policy demands of the holders of such assets only at their own great peril. What explains this contrast between expectation and observation? In this book, I argue that the standard interpretation of the convergence argument—both the version put forth by its proponents and that put forth by its opponents—is deeply flawed. Specifically, existing studies find no evidence of a growing convergence between parties as a result of increased capital mobility because, as the quotations from Przeworski at the beginning of this chapter imply, the convergence between parties is a hallmark of economic policy-making in democratic capitalist societies and, consequently, predated the recent increase in capital mobility. Recent empirical studies have produced confusing results because they were looking for the effects of capital mobility on a phenomenon that does not exist—namely, partisan differences in policies or outcomes.

One theme that emerges from my analysis of the politics of macroeconomic policy in the late twentieth century is that many of the domestic political consequences of "globalization"—partisan convergence, constraints on the choices of democratically elected governments, the need for governments to anticipate the response of "footloose" capital, and so on—are not the recent effects of changes in the international economy. Instead, they appear to be the enduring features of the process of economic policy choice in polities dominated by private investment and electoral politics. Such sweeping claims are typically accompanied by equally sweeping surveys of history. In this volume, however, I choose to examine just enough of recent history to get a glimpse of macroeconomic policy and performance before and after "globalization." Comparisons with earlier periods of mobile capital and experiments with central bank independence would be informative but will not be pursued here.[1]

Much has been written about the effects of international capital mobility and central bank independence and the way in which they may or may not constrain economic policy choice. International capital mobility, it has been argued, has torn down barriers between countries, barriers that had (depending on your perspective) prevented resources from being optimally allocated or served as a buffer between a nation's citizens and the risks of the international economy. Central bank independence has been declared to be a nearly magical technology that provides price stability without losses in output. But it has also been seen as a threat to democratic control over economic policy. Many such propositions are advanced—and accepted or rejected—with very little reference to empirical evidence. What empirical evidence does exist to support or challenge such broad claims tends to rest on one or another model (often implicit) of the political control of the macroeconomy. The results of such studies are, therefore, meaningful only to the extent that the appropriate underlying model of the political economy has been identified. Since the veracity of these models is highly contested, the conclusions about the effects of capital mobility or central bank independence are much more provisional than is typically admitted.

This book examines competing claims about the political sources of macroeconomic policy and performance in a manner that allows us to evaluate the ways in which central bank independence and increased capital mobility structure the interaction between political goals and macroeconomic policy outputs. Specifically, I compare the two main models of the political control of the economy—the partisan and the electoralist models[2]—and find more support for the latter. I argue that close attention to how these structural factors influence the behavior of policymakers reveals new insights about competing models of political processes within countries, and that, at the same time, an examination of the effects of international capital mobility and central bank independence in the context of the electoralist model sheds new light on their political and economic consequences.

The partisan model of the political control of the macroeconomy predicts that political parties with different ideological orientations will enact systematically different policies and produce systematically different macroeconomic outcomes (Hibbs 1977; Tufte 1978). Parties of the right will choose policies that maximize price stability, even at the expense of growth and employment, while parties of the left will be more inclined to trade away price stability to achieve higher levels of employment and faster rates of growth. In contrast to the partisan model, the electoralist model asserts that electoral constraints force politicians of all stripes to behave in much the same way—they must select policies and produce outcomes that please the median voter (Downs 1957). The electoralist political business cycle model adds to the Downsian model a number of assumptions about the way voters form expectations and yields predictions that tie the behavior of policymakers to the electoral calendar. Incumbents will do their best to create growth and employment in the period leading up to elections, even if such behavior leads to future inflation (Nordhaus 1975).

One assumption that the electoralist and partisan models share is that policymakers have sufficient control over the instruments of monetary and fiscal policy to determine inflation, growth, and employment outcomes. This book explores two structural factors that call that assumption into question. Central bank independence is specifically designed to shelter the instruments of monetary policy from the control of politicians. International capital mobility has also been thought of as a constraint on effective manipulation of monetary or fiscal (depending on the exchange rate regime) policy.[3] By relaxing this assumption, it is possible to produce a more nuanced set of expectations about the conditions under which partisan or electoralist behaviors might occur and, at the same time, an appreciation for the political and economic consequences of changes in the environment in which policy is made.

I find there is little evidence of partisan differences in either macroeconomic policies or performance—regardless of the degree of central bank independence or the degree of capital mobility. Consequently, it is difficult, if not impossible, to understand the consequences of central bank independence or capital mobility when peering through the lens of the partisan model. Electoralist political business cycles are also not ubiquitous, but when one pays close attention to the ways in which the degree of central bank independence and the degree of national policy autonomy structure the choices of politicians, electoralist behavior begins to come into sharper focus. Specifically, electoralist cycles in growth and unemployment, as well as budget deficits and money supply, occur under a specified set of conditions—that is, when incumbents retain sufficient control over the policy instruments necessary to engineer them. The frequent absence of such control explains why such cycles are relatively rare.

While a comparison of the partisan and electoralist models informs debates about the determinants of macroeconomic policy within countries, it also has clear implications for debates about the consequences of recent changes in the international economy. As already noted, a commonplace assertion is that increasingly mobile capital places new constraints on the choices available to policymakers. Attempts to evaluate this argument, however, have failed to find evidence of the predicted effects of globalization (Garrett 1995, 1998; Rodrik 1997; Iversen 1997). I argue that this is because such studies are looking in the wrong place. The consequences of increased international capital mobility cannot be seen in a convergence in the policies or performance of political parties because, the evidence suggests, partisan differences did not exist before capital mobility. International capital mobility has, however, had two important consequences. First, it has altered the circumstances under which incumbents may use macroeconomic policies for electoral purposes. Second, it appears—under certain circumstances—to have shifted the content of policies. The policies produced after capital mobility may be more deflationary than they were before.

Taken together, these findings have complex normative implications. If the consequence of capital mobility were the end of meaningful partisan differences and convergence around the policy preferences traditionally associated with right-wing parties and their voters, then one's assessment of international capital mobility would be a strict function of one's affinity for such policies. But the finding that politicians are discouraged from manipulating the economy for electoralist purposes agrees with what all citizens could be reasonably expected to support. Macroeconomic policy should be used to produce economic benefits for the people, not political benefits for officeholders. This normative conclusion, however, assumes a zero-sum relationship between those who govern and those who are governed—a radically predatory view of the state. If, on the other hand, democratic institutions are set up in a manner such that incumbents help society when helping themselves, then constraints on electoralist behavior are not necessarily socially optimal. In fact, I find that the conditions that discourage electoralist behavior have a tendency to push policy in the direction that partisan models argue is favored by right-wing parties and their constituencies. Whether this is good or bad for society as a whole is logically independent from whether it is helpful to survival-maximizing incumbents. Such normative issues are not the central focus of this book, but they will be explored in the conclusion.

In the remainder of this introductory chapter, I will briefly compare alternative versions of the partisan and electoralist models, discuss the overall structure of the book, and compare this work to other recent volumes that address similar topics.

Comparing Partisan and Electoralist Models of the Political Economy

One can organize the literature on the domestic political sources of macroeconomic policy by comparing the assumptions scholars make about the motivations of politicians and the process of belief formation employed by voters. Electoralist political business cycle (PBC) models assume that politicians are survival maximizers, whereas partisan models emphasize candidates' ideological motivations. "Adaptive expectations" arguments characterize voters as retrospective, whereas "rational expectations" models assume that voters consider the expected future effects of policy decisions.

Adaptive Electoral Cycles

In the founding works of the PBC literature, William D. Nordhaus (1975) and Duncan MacRae (1977) assume that politicians are "opportunistic" survival maximizers. That is, they care only about being elected and can control macro-economic policy outcomes in a manner that maximizes the probability of re-election. Voters are assumed to be "retrospective" and "pocketbook"; that is, they assess candidates' performance on the basis of economic outcomes they produce without regard to the future consequences of these policies.[4] These assumptions imply that incumbents will lower the rate of unemployment prior to elections and raise it "to some relatively high level in order to combat inflation" in the period just after the election (Nordhaus 1975, 184; see also 1989).[5]

Nordhaus's model is controversial on both theoretical and empirical grounds.[6] His own results were weak: he found partial evidence for the existence of PBCs in only four of the nine countries he examined. Edward R. Tufte (1978) also predicts unemployment cycles tied to the electoral calendar, but his evidence based on U.S. presidential elections is less than robust. Similarly, Michael S. Lewis-Beck's test (1988) of key implications of the Nordhaus model shows no systematic relationship between the timing of elections and changes in unemployment, growth, or inflation in Britain, France, West Germany, Italy, or the United States. Studies that pool observations across countries of the OECD (Organization for Economic Cooperation and Development) also fail to provide substantial evidence that unemployment or output fluctuates with the electoral calendar (Alesina and Roubini 1992; Alesina, Cohen, and Roubini 1992).

Rational Electoral Cycles

The electoralist model has come under increased fire since the rational expectations revolution in macroeconomic theory. Rational expectations are germane in two ways. First, if private actors use all relevant information except the "competence" of different policymakers to predict the inflation rate, politicians should not be able to create preelectoral inflationary surprises in equilibrium. Second, if voters are rational, they should include the expected future costs of politically motivated expansions beyond the natural rate when formulating expectations of the incumbents' postelection macroeconomic performance (Cukierman and Meltzer 1986; McCallum 1978; Persson and Tabellini 1990; Rogoff and Sibert 1988). The primary empirical implication of the rational electoralist model is that, though informational advantages enjoyed by politicians may provide some incentive for the manipulation of policy instruments in the preelectoral period, this will not necessarily result in an association between elections and employment or output (Alesina and Roubini 1992).

Although the lack of systematic evidence linking macroeconomic outcomes to the electoral calendar is consistent with the rational expectations variant of the electoralist approach, evidence of preelectoral manipulation of policy instruments would lend more direct support. As it turns out, there is considerably more evidence of a connection between elections and the manipulation of policy instruments than has been the case for macroeconomic outcomes. Some evidence indicates that budget deficits and money growth tend to increase in preelectoral periods in several OECD countries (Alesina 1989; Alesina, Cohen, and Roubini 1992), and similar monetary cycles (Greir 1987, 1989) and budgetary cycles (Tufte 1978; Alesina 1988b; Nordhaus 1989) have been found in the United States.

Adaptive Partisan Cycles

The partisan explanation of economic policy choice departs from the Downsian approach to politics because it assumes that political parties differ in their evaluation of policy outcomes and, therefore, set policy in an effort to achieve their preferred outcome. Typically, parties of the left are assumed to be more sensitive to unemployment than parties of the right, while the latter place a higher value on price stability than do parties of the left (Hibbs 1977, 1987). Expectations are adaptive, and voters are assumed to vote for the party that they expect to implement the policy closest to their ideal point. Unlike in the Downsian model, however, this does not lead candidates' positions or incumbents' policies to converge on the preferences of the median voter. Many reasons have been offered for a lack of convergence, including the attempt to make campaign promises credible (Alesina and Rosenthal 1995), the need to deter entry of new parties (Palfry 1984), and the possibility that some voters will abstain (Calvert 1985).[7] The primary implication of the partisan approach is that parties of the left should produce consistently higher levels of output and inflation and lower levels of unemployment than parties of the right.

The evidence in support of the partisan hypothesis has been more consistent than that for its electoralist alternative. In early studies, Hibbs (1977) found support for the partisan hypothesis in the United States and Great Britain, and Alt (1985) found a link between decreasing unemployment and left government control in a sample of twelve OECD countries. Using a sample of eighteen OECD countries for the period 1960–87, however, Alesina and

Roubini (1992) find no evidence of permanent partisan differences in output and unemployment.

Rational Partisan Cycles

Alesina's 1987 analysis of macroeconomic policy choice in two-party systems suggests that partisan differences in policy outcomes can exist despite rational expectations (see also Chappell and Keech 1986). This is the case because wage contracts signed under one regime cannot automatically be adjusted to incorporate changes in inflationary expectations induced by the election of a government with different preferences over outcomes. Thus, the rational partisan model predicts partisan differences in macroeconomic policies in the period immediately following elections, but these differences are not expected to persist beyond the initial period of adjustment. This conclusion receives empirical support from Alesina and Roubini's failure (1992) to find a link between partisanship and permanent differences in macroeconomic outcomes.

PBCs and Endogenous Elections

The approaches to the politics of macroeconomic policy discussed up to this point either embrace the assumptions of the Nordhaus model or relax one or more of the original model's assumptions related to the preferences actors hold and the way in which they formulate their beliefs (see the comparison of alternative models in table 1, derived from Alesina and Roubini 1992). In so doing, these studies pay little attention to the extent to which behaviors associated with PBCs are influenced by the institutional structure in which politicians and voters operate. Studies examining the effect of endogenous election timing on PBCs are an important exception to this general trend. The empirical implications of endogenous elections for PBCs are not clear-cut, however. If voters' expectations are adaptive, it is possible that incumbents can take advantage of favorable economic conditions by calling early elections.[8] Note that the main empirical implication of the Nordhaus model holds both when elections are exogenous and when they are endogenous, despite the operation of different causal logics. For Japan, Thomas F. Cargill and Michael M. Hutchison (1991) use a simultaneous equation procedure and find evidence for a "two-way interaction" in which causation runs in both directions. In addition, multinational studies that use macroeconomic outcomes to predict the timing of elections find some evidence that early elections are more likely to be called when economic conditions are favorable (Alesina, Cohen, and Roubini 1993; Palmer and

TABLE 1. Alternative Models of the Domestic Political Economy

	Traditional Electoralist Model[a]	Rational Electoralist Model[b]	Partisan Model and Rational Variant[c]	Context-Dependent Partisan Model
		Assumptions		
Structure of macroeconomy	Output and employment are driven by changes in inflation	Output and employment are driven by changes in unanticipated inflation	Output and employment are driven by changes in unanticipated inflation	Output and employment are driven by changes in inflation
Inflation controlled by	Elected politicians	Elected politicians	Elected politicians	Elected politicians only under certain institutional arrangements
Politicians are	Electoralist	Electoralist	Partisan: Left-wing incumbents attribute higher cost to unemployment relative to inflation than right-wing parties	Partisan
Voters are	Homogenous, retrospective, and "pocketbook"	Homogenous, forward-looking, and "pocketbook"	Heterogenous, forward-looking, and "pocketbook"	Heterogenous, retrospective, and "pocketbook"
		Implications		
	Increase in growth and employment prior to elections. Increase in inflation either before or after elections	Monetary and fiscal variables may exhibit short-lived and irregular cycles, but growth and unemployment are all but unrelated to elections	Output growth and inflation should be permanently (temporarily, for rational variant) higher and unemployment lower under left governments	Output growth and inflation should be permanently high and unemployment lower under left governments, unless (a) central bank is highly independent; or (b) country pursues a fixed exchange rate amid highly mobile capital

[a]For example, see Nordhaus 1975.

[b]For example, see Rogoff and Sibert 1988; and Persson and Tabellini 1990.

[c]For example, see Hibbs 1977; Alesina 1987; and Alesina and Rosenthal 1995.

Whitten 1995). Although Cargill and Hutchison's study suggests that endogenous elections do not represent a barrier to a correlation between elections and increased growth, one cross-national study (Terrones 1989) finds evidence that macroeconomic policy cycles are more pronounced in countries with fixed-term elections than in countries where election timing is endogenous.

Alastair Smith's model (1996) of endogenous election timing in majoritarian systems has implications that are consistent with the rational expectations version of the electoralist model. Smith argues that it is difficult for governments to benefit from a strong economy by calling early elections because of the signal that this behavior sends to the electorate; voters are likely to infer that incumbents have called early elections because they expect the economic situation to deteriorate.

Context-Dependent Electoral Cycles

Although I would not argue that close attention to actors' preferences and beliefs is misplaced, I do argue that relative inattention to the structure in which actors operate explains, in part, why existing models have failed to receive robust empirical support. In this book, I relax one assumption of the traditional electoralist and partisan models that has been accepted in other models. I argue that the extent to which elected officials control the instruments necessary for guiding the economy can vary significantly depending on prior institutional choices. These choices can severely limit the ability of politicians to steer the economy in electorally advantageous directions.[9] In some cases the steering column may be locked, and in others elected officials may not even be in the driver's seat.[10]

In the next chapter, I present two different models that capture alternative ways in which central bank independence and the loss of national policy autonomy could be expected to influence partisan and electoralist behavior. I also address conceptual and measurement issues related to these structural factors, which will play a big role in the empirical tests in chapters 3 through 6. Chapter 3 uses time-series cross-sectional data to evaluate competing arguments about the effects of international capital mobility and central bank independence on partisan differences in fiscal and monetary policies. Chapter 4 uses similar data to test arguments about the existence of context-dependent electorally induced cycles in monetary and fiscal policy. Chapter 5 examines the evidence for context-dependent partisan differences in macroeconomic outcomes. Chapter 6 looks at the conditions under which we find a link between macroeconomic outcomes and the electoral calendar. Chapter 7 concludes by summarizing my findings and briefly addressing their normative implications.

Since there have been a number of excellent book-length treatments of issues closely related to the ones addressed here, it may be helpful to point out how this book differs from those. Keech 1995, which explores the logics behind and evidence for partisan differences and electoral cycles in macroeconomic policies, does a particularly fine job of linking positive analysis to normative questions about the costs and benefits of democratic governance. Along with Alesina and Rosenthal 1995, Keech's book is currently the definitive statement on the politics of macroeconomic policy choice in the United States. Alesina and Roubini (1992) extend the comparison of partisan and electoralist sources of macroeconomic policy and performance to the study of most OECD countries. They also present formal models of the variants of the partisan and electoralist models discussed above. The current volume also compares partisan and electoralist models and is cross-national in scope, but, unlike Alesina and Roubini 1992, it is self-consciously open-economy and institutionalist in spirit. In addition, while I present game-theoretic models in the next two chapters and rely on quantitative evidence to evaluate these models, it is my hope that less prior technical knowledge will be needed to follow the argument here than is the case for Alesina and Roubini's book. As a consequence, the current book may be a bit less daunting to those new to formal analysis than theirs is. This should not be construed as a criticism of formal analysis in general or of Alesina and Roubini in particular; the argument presented simply does not require much formalism.

This book is also quite close in spirit and substance to Garrett 1998, but there are important differences. Most obviously, I extend the analysis of the influence of capital mobility on the political sources of macroeconomic policy to the electoralist model. In addition, I examine the potentially perturbing effects of central bank independence and examine the ways in which the choice of exchange rate regime modifies the effects of capital mobility. Finally, unlike Garrett, I argue that the dearth of evidence in support of the partisan model—before, after, or during the recent increase in global financial integration—means it should be dispensed with entirely. I argue that the electoralist model instead is the appropriate baseline for understanding the politics of macroeconomic policy in rich democracies and, therefore, the effects of central bank independence and increased capital mobility in those countries.

CHAPTER 2

The Structural Context of Macroeconomic Policy Choice

Both the partisan and electoralist models tend to assume that incumbents have sufficient control over the instruments of monetary and fiscal policy that they can produce the macroeconomic outcomes they desire. In the partisan model, this means manipulating monetary and fiscal instruments so as to produce the combination of growth, employment, and inflation most preferred by the incumbent's constituency. In the electoralist model, each member of the electorate is assumed to have the same preferences over macroeconomic outcomes (which can be thought of as the bliss point of the median voter), and the incumbent steers the economy toward this most preferred point. So in the standard model, the incumbent sets policies that produce survival-maximizing macroeconomic outcomes, the electorate observes the incumbent's behavior, and the electorate then votes. These models typically assume a mechanism that transmits the movement of policy instruments frictionlessly into changes in macroeconomic outcomes. This assumption, of course, abstracts from the real world, because policymakers do not, in fact, have deterministic control over macroeconomic outcomes—in part because the world is fundamentally stochastic, but also because they are operating under limited information and are engaged in a complicated strategic interaction with market actors.

Each of these sources of friction in the transmission mechanism is likely to be consequential for the interaction between incumbents and voters, but I will focus on two factors that have been argued to affect the incumbent's control over macroeconomic policy: central bank independence and the loss of national policy autonomy resulting from increased capital mobility.

In the first two sections of this chapter, I will discuss why I believe that the structures examined in this book are important to our understanding of the political control of the economy. In the first section, I use a decision-theoretic model to show why central bank independence and the combination of capital mobility and exchange rate arrangements are each important constraints on the political control of the macroeconomy. Building on the standard model of open-economy macroeconomics, this model departs from much of the literature on "globalization" by emphasizing the fact that the impact of increased capital mobility on national monetary policy autonomy is modified by a nation's choice of exchange rate regime. I then present a game-theoretic model that integrates both the domestic and international constraints and shows how they interact to affect the conditions under which political manipulation of the macroeconomy by incumbents can be expected to occur. By emphasizing the conclusion of the standard open-economy macroeconomic model that a decline in national monetary policy autonomy can be accompanied by enhanced fiscal policy autonomy, the game-theoretic model departs from the globalization literature even further. In addition, the game-theoretic model allows for an examination of the strategic interaction between monetary and fiscal policymakers and, as a result, a richer analysis of the complex interaction between international and domestic institutions. In the third section of this chapter, I will classify OECD countries according to the relevant domestic and international constraints.

A Decision-Theoretic Model

Central Bank Independence

The degree of central bank independence is important because incumbent politicians typically do not actually have their hands on the levers of all macroeconomic policy instruments. Usually, technocrats at the central bank are in control of day-to-day monetary policy decisions. Consequently, it is only when the relationship between the bank and the government is such that the officials of the central bank are dutiful agents of the government that the fiction that incumbents have their hands on the levers of monetary policy can be maintained without much damage to the truth. If, however, the relationship between the bank and the government is structured in such a way as to grant central bankers considerable autonomy in choosing policy targets or the means for achieving them, then it is easy to imagine considerable friction in the mechanism between the desires of incumbents and policy outputs.

If one is willing to assume that the incumbent's already complicated task of producing macroeconomic outcomes is made more difficult when he or she does not control monetary policy instruments, then it is plausible that both partisan differences and electorally timed cycles in macroeconomic outcomes become less likely as central bank independence increases. Assume for a moment that left parties are more expansionary than right parties and that central bankers have macroeconomic preferences that are much closer to those of right parties than left. In the absence of central bank independence, monetary policy would be set at the government's ideal point—in figure 1, L when a left party controls the government and R when a right party governs. If central bank independence were complete, monetary policy would be set at the central bank's ideal point, CB. Most of the literature on central bank independence, however, suggests that independence is never complete. No matter how independent from political control the bank is on paper, some degree of responsiveness to the wishes of elected officials will exist—either to deter encroachments on independence or to lend legitimacy to the bank's actions, or both. Thus, unless there is no independence whatsoever, monetary policy will always reflect a compromise between the wishes of the government and the wishes of the bank. Policy will be set somewhere between L and CB (at, say, x^L) when a left government is in power and somewhere between R and CB (at, say, x^R) when a right party is in power. As central bank independence increases, the distance between monetary policies implemented under left governments and right governments gets smaller (note that the distance between x^L and x^R is smaller than the distance between L and R—the policies that would be implemented in the absence of independence). If independence were to be complete, the monetary policy enacted would be CB under both left and right governments. Thus, given an exogenously determined difference in the preferred policies of governments with different partisan compositions, an increase in central bank independence reduces the differences in behavior that parties will engage in.

A similar story can be told about the effect of central bank independence on electoralist cycles. Since electoralist models typically assume that incumbents of both parties have the same policy preferences, we need only compare the preferences of the central bank with the preferences of a representative incumbent. Electoralist models, both the traditional and rational expectations variants, conclude that incumbents have incentives to try to push growth above the natural rate during electoral periods. Central bankers have no such incentive; and, let us assume, neither do politicians in nonelectoral periods.

A shorthand way of describing this situation is that incumbents prefer more expansionary policies during electoral periods than they do during nonelectoral periods (I^E, the ideal point of an independent central banker during an

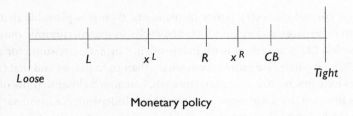

Monetary policy

Fig. 1.   The effect of central bank independence on the relationship between preferences and policies in the partisan model

electoral period, is to the left of $I^{\sim E}$ in fig. 2) and that they prefer more expansionary policies than central bankers only when electoral pressures are acute (I^{E} is to the left of CB, but $I^{\sim E}$ is not). Thus, when the central bank is the dutiful agent of the government, we would expect to see a change in policy during electoral periods of $I^{E} - I^{\sim E}$. When some degree of independence exists, electoral period policy will be a compromise between the wishes of the government and the wishes of the bank (say, x^{E}), so that electorally induced changes in policy will be smaller as independence increases.

International Capital Mobility

Central bank independence does not influence the effectiveness of policy instruments; rather, it determines the government's effective control over those instruments. In contrast, increased capital mobility influences the effectiveness of policy instruments that may or may not remain in the hands of election-seeking incumbents. According to the Mundell-Fleming framework, the consequence of international capital mobility on the effectiveness of fiscal and monetary policy depends on the exchange rate mechanism in place.[1]

When the exchange rate is fixed, increased capital mobility reduces the effectiveness of monetary policy but enhances the effectiveness of fiscal policy. To understand why an increase in capital mobility erodes national monetary policy autonomy, it is instructive to consider the effect of a macroeconomic expansion through a drop in interest rates. When capital is mobile, a drop in interest rates will lead to an outflow of capital, putting downward pressure on the exchange rate. If monetary authorities are committed to maintaining the value of the currency, they must sell foreign exchange to prevent a depreciation. The result is a tightening of the money supply until the original interest rates are restored. Less emphasized in the globalization literature is the contention of the Mundell-

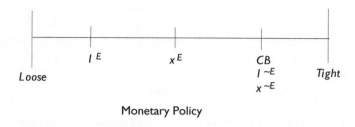

Fig. 2.   The effect of central bank independence on the relationship between preferences and policies in the electoralist model

Fleming model that increased capital mobility actually increases the effectiveness of fiscal policy. The reasoning goes like this: Fiscal expansion (or any other increase in autonomous expenditure) leads to an increase in both income and interest rates. If capital is mobile, the rise in interest rates attracts an inflow of capital, which leads to a currency appreciation. If the exchange rate is fixed, the central bank has to expand the money supply to offset the effects of the capital inflow on the exchange rate. Thus, under fixed exchange rates and mobile capital, a fiscal expansion induces a reinforcing monetary expansion.[2]

When the exchange rate is allowed to fluctuate, international capital mobility has exactly the opposite effect—fiscal policy becomes less effective and monetary policy becomes more effective. Again, an example may be helpful. When capital is mobile, an increase in net government spending will lead to an increase in interest rates. The resulting capital inflow will put upward pressure on the exchange rate. Absent sustained intervention in currency markets, an appreciation will occur, resulting in a loss in competitiveness and a drop in exports—thereby offsetting the effects of the fiscal expansion. Monetary policy, however, is expected to be effective when capital is mobile as long as the exchange rate is allowed to fluctuate. As already mentioned, a drop in interest rates is expected to produce an outflow of capital and downward pressure on the exchange rate. As long as monetary authorities do not intervene to defend the value of the currency, the result is a competitiveness-enhancing depreciation. As a result, an increase in demand for exports can be expected to reinforce a monetary expansion. Thus, as long as the exchange rate is allowed to fluctuate, monetary policy is expected to be at least as effective after capital mobility as it is before.

This discussion of the influence of capital mobility on the effectiveness of monetary and fiscal instruments for stabilization purposes can be extended to the question of the political control of the economy. For example, since an

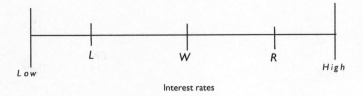

Fig. 3.   The effect of eroding monetary policy autonomy on interest
rates in an open economy partisan model

increase in capital mobility leads to an erosion of national monetary policy
autonomy when the exchange rate is fixed, incumbents that wish to use monetary policy for electoral or partisan purposes under such conditions are likely
to be frustrated in their attempts to do so.[3] Assume, for example, that incumbents are partisan, in the sense that they would push monetary policy in the
direction predicted by the partisan model if structural conditions allowed.
When capital is not very mobile, left and right governments would set interest rate policy in line with their preferences (L and R in fig. 3). In contrast, the
Mundell-Fleming framework suggests that when capital is fully mobile, interest rates are determined by international conditions unless the government is
prepared to let the value of the currency change. Thus, if capital is mobile and
the exchange rate is fixed, the interest rate is no longer controlled by the incumbent. If, after accounting for country-specific risks, the world interest rate
(W) is between the interest rates most preferred by parties of the left and
right, incumbents of either party could implement a different interest rate
only if they were willing to forgo the existing commitment to exchange rate
stability. Thus, we would expect to see interest rates of W whether a left or a
right government was in power.

A similar logic ties the existence of electorally induced cycles to the existence of national policy autonomy. If we can say that incumbents prefer lower
interest rates in preelectoral periods than in other periods, then figure 3 can be
reinterpreted in an electoralist light as well. Suppose the incumbent's preferences during nonelectoral periods are like R's, the incumbent's electoral period
preferences are like L's, and the world interest rate is once again W. When capital is not mobile, or when capital is mobile and the exchange rate is allowed to
fluctuate, interest rates will be lower during electoral periods (L) than in nonelectoral periods (R). But if capital is mobile and the exchange rate is fixed, interest rates will be set at W in both electoral and nonelectoral periods, and so
there will be no electorally induced cycle in monetary policy.[4]

The main conclusion of the decision-theoretic model is that when either constraint on monetary policy autonomy occurs, politically induced changes in monetary policy and/or macroeconomic outcomes are not expected to occur. As noted earlier, however, this result depends on the assumption that constraints on monetary policy will not be offset by fiscal activism. This assumption is relaxed in the game-theoretic model outlined in the next section, which examines the strategic interaction between monetary and fiscal policymakers.

A Game-Theoretic Model

While the preceding discussion conveys some simple intuitions about why these institutional structures might constrain political use of the macroeconomy, these intuitions can be misleading, in part because they fail to capture the potentially complex ways in which the institutions combine to affect policy behavior and economic outcomes. Clark and Nair Reichert (1998), for example, use reasoning similar to these intuitions to argue that if central bank independence constrains monetary policy and if the combination of fixed exchange rates and mobile capital constrains monetary policy, then a combination of these forms should be no less constraining. The model presented in Clark and Hallerberg 2000 suggests otherwise. Consequently, it may be worth examining this model more carefully.[5]

Central Bank Independence

"Government," broadly construed, can use some combination of monetary and fiscal policy to affect the country's economy. Monetary policy consists of the aiming of policy instruments (the discount rate, the purchase and sale of government securities and foreign currencies) at policy targets (such as interest rates, the money supply, and exchange rates) in an attempt to produce desired macroeconomic outcomes (growth, price and exchange rate stability, and/or a stable balance of payments). In all cases it is the central bank (CB), not elected politicians, that ultimately sets the policy instruments. This is not to say that elected officials are irrelevant to the conduct of monetary policy. The extent to which the central bank is obliged to pursue targets chosen, or goals preferred, by elected officials varies from country to country and across time. Central banks in Germany and the United States, for example, have considerable latitude both in selecting instruments and in choosing targets and goals, while the British and Norwegian banks have traditionally had much less freedom of action. While statute and tradition support a high degree of autonomy, one should not forget that even the Federal Reserve and the Bundesbank are *relatively* autonomous. Central bankers are appointed by elected officials, and to the extent that they enjoy autonomy, it is an autonomy that is granted by (and potentially taken away by) elected officials.[6]

Fiscal policy consists of the manipulation of taxation and expenditures in an attempt to produce desired macroeconomic outcomes. This task is accomplished primarily through the taxing and spending powers of the central government. While elected officials exercise direct influence over the fiscal process, they rely upon the finance ministry for crucial information, analysis, and day-to-day implementation. I adopt the simplifying assumption that the minister of finance is the dutiful agent of the government. There is reason to believe that, in addition to having separate responsibilities and information, there are differences between the Central Bank and the minister of finance in the way they evaluate alternative macroeconomic outcomes. Minsters of finance are assumed to be elected officials and, therefore, to feel the same political pressures as all officeholders. From the standpoint of the electoralist model, elected officials are assumed to derive sufficient benefits from electorally timed increases in growth and employment that they heavily discount the negative impact such behavior may have on inflation rates. From the standpoint of the partisan model, elected officials are expected to feel greater pressure to expand growth and employment if they belong to left-wing parties. Much of the literature on central banks argues that decision makers in these institutions tend to be more inflation-averse than their principals and are, therefore, likely to discount the value of such politically induced expansions.[7]

I represent actor preferences over macroeconomic outcomes with the following quadratic loss function, which describes the way actors assess deviations from their ideal values for unemployment and inflation:

$$L_i = (y - y^{*i})^2 + \alpha^i(\pi - \pi^{*i})^2, \tag{1}$$

where π and y are inflation and output, π^* and y^* are the actor's ideal points, α is the weight that the actor attaches to inflation stabilization relative to achieving his or her output goals, and i indexes the actor. Deviations from ideal points are squared to capture the intuition that small deviations from ideal points result in a proportionately smaller utility loss than large ones.

Differences among actors in their preferences for macroeconomic outcomes can be captured by varying assumptions about particular parameters in the model. I emphasize differences between the government and the central bank concerning their assessment of the ideal rate of growth, but I assume that actors share an ideal point of zero inflation.[8] In addition, both central bankers and governments would like to stabilize the economy at the natural rate of growth, that is, the rate of growth that is consistent with price stability. Political sources of macroeconomic policy, however, can be thought of as factors that induce in policymakers a desire to push growth above the natural rate. This desire can stem from either electoralist or partisan motivations. In the former case, incumbents will be tempted to try to push output above the natural rate just prior to elections in an effort to increase electoral support before inflationary consequences are felt. In the latter case, the employment goals of left-wing parties may make them more prone to attempt to push growth above the natural rate than their right-wing competitors. Whatever the motivation, political pressures can induce a change in preferences such that

$$y^{*gov} = k^{gov}y^n, \tag{2}$$

where y^n is the natural rate of growth and k is, if viewed from the standpoint of the electoralist model, a coefficient that equals 1 during nonelectoral periods and is greater than 1 in electoral periods (alternatively, if viewed from the standpoint of the partisan model, k is greater than 1 when there has been a leftward change in government).[9] In the absence of central bank independence, these inflationary pressures are transmitted to the central bank through rewards and punishments the government has at its disposal. Under such circumstances, the central banker then acts "as if" he or she were minimizing the government's politically induced loss function.[10] In the absence of central bank independence, the central bank's growth target is as defined in equation (2). If, however, the central bank is independent, I assume that it is insulated from government pressure.[11] The bank's growth target will then be the same in electoral periods (or under left-wing governments) as in nonelectoral periods (or under right-wing governments), such that

$$y^{*cb} = k^{cb}y^n, \qquad k = 1. \tag{3}$$

The government and central bank both bring about changes in macroeconomic outcomes through the manipulation of a short-term, expectations-enhanced Phillips curve:

$$y = y^n + \mu(\pi - \pi^e) + \phi g, \tag{4}$$

where π^e is the rate of inflation expected to prevail at time t embodied in sticky contracts signed at time $t - 1$, g is net government spending, and μ and ϕ are coefficients that characterize the effectiveness of fiscal and monetary policy transmission. The central bank is assumed to control inflation directly,[12] while the government controls spending.

International Capital Mobility

According to the standard Mundell-Fleming model, the effectiveness with which a government or central bank can manipulate these instruments depends upon the level of capital mobility as well as the exchange rate regime. The Mundell-Fleming model indicates that both instruments are somewhat effective when there is no capital mobility. When capital becomes mobile, however, fiscal policy is effective only when exchange rates are fixed, while monetary policy is effective only when exchange rates are flexible (Mundell 1963; Dornbusch 1976; Branson and Buiter 1983).

The current model captures the salient aspects of the international environment in the following ways. When capital is immobile, fiscal and monetary policy are only partially effective ($0 < \mu < 1, 0 < \phi < 1$). If capital is fully mobile and exchange rates are fixed, monetary policy is assumed to be ineffective and fiscal policy is assumed to be hypereffective (standardized here so that $\mu = 0$ and $\phi = 1$). When capital is fully mobile and exchange rates are not fixed, fiscal policy is ineffective and monetary policy is hypereffective ($\mu = 1$ and $\phi = 0$).[13]

Order of Play

At the start of the game, the players learn about the structure of the game—that is, they learn whether it is an electoral period, whether the central bank is independent, whether capital is mobile, and whether the exchange rate is fixed. After learning this information, the government chooses the level of net government spending by passing a budget. The central bank observes the budget and then chooses the rate of inflation by manipulating interest rates or the money supply.

Equilibria

I will solve the game for electoral and nonelectoral periods under alternative assumptions about the independence of the central bank. I first address the closed-economy case, then consider the conditional effects of capital flows.

PROPOSITION 1. *In general, the government adopts a budget (g) with net spending an increasing function of the propensity to push growth above the natural rate and a decreasing function of unanticipated inflation:*

$$g = \frac{1}{\phi}\left[y^n(k-1) - \mu(\pi - \pi^e)\right];$$

(5)

and the central bank responds by setting inflation (π) such that it is increasing in inflationary expectations and the propensity to push output above the natural rate and decreasing in the net budget deficit.

$$\pi = \frac{1}{\mu + \frac{\alpha}{\mu}}\left[\mu\pi^e + y^n(k-1) - \phi g\right].$$

(6)

Derivation: See appendix 1.

Proposition 1 can be used to derive predictions about central bank and government behavior under different sets of (ideal typical) structural conditions (table 2). Specifically, I consider the effects of political change (understood as either an increase in left governance or the occurrence of an election) on government and bank behavior and examine whether this effect is modified in important ways by the existence of central bank independence and the satisfaction of Mundell-Fleming conditions for national policy autonomy. Equilibrium policies before and after political change are presented in columns 4 and 5; the effect of political change on monetary and fiscal policy is simply the difference between these two columns (presented in column 6). I will discuss the implications of the model for fiscal policy, monetary policy, and national income in turn. I will focus my attention on the broadest implications of the model; for a more detailed discussion, see Clark and Hallerberg 2000.

Politically Induced Fiscal Expansions
First, recall that all of the parameters in table 2 are, by assumption, nonnegative. Consequently, any term that does not have a negative sign in front of it is positive. With this in mind, it is easy to see that the effect of either a shift to the left or the onset of an election is expected to lead to an *increase* in net government spending when the economy is closed, whether or not the central bank is independent, although the magnitude of the political effect may change when the degree of central bank independence changes. The effect of an increase in central bank independence on the size of politically induced fiscal expansions depends

TABLE 2. Comparative Static Implications of the Game-Theoretic Model

Condition (1)	International Conditions (2)	Central Bank Independence (3)	Policy before Political Change (4)	Policy after Political Change (5)	Politically Induced Policy Change (6)	Politically Induced Change in Income (7)
1	Closed economy	No	$g = \frac{1}{\phi}\left[y^n(k-1) + \mu\pi^e\right]$ $\pi = 0$	$g = \frac{1}{\phi}\mu\pi^e$ $\pi = 0$	$\frac{1}{\phi}y^n(k-1)$	$y^n(k-1)$
2		Yes	$g = \frac{1}{\phi}\left[\left(\frac{\mu^2}{\alpha}+\mu\right)y^n(k^G-1) + \mu\pi^e\right]$ $\pi = -\frac{1}{\mu+\frac{\alpha}{\mu}}\left[\left(\frac{\mu^2}{\alpha}+\mu\right)y^n(k^G-1)\right]$	$g = \frac{1}{\phi}\mu\pi^e$ $\pi = 0$	$\frac{1}{\phi}\left(\frac{\mu^2}{\alpha}+\mu\right)y^n(k-1)$ $-\frac{1}{\mu+\frac{\alpha}{\mu}}\left(\frac{\mu^2}{\alpha}+\mu\right)y^n(k-1)$	$\frac{\mu(\mu+\alpha)}{\mu^2+\alpha}y^n(k-1)$
3	Fixed rates and mobile capital	No	$g = y^n(k-1)$ $\pi = 0$	$g = 0$ $\pi = 0$	$y^n(k-1)$	$y^n(k-1)$
4		Yes	$g = y^n(k-1)$ $\pi = 0$	$g = 0$ $\pi = 0$	$y^n(k-1)$	$y^n(k-1)$
5	Flexible rates and mobile capital	No	$g = \frac{1}{1+\alpha}(\pi^e + y^n(k-1))$ $\pi = \frac{1}{1+\alpha}\pi^e$	$g = 0$ $\pi = \frac{1}{1+\alpha}\pi^e$	$\frac{1}{1+\alpha}y^n(k-1)$	$\frac{1}{1+\alpha}y^n(k-1)$
6		Yes	$g = 0$ $\pi = \frac{1}{1+\alpha}\pi^e$	$g = 0$ $\pi = \frac{1}{1+\alpha}\pi^e$	0 0	0

on the weight that policymakers place on hitting their monetary target (α) and the effectiveness of monetary policy (since an independent central bank is expected to counter fiscal expansions with monetary contractions). The greater the weight that policymakers place on hitting their monetary target, the smaller the politically induced fiscal expansion when the central bank is independent. The greater the effectiveness of monetary policy, the larger the fiscal expansion when the central bank is independent. The net effect of an increase in central bank independence, therefore, depends on the interaction between these factors, but for most reasonable parameterizations, an increase in central bank independence is expected to lead to a decrease in the magnitude of politically induced fiscal expansions. When policymakers place a great deal of weight on hitting their inflation target, politically induced fiscal expansions under immobile capital can be expected to be half as large when the central bank is independent as they are when the central bank is the obedient agent of elected officials.[14]

As one might expect in light of the Mundell-Fleming model, when capital is mobile, the effect of politics on net spending depends on the exchange rate regime. Spending is expected to increase as a result of elections or leftward shifts in government if and only if there is a commitment to maintain a fixed exchange rate. Note that this result is unaffected by the degree of central bank independence. The implications of the model for the existence of politically induced fiscal expansions can be summarized as follows.

HYPOTHESIS 1F. *When capital is immobile, politically induced fiscal expansions are expected to occur regardless of the exchange rate regime and the degree of central bank independence. But they are likely to be smaller in magnitude when central bank independence is high.*

HYPOTHESIS 2F. *When capital is mobile, politically induced fiscal expansions are expected to occur when the exchange rate is fixed, but not when it is allowed to fluctuate. This result is independent from the degree of central bank independence.*

Politically Induced Monetary Expansions

When the central bank is not independent and capital is immobile, there is no politically induced change in monetary policy. In effect, a compliant central bank "gets out of the way" and allows the government to pursue its goals through the use of fiscal policy.[15] When the central bank is independent, however, we expect a *decrease* in the money supply as conservative central bankers attempt to deter or, failing that, counteract politically induced fiscal expansions.

As with fiscal policy, when capital is mobile, the existence of politically induced monetary expansions depends on the exchange rate regime that is in place, but unlike with fiscal policy, the effect of the exchange rate regime on monetary policy depends on the degree of central bank independence. Specifically, when capital is mobile, politically induced expansions never occur when the exchange rate is fixed, but they occur when the exchange rate is flexible—if and only if the central bank is not independent.

The model's predictions about the existence of politically induced changes in monetary policy can be summarized as follows:

HYPOTHESIS 1M. *When capital is immobile, politically induced monetary contractions are expected to occur if and only if the central bank is independent.*

HYPOTHESIS 2M. *When capital is mobile, politically induced monetary expansions are expected to occur if and only if the exchange rate is flexible and the central bank is not independent.*

Politically Induced Expansions in National Income

Recall that the equilibrium fiscal and monetary policies presented in table 2 are derived from a model in which national income is assumed to be a function of both the rate of inflation chosen by the monetary authority and the level of net spending chosen by the fiscal policy through a Phillips curve mechanism. This same Phillips curve mechanism can, therefore, be used to derive various context-dependent predictions about politically induced changes in national income. We need only plug the equilibrium changes in policy in column 6 into the Phillips curve (equation (4)). The resulting changes in national income are reported in column 7 of table 2.

When capital is immobile, a politically induced increase in income is expected both when the central bank is independent and when it is not. When the central bank is not independent, this increase in growth is due to the increase in government spending (condition 1, column 6 in table 2). When the central bank is independent, however, the effect of political change is the net result of a fiscal expansion and a monetary contraction (condition 2, column 6). The model tells us, however, that the former will always be larger than the latter, and, as a result, a shift to the left or the onset of an election will lead to an increase in growth in a closed economy—even when the central bank is independent. However, because for all values of μ and α consistent with the model assumptions,

$$0 < \frac{\mu(\mu + \alpha)}{\mu^2 + \alpha} < 1, \tag{7}$$

a switch to an independent central bank can be expected to lead to a decrease in the magnitude of the politically induced change in growth (compare conditions 1 and 2, column 7).[16]

As predicted by the decision-theoretic model in the first part of this chapter, when capital is mobile, the occurrence of politically induced expansions in growth depends both on the degree of central bank independence and the exchange rate regime, but the interaction of these domestic and international contexts is a bit more subtle than expected. First, note that a politically induced increase in growth is expected when the exchange rate is fixed both when the central bank is independent and when it is not (conditions 3 and 4, column 7). Thus, contra Clark and Nair Reichert 1998, the presence of both constraints on the political control of monetary policy (central bank independence on the one hand and the combination of fixed exchange rates and mobile capital on the other) is not more constraining on the political manipulation of the macroeconomy than the presence of just one constraint. Consider, for example, the case where central bank independence is high and capital is immobile (condition 2, column 7). When the exchange rate is fixed, an increase in capital mobility erodes national monetary policy autonomy, and, as a result, the independent central bank loses its ability to counteract or deter politically motivated fiscal expansions (condition 4, column 7). Consequently, there will be an *increase* in the size of politically induced expansions in income.[17] Next, consider the case where capital is mobile and the exchange rate is fixed (condition 3, column 7). An increase in central bank independence under these circumstances (condition 4, column 7) is expected to have no effect on the size of politically induced macroeconomic expansions because in the absence of national monetary policy autonomy, an independent central bank has no effective instrument with which to counteract or deter politically motivated fiscal expansions.

In contrast, when the exchange rate is flexible, central bank independence is particularly effective for reducing politically induced expansions in national income. This is because when the exchange rate is allowed to fluctuate, an increase in capital mobility erodes national fiscal policy autonomy. As a result, the only way to bring about an expansion in growth is through monetary policy. If, however, the central bank is independent (condition 6, column 7), it will be able to resist political pressures to do so. Even when the central bank is compliant, politically induced macroeconomic expansions may not occur when capital is mobile and the exchange rate is flexible. The extent to which this is true depends on the weight that policymakers place on hitting their inflation target. For example, if policymakers place as much weight on hitting their inflation target as on hitting their growth target, then the size of politically motivated macroeconomic expansions will be cut in half (condition 5, column 7).

The main implications of the model for politically induced changes in income can be summarized as follows.

HYPOTHESIS 1P. *When the exchange rate is fixed, politically induced increases in growth are expected to occur both when capital is mobile and when it is not, and when the central bank is independent and when it is not (though the size of such increases will be smallest when capital is immobile and the central bank is independent).*

HYPOTHESIS 2P. *When the exchange rate is allowed to fluctuate, politically induced changes in growth are expected when capital is immobile. Smaller politically induced expansions may occur when capital is mobile or the central bank is independent, but no politically induced expansions are expected when capital is mobile and the central bank is independent.*

Summary of the Model's Implications

The model's implications for politically induced changes in monetary and fiscal policy and growth are summarized in table 3. Notice that politically induced expansions in fiscal policy are expected to occur except when the com-

TABLE 3. **The Expected Effect of an Increase in Left Governance or the Onset of an Election under Various Conditions**

	No Central Bank Independence	Central Bank Independence
No capital mobility	*Fiscal policy:* expansion *Monetary policy:* indeterminate *National income:* expansion	*Fiscal policy:* (smaller) expansion *Monetary policy:* contraction *National income:* (smaller) expansion
Capital mobility and fixed exchange rates	*Fiscal policy:* (larger) expansion *Monetary policy:* none *National income:* expansion	*Fiscal policy:* (larger) expansion *Monetary policy:* none *National income:* expansion
Capital mobility and flexible exchange rates	*Fiscal policy:* none *Monetary policy:* expansion *National income:* (smaller) expansion	*Fiscal policy:* none *Monetary policy:* none *National income:* none

bination of mobile capital and flexible exchange rates has eroded fiscal policy autonomy. The situation is a bit more complicated when it comes to monetary policy. First, the model rules out politically induced monetary expansions whenever the central bank is independent—in fact, when the central bank is independent and capital is immobile, we expect to observe politically induced monetary contractions aimed at offsetting politically induced fiscal expansions. In addition, the model rules out politically induced monetary expansions whenever the exchange rate is fixed. The model predicts politically induced monetary expansions only when the exchange rate is allowed to fluctuate and the central bank is not independent. When capital is mobile, the model tells us to expect such expansions; when capital is immobile, the model does not rule out such expansions.[18]

Notice that politically induced increases in income should be ubiquitous under fixed exchange rates and relatively rare under flexible exchange rates. When the exchange rate is fixed, incumbents are expected to use fiscal policy to engineer preelectoral macroeconomic expansions. Central bank independence can impede these efforts when capital is immobile, but not when it is mobile.

When the exchange rate is flexible, politically induced macroeconomic expansions are unambiguously expected only when capital is immobile and the central bank is not independent. When capital is immobile and the central bank is independent, politically induced macroeconomic expansions may occur, but they can be reduced in size by as much as 50 percent. When capital is mobile and the exchange rate is flexible, politically induced macroeconomic expansions can occur as long as the central bank is not independent, though they are expected to be smaller in magnitude than would have been the case under immobile capital. Finally, no politically induced macroeconomic expansions are expected to occur when capital is mobile and the central bank is independent. Under such circumstances, the combination of mobile capital and flexible exchange rates leads to an erosion of fiscal policy autonomy and enhances the effectiveness of monetary policy. Unfortunately, from the standpoint of a survival-maximizing incumbent or a left-wing incumbent seeking to implement expansionary policies, monetary policy is controlled by a central bank that is relatively indifferent to such concerns.[19] Note that this conclusion is at odds with the argument in Clark and Nair Reichert 1998 and the decision-theoretic model earlier in this chapter. Those arguments implied that if central bank independence on the one hand and the combination of fixed exchange rates and mobile capital on the other were each constraints on the political manipulation of the macroeconomy, then their combination should be at least as constraining. According to the game-theoretic model, however, this "additive" effect of institutional constraints seems to apply only in the case of flexible exchange rates. Under fixed exchange rates, mobile capital constrains monetary policy but does not constrain fiscal policy—so there is nothing to prevent incumbents from using fiscal policy to pursue their political goals. Furthermore, since monetary policy is ineffective under these conditions, independent central bankers can neither deter nor offset politically induced expansions, as they can when capital is immobile.

It should be noted that the theoretical models discussed in this chapter both assume that the variables that modify partisan and electoral influences on macroeconomic policy and outcomes are exogenous to the model. It is possible, of course, that capital mobility, the exchange rate, and even central bank independence are themselves choice variables and are endogenous to the decisions of the very actors whose behavior we are attempting to explain. If the exchange rate regime prevents a policymaker from using an instrument for electoral purposes, and the nature of the exchange rate regime is also under the control of the politician, why would an opportunistic politician not just drop the commitment to the exchange rate regime when it became inconvenient? Bernhard and Leblang (1999), for example, argue that incumbents that inhabit domestic political institutions that create incentives for survival maximizing will be less likely to adopt pegged exchange rates. The Mundell-Fleming model and the models in this chapter, however, can be used to challenge this argument. If, in a world of mobile capital, the choice of the exchange rate regime has implications for *which* macroeconomic policy will be used to pursue electoral or partisan objectives, not *whether* some instrument will be used, it is not clear why incumbents facing an election would have a systematic incentive to switch from one exchange rate regime to another.[20] While central bank independence seems to have a more clearly constraining effect on the political manipulation of the economy, changes in the degree of central bank independence in OECD countries are rare events. More generally, we simply do not observe instances where governments systematically change the exchange rate regime, the level of capital mobility, or central bank independence before elections.[21] It is unlikely, therefore, that we will encounter the type of endogeneity problem that would bias our tests of the link between policy and elections, despite the fact that the modifying institutions examined here are the product of human choice.

Classifying Contexts

More generally, the game-theoretic model demonstrates that equilibrium policies and macroeconomic outcomes are quite sensitive to the context in which

policymakers operate. Attempts to test arguments (both partisan and electoralist) about the political determinants for macroeconomic policy without
taking careful account of that context will be misleading at best. Consequently,
it will be necessary to devise context-specific tests of the partisan and electoralist arguments. To do so will require an attempt to classify observations in
terms of the degree of capital mobility and central bank independence present
and the nature of the exchange rate regime in place.

The remainder of this chapter will explain the process used to accomplish
such classification for about nineteen OECD countries from 1960 to 1989.
Chapters 4 through 7 will evaluate the hypotheses produced above as they pertain to both electoralist and partisan incentives for the political control of the
economy.

The Determinants of National Policy Autonomy[22]

According to the Mundell-Fleming approach to open-economy macroeconomics, the effects of increases in international capital mobility are moderated
by the nature of the exchange rate commitments maintained by individual
countries. Thus, changes in the global economy may have very different consequences in different countries, because these changes are refracted by the
choices of individual governments—both by their attempts to constrain capital movements and by the exchange rate system they adopt.

International Capital Mobility

Capital mobility is commonly conceptualized in two ways: first, as a characteristic of the international system or an attribute of individual countries; and
second, as a legal or behavioral phenomenon (Hallerberg and Clark 1997). Recent works have identified three sources of the increase in capital mobility: ad-
vances in communications and information technologies, the creation of in-
novative financial instruments (such as the "Euro" money markets) capable of
facilitating cross-border capital flows, and the removal of legal barriers to trade
by national authorities. In addition to these sources, Michael C. Webb (1991)
traces the increase in capital flows in the 1970s to the rapid increase in trade
flows in the 1960s. Since only one of these recognized sources of capital mobility is under the direct control of policymakers—namely, deregulation—and *it*
has largely been a response rather than a stimulus to the other sources of the
increase, some observers have concluded that the level of capital mobility is
appropriately viewed as a structural characteristic of the international system
rather than the product of national choice (Andrews 1994; Webb 1991).

Although there is broad consensus that the degree of financial integration among advanced capitalist nations increased tremendously between the 1960s and the 1980s, it is difficult to say more precisely when the transition from the "before capital mobility" world to the "after capital mobility" world took place.[23] The 1970s were clearly a decade of transition. The increase in trade flows that resulted from the reduction of tariff barriers in the 1960s required the support of an almost immediate increase in capital flows. This initial increase in capital flows did not require state action to liberalize capital controls; in fact, the flows occurred despite the best efforts of governments to curtail them.[24] Webb argues that by 1978 the nature of the international system had changed to a situation where there was a "striking unwillingness of governments to use trade and capital controls to limit the external imbalances generated by different macroeconomic politics in different countries" (1991, 309). A key turning point had occurred several years earlier, however, when the Bretton Woods exchange rate system staggered and then died between 1971 and 1973. Although many factors contributed to the decline of the Bretton Woods system, increasing capital mobility, which "made it impossible for governments to stabilize exchange rates without subordinating monetary policy to that end," was certainly a significant factor (Webb 1991, 311; see also Gowa 1983; and Odell 1982).

A quantitative indication of the increase in international capital mobility that occurred during the 1970s can be seen in changes in savings–investment coefficients. Feldstein-Horioka coefficients measure the extent to which an economy's rate of domestic investment is determined by its domestic savings rate. When capital is perfectly immobile, domestic investment should be fully determined by domestic savings. In contrast, when capital is perfectly mobile, domestic investment should be less dependent on domestic savings. Thus, when domestic investment is regressed on domestic savings, the resulting coefficient can be interpreted as a systemwide measure of capital mobility that would equal 0 when capital is perfectly mobile and 1 when capital is wholly constrained.[25]

The use of savings–investment coefficients as an indicator for capital mobility has been controversial.[26] First, since both savings and investment are procyclical, estimates of the relationship between them may be inflated. Second, because the world interest rate is likely to be influenced by changes in the savings rates of large countries, the assumption that capital mobility will lead to a decoupling of domestic investment from domestic savings will not hold for large countries. Finally, in contrast to a broad consensus that capital mobility has been increasing in recent decades, many studies have found that savings–investment ratios show little, if any, sign of decline during the last thirty years. These concerns, however, do not necessarily rule out the Feldstein-Horioka coefficient as a measure of capital mobility. Martin Feldstein and Charles Horioka were well aware of the procyclical problem and sought to ameliorate it by averaging savings and investment over a long enough period to control for cyclical variations. Jeffrey A. Frankel argues that the "large country" problem is not an issue in cross-sectional tests, "because all countries share the same world interest rate" (1991, 230). Finally, evidence that Feldstein-Horioka coefficients have not declined as expected may be due to the repeated use of observation periods that were not necessarily representative.

I calculated cross-sectional savings–investment coefficients by regressing five-year averages of savings and investment for eighteen OECD countries. Five-year averages are used here because they are, for the reasons stated earlier, preferred to annual observations, and they yield twice as many observations as ten-year averages. Figure 4 displays estimates of Feldstein-Horioka coefficients for twenty-six periods, beginning with 1960–64, and the 95 percent confidence interval around particular estimates. Note that these coefficients tend to decline over time.[27] In addition, the null hypothesis that the savings–investment coefficient equals 1 (that is, capital is perfectly immobile) can be rejected in those years for which the upper bound of the confidence interval falls below the line emanating from "1.0" on the right-hand axis. Note also that this occurs for the first time in the five-year period ending in 1971, which is in line with the argument that increasing capital mobility played a role in the breakup of Bretton Woods. By the five-year period ending in 1974, however, the coefficient is no longer distinguishable from 1. This might suggest that the initial increase in international capital mobility was fleeting, but it is worth noting that the failure to reject the null hypothesis in the mid-1970s seems to be driven more by a marked increase in the standard error (perhaps reflecting diverse national investment responses to the first oil price shocks) than by a change in the coefficient itself.

Although figure 4 supports the common perception that a systemic increase in capital mobility began in the 1970s and continues today, important differences may exist among OECD countries in the barriers to capital flows. Unfortunately, establishing evidence of cross-national differences in barriers to capital flows is fraught with difficulties. One option is to examine country-specific time series to generate a Feldstein-Horioka savings–investment coefficient for each country. The cyclical nature of savings and investment makes this difficult unless long time-series data are available (Feldstein and Horioka 1980; Frankel 1991).[28] Another alternative is to use government restrictions on

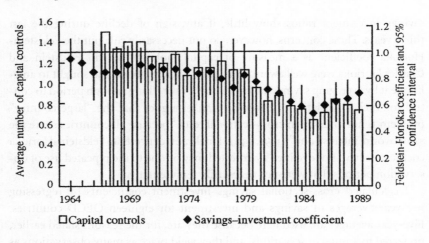

Fig. 4.   Alternative measures of capital mobility for 18 OECD countries. (From Clark and Nair Reichert 1998.)

capital flows as an indicator of barriers to cross-national capital movements. Numerous scholars have adopted this approach by aggregating a number of qualitative indicators of alternative government restrictions (Rose 1994; Garrett 1995; Simmons 1996). Restrictions on capital can be used to indicate barriers to movements across particular borders or averaged across a group of countries. The bars in figure 4 display annual averages of an index constructed for seventeen of the countries in the sample.[29] Note that, like the savings–investment coefficients, capital restrictions declined through the 1970s and 1980s.[30] Together, savings–investment coefficients and restrictions on capital movements provide some evidence supporting the notion that the increase in capital mobility dates back to the breakup of the Bretton Woods system.

There are alternatives to the indicators of capital mobility discussed here, but each presents problems, either conceptually or in terms of data availability. Conceptually, covered interest rate parities capture important aspects of financial integration (Frankel 1991), but data availability poses a serious problem.[31] Actual capital flows are a poor indicator, because if financial integration reduces interest rate differentials, few arbitrage opportunities are available to motivate capital flows. Finally, measures based on the long-term implications of capital mobility, such as cross-country consumption correlations and the convergence in capital–output ratios, are difficult to estimate for the shorter time periods addressed here (Rose 1994).

Both of the systemic measures reported here point to an increase in capital mobility beginning in the early 1970s, around the time of the breakup of Bretton Woods. I believe that considerable evidence indicates that a qualitative change in the level of capital mobility occurred at this time. Consequently, I identify the end of the Bretton Woods period as the divide between the "before capital mobility" and "after capital mobility" worlds. Clearly, this division ignores important incremental changes in the degree of capital mobility over time and between countries. Consequently, I also report results in the pooled time-series analysis in chapters 3 through 6 that utilize a continuous measure of capital mobility based on savings–investment coefficients and capital controls.

Changing Exchange Rate Arrangements

Clearly, the decline of Bretton Woods was the single most dramatic change in the exchange rate regime since the collapse of the interwar gold standard. Before 1971 all OECD countries, with the partial exception of Canada, pegged their currencies to the dollar, which in turn was linked to gold. After President Richard Nixon "closed the gold window" in August 1971, however, individual countries were again faced with a set of choices regarding the exchange rate mechanism. Since that time, exchange rate relationships have been heterogeneous. Important subsets of the OECD nations have made various attempts to resurrect the stabilizing potential of the Bretton Woods system by implementing regional systems of quasi-fixed exchange rates. Some nations have unilaterally chosen to peg their exchange rates either to particular currencies or to a composite of currencies. Others have maintained a "dirty float"; that is, they have not systematically pegged their exchange rates to other currencies but have intervened in foreign exchange markets when they considered it necessary to protect other policy goals. Since 1978, governments have also used various forums (such as G-7 meetings) to engage in ad hoc coordination of exchange rate interventions (Webb 1991, 1995; Putnam and Bayne 1984; Cohen 1993; Henning 1994). For the purpose of this discussion, it is important to identify those countries whose exchange rates were "formally or informally pegged" to another currency (Cohen 1993, 147), because in those cases high levels of capital mobility caused monetary policy autonomy to be significantly curtailed.

The European Exchange Rate System (the "snake"), established on April 24, 1972, restricted the exchange rate fluctuations between participating countries (West Germany, France, Italy, the Netherlands, Belgium, and Luxembourg) to ±2.25 percent (Denmark, Ireland, Norway, and the United Kingdom joined the next month). Participation in the snake, which remained in effect until 1978, was highly unstable. By the beginning of 1973, Italy, Ireland, and Britain had dropped out, and France participated only intermittently. Sweden dropped out of the snake in 1977, choosing instead to peg its exchange rate to a composite.[32]

The Exchange Rate Mechanism of the EMS came closer to creating a stable currency zone than the snake, which it replaced in March 1979. The variability of intra-EMS exchange rates declined over time, and participation has been both expanding and more stable (Nolling 1993, 51–52). All the original members of the snake joined the EMS in 1979 and remained members throughout the 1980s. The United Kingdom was conspiciously absent. Table 4 lists each country's participation in fixed exchange rate regimes in the post–Bretton Woods era. In most cases, regime membership was clear-cut. Denmark, West Germany, and the Benelux countries were consistent participants in fixed-rate regimes. France was an on-again, off-again member of the snake and joined the EMS. Italy and Britain left the snake shortly after its conception. Norway and Sweden participated in the snake but not the EMS and, like Ireland, maintained a pegged rate when not participating in multilateral regimes. Austria, Finland, and New Zealand did not participate in either the snake or the EMS but maintained pegged exchange rates for significant periods. In all, twelve of the nineteen countries examined have been participants in fixed exchange rate arrangements for a significant portion of the post–Bretton Woods period.

TABLE 4.   **Participation in Fixed Exchange Rate Regimes after 1972 and before 1990**

	Snake	EMS	Pegged
Australia	—	—	—
Austria	—	—	1973–89
Belgium	1973–78	1979–89	—
Canada	—	—	—
Denmark	1973–78	1979–89	—
Finland	—	—	1977–89
France	Intermittent	1979–89	—
Great Britain	—	—	—
Greece	—	—	—
Ireland	—	1979–89	1973–78
Italy	—	1979–89	—
Japan	—	—	—
Netherlands	1973–78	1977–89	—
New Zealand	—	—	1973–79
Norway	1973–78	—	1979–89
Spain	—	—	—
Sweden	1973–77	—	1977–89
United States	—	—	—
West Germany	1973–78	1979–89	—

Source: Coffey 1984; IMF, *International Financial Statistics,* various years; OECD 1985.

Central Bank Independence

The literature on central bank independence has identified two distinct dimensions of independence—de jure and de facto. De jure independence involves the legal relationship between central bank decision makers and the government, whereas de facto independence is gauged by examining the actual behavior of the central bank. Alex Cukierman, Steven B. Webb, and Bilin Neyapti (1992) provide evidence that measures of de facto independence are correlated with price stability in developing nations, and measures of legal independence are correlated with price stability in advanced industrialized nations.[33] The key aspects of legal independence concern the appointment, dismissal, and length of tenure of the chief executive officer; procedures governing the resolution of conflicts between the executive branch and the bank; the policy objectives of the bank enshrined in its charter; and the extent to which the public sector is restricted in its ability to borrow from the bank (Cukierman et al. 1993, 98–99; Cukierman, Webb, and Neyapti 1992). Among OECD nations, central banks exhibit considerable cross-national variance in independence, ranging from those in the United States and Germany, which are among the most independent in the world, to the French central bank, which has traditionally been subordinate to the finance ministry (Coffey 1984). Until recently, changes in the degree of central bank independence were rare in OECD countries.[34]

There have been several attempts to quantify the degree of central bank independence in advanced capitalist countries (Bade and Parkin 1982; Alesina 1988b; Grilli, Masciandaro, and Tabellini 1991; Cukierman, Webb, and Neyapti 1992; Alesina and Summers 1993). Table 5 reports the central bank independence scores for nineteen OECD countries according to various indexes.[35] The indexes display a fair amount of agreement among them. If we compare each country's scores with the median score of independence, we see only a few points of disagreement. Australia ranks equal to or above the median on every scale except the Bade and Parkin index. Japan ranks above the median according to the Bade and Parkin index and the Alesina and Summers index but is below the median according to the Grilli, Masciandaro, and Tabellini index and the Cukierman, Webb, and Neyapti index. Greece is below the median on the Grilli, Masciandaro, and Tabellini index but above the median according to the Cukierman, Webb, and Neyapti index. Since the Cukierman, Webb, and Neyapti measure has the widest coverage of cases and is fairly consistent with the other measures, I have used it as the primary indicator of central bank independence in this study.

TABLE 5.   Alternative Measures of Central Bank Independence

	AS^a	BP^b	GMT^c	CWN^d
West Germany	4	4	14	0.69
Austria	—	—	9	0.63
Greece	—	—	4	0.53^e
Denmark	2.5	2	8	0.50
United States	3.5	3	13	0.49
Canada	2.5	2	11	0.45
Ireland	—	—	7	0.44
Netherlands	2.5	2	10	0.42
Australia	2	1	9^e	0.36^e
United Kingdom	2	2	6	0.34
Sweden	2	2	—	0.29
France	2	2	7	0.29
Finland	—	—	—	0.28
Italy	1.75	1.5	5	0.25
New Zealand	1	1	3	0.24
Japan	2.5^e	3^e	6	0.18
Spain	1.5	1	5	0.17
Norway	2	2	—	0.16
Belgium	2	2	7	0.16
Median	2.0	2.0	7.0	0.30
Mean	2.23	2.03	7.6	0.36

Note: All indexes are constructed so that higher numbers indicate greater central bank independence.

[a]Index created by Alesina and Summers (1993) by rescaling and combining the Bade and Parkin (BP) and Grilli, Masciandaro, and Tabellini (GMT) indexes.

[b]Index proposed by Bade and Parkin (1982) and extended by Alesina (1988b).

[c]Sum of economic and political indexes provided by Grilli, Masciandaro, and Tabellini (1991).

[d]Index created by averaging Cukierman, Webb, and Neyapti's (1992) aggregate legal measure for the period 1960–89.

[e]Indicates an above-median score for a country that is below the median on at least one other index.

Conclusion

In this chapter I have attempted to clarify the reasons that I expect the behaviors predicted by the partisan and electoralist models to be influenced by the degree of central bank independence and the level of national policy autonomy, and I have discussed the observable manifestations of these structural conditions and summarized their cross-national and cross-temporal variance. I maintain that these factors influence the control that policymakers have over macroeconomic policy instruments and that such control is a functional prerequisite for the political control of the economy.

The decision-theoretic model yields predictions about the influence of domestic and international institutions on the incentives for incumbents to use monetary policy to engineer politically motivated macroeconomic expansions, predictions consistent with the empirical results in Clark and Nair Reichert 1998. The model predicts that monetary policy will be used to create such expansions except when the central bank is independent or when capital is mobile and the exchange rate is fixed. The predictions from this model are intuitive, straightforward, and additive—either constraint on the effective control of monetary policy by elected officials will make it difficult for incumbents to engineer macroeconomic expansions. While the model is suitable as a baseline for analyzing context-dependent politically induced cycles, the underlying assumption that fiscal policy will be constrained whenever monetary policy is constrained, should, and has, been questioned (Clark and Hallerberg 2000).

The game-theoretic model relaxes this ad hoc assumption about the relationship between monetary and fiscal policy by viewing policy as the product of the strategic interaction between fiscal and monetary policymakers and by using the Mundell-Fleming model of the open economy to predict when fiscal and monetary instruments will be effective. Some, but not all, of the resulting predictions are the same as those of the decision-theoretic model. The models yield their most dramatically different predictions for the case where the central bank is independent, capital is mobile, and the exchange rate is fixed. Because both the international and domestic constraints on the political use of monetary policy are present, the decision-theoretic model predicts that this is the context in which political control of the economy is most difficult. In contrast, because independent central bankers cannot use monetary policy to deter or counteract fiscal policy when the exchange rate is fixed and capital is mobile, the game-theoretic model predicts that incumbents will be relatively free to use fiscal policy to pursue their goals—be they ideological or electoral—under such circumstances.

The decision-theoretic and game-theoretic models are both potentially useful tools for understanding the ways in which the political control of the economy depends on the context in which incumbents find themselves. Because the game-theoretic model explains, rather than makes assumptions about, the way in which fiscal and monetary actors will interact, it can be said to have greater empirical content. It arrives at this additional content, however, at the cost of increased complexity. In the end, the choice between these models is an empirical question. While they are both useful rubrics for thinking about the context-dependent nature of the political control of the economy, ultimately we would like to place our confidence in the model that is most consistent with observation. Determining the answer to this empirical question will be the central focus of the remainder of this book.

CHAPTER 3

Partisanship and Fiscal and Monetary Policy

There is not a dime's worth of difference between the Republicans and the Democrats.

—George Wallace, 1968 American Independent Party presidential candidate

At the beginning of this book, I pointed to the apparent rightward leaning of British prime minister Tony Blair and German chancellor Gerhard Schroeder as two instances of the popular view of the effects of globalization. It is frequently argued that in today's global economy, left-wing politicians have had to mimic the policy actions of right-wing governments. But is this apparent consequence of globalization really a new development? The infamous "policy U-turn" of the socialist government of French president François Mitterrand suggests that international capital markets have possessed the ability to discipline aggressively interventionist left-wing governments for some time. On the other hand, it could be argued that the Mitterrand experience in the early 1980s was the opening bell for the brave new world of global capital. But was the Mitterrand U-turn the first example of a left government's interventionist plans being checked by international investors? Many observers of the austerity plan adopted by the Wilson government during the sterling crisis in Britain would argue that it was not. While many lessons can be drawn from important individual cases, the goal of this chapter is to examine in a systematic fashion whether and when left-wing governments have enacted distinguishably more interventionist policies than their right-wing competitors.

The notion that policy outputs reflect and are, at least in part, determined by the ideologically driven preferences of either policymakers or their constituents has become a common way of understanding the influence of politics on macroeconomic policy.[1] Recent studies have shown that increased economic integration has, contrary to the predictions of convergence theorists, not eroded partisan differences (Cusack 1997; Oatley 1999). In fact, it has been argued that the forces of market integration have created new pressures for partisan differentiation (Garrett 1995, 1998). In this chapter, I assess the evidence for partisan differences in fiscal policy in the existing literature, reanalyze data from an exemplary study in this tradition (Garrett 1998), and conclude that there is little evidence of partisan differences and that the recent increase in international integration has done little to change this. I interpret these results as indirect evidence in support of the partisan model's main political economic competitor— the electoralist model—and argue that future research on the effects of internationalization would do well to examine the effects of increased capital mobility on behaviors consistent with the electoralist model.

The chapter begins with a review of the literature employing the partisan approach to macroeconomic policy. I then specify my plan to conduct an open-economy test of the partisan hypothesis that differs from most prior tests in that it pays close attention to the theorized interaction between capital mobility and exchange rate regime. The third section presents the results of these tests.

The Partisan Approach to Macroeconomic Policy Choice

The partisan model is a set of loosely connected assumptions about the ways in which the goals of voters and policymakers interact with the structural environment to produce partisan differences in policies and/or macroeconomic outcomes.[2] Typically, these partisan differences are thought to be the result of the policymakers' concerns over the content of policy. These concerns can stem from the policymakers' intrinsic preferences over macroeconomic outcomes or from the fact that their political survival depends on pleasing distinctive constituencies. Thus, partisan models are typically compared to arguments that predict convergence in party platforms because political survival comes to overwhelm concerns about other goals (Downs 1957), leading policymakers to act "as if" they were maximizing votes or pluralities.[3] While it is tempting to summarize the differences between these approaches as differences over the means and ends of political behavior, Alesina and Rosenthal's pithy formulation is that "in a Downsian model, the parties choose policy in order to win elections, whereas in a partisan model, the parties want to be elected in order to choose policies" (1995, 17). There is, however, nothing in the Downsian approach that suggests that parties do not differ in the policies that, absent the need to win votes, they would like to see implemented. The difference between the two schools involves the question of whether the structural environment the parties operate in compels their *behavior* to converge.

Hibbs (1977) argued that distinctive constituencies exist in advanced democratic states that differ in their assessment of macroeconomic outcomes and that these differences are reflected in the platforms and behavior of parties that arise to represent them. As a result, "working-class-based Socialist and Labor parties typically attach far greater importance to full employment than to inflation, whereas business-oriented, upper middle-class-based Conservative parties generally assign higher priority to price stability than to unemployment" (1470). Precisely why parties decide to specialize in serving these separate constituencies rather than alter their products in order to lure customers away from their competitors, as the Downsian model proposes, is not stated by Hibbs, but others have offered explanations for a lack of convergence.[4]

To evaluate his argument, Hibbs pursued two strategies that structured empirical studies for twenty years. First, he compared long-run averages in unemployment and inflation across countries and found that countries where left-wing control of government was commonplace tended to have lower unemployment and higher inflation than those where left-wing participation in government was rare. While this result is broadly consistent with the assertion that left- and right-wing parties implement different policies, it is not *inconsistent* with the Downsian hypothesis—which predicts that the Conservative Party will act like the Labour Party and the Democrats will act like the Republicans but which says nothing at all about the relationship between British and American policy.[5] Cross-national differences in physical geography, risk propensities, historical experiences, production profiles, stages of development, exposure to trade, and so forth are likely to produce cross-national differences in the policy preferences of the median voter and, by Downsian logic, differences in policy behavior and macroeconomic outcomes.[6] If, as is easily imagined, these cross-national structural differences turn out to be correlated with the frequency with which parties operating under particular banners are elected, cross-national tests could produce correlations between partisanship and macroeconomic variables even when convergence upon the preferences of the median voter within a country is complete.

In light of this, comparisons of partisan behavior over time *within* countries would seem to be a more direct method for deciding between the Hibbsian and Downsian models. Hibbs, in fact, did just this for the U.S. and British cases and found partisan differences in unemployment rates consistent with his argument. The problem with testing the partisan hypothesis with individual-country time series is, of course, that in many countries movements between right and left are rather rare. As a consequence, the pooling of time-series and cross-sectional data has become the standard technique for evaluating these arguments. As we will see, this research strategy is also not without its difficulties.

There are at least three distinct branches of partisan research that bear on the question at hand. The Hibbsian, or pluralist, approach examines the direct and unconditional relationship between the ideological orientation of government and macroeconomic policy and outcomes. The social democratic corporatist approach argues that the incentives for, and the effectiveness of, partisan policies depend on the strength and centralization of labor-market institutions. Finally, the open-economy partisan approach examines the interaction between partisan behavior and the degree to which a nation's goods and capital markets are integrated with the international economy.

The Hibbsian Partisan Model

Since my current focus is on partisan differences in fiscal policy rather than on outcomes, I will, for the rest of this chapter, restrict my attention to the literature that examines the former. I will also focus exclusively on broadly cross-national empirical studies. The primary empirical implication of the partisan approach is that parties of the left should produce consistently higher levels of output and inflation, and lower levels of unemployment, than parties of the right, but many analysts have inferred that the pursuit of this goal will lead to systematic differences in fiscal *policies* as well. Specifically, left governments have been argued to be more aggressive in the taxation of capital and more reliant upon progressive income taxes; to be quicker to expand social welfare programs and other mechanisms that redistribute wealth (and to raise the revenues necessary to fund them); and to exhibit a greater enthusiasm for countercyclical demand management, which they are expected to implement in a particularly expansionary manner. The notion that left governments will be more willing to raise taxes than right governments stems from the assumption that their constituency will be net recipients of government services and, therefore, less resistant to the tax increases that fund them than the supporters of right-wing parties. There is considerable indeterminacy, however, with respect to the approach's bottom-line prediction about the relationship between total revenues and left governance. Will the left's expansionary impulse make it more likely to *cut* taxes than the right, or will the left's desire to expand the size of the government and fund redistributive programs make it more likely to *raise* taxes than the right? If the former dominates the latter, the left's pursuit of expansionary policies and generous welfare provisions is expected to lead to a propensity for deficit spending and, over time, greater public indebtedness.

For two decades, scholars have been attempting to establish an empirical relationship between the ideological orientation of government and various aspects of fiscal policy. These studies can be usefully divided into three groups based on their conceptualization of the dependent variable. There are studies that look for partisan differences in the propensity to raise taxes (especially taxes on capital), those that focus on spending behavior (especially spending related to "welfare effort"), and those that emphasize overall fiscal stance (typically conceived of as the propensity toward deficit spending or indebtedness).

Revenue Collection and the Taxation of Capital

In perhaps the first cross-national study of the effect of partisan politics on economic *policy,* Cameron (1978) argued that as the partisan composition of government changed over time, so too did the policies that government implemented (Hibbs 1977; Wildavsky 1974). Indeed, over time these changes could produce a redefinition of the boundaries between public and private, and such a redefinition, Cameron argued, was likely to be reflected in the share of the economy extracted by public authorities in the form of taxation. To evaluate this argument, Cameron conducted a cross-sectional test and found that government revenues were a larger share of GDP (gross domestic product) in countries where social democratic or labor parties were more influential. Since Cameron was explicitly attempting to analyze the long-term effects of cross-national differences in the propensity to elect parties connected to working-class groups, his decision to test his argument using cross-national differences in long-run averages in his variables of interest was appropriate. Unfortunately, the relatively small number of countries with arguably comparable data meant that the degrees of freedom for such tests were extremely limited and that, as a result, fully specified multivariate tests were not possible. Huber, Ragin, and Stephens (1993), however, used cross-sectional time-series data from OECD countries between 1956 and 1988 and found considerable support for Cameron's hypothesis. In both ordinary least squares (OLS) and generalized least squares (GLS) specifications, revenues as a share of GDP were consistently found to be positively related to left and Christian Democratic cabinet participation.

Since Cameron, most studies have sought to gauge the effects of left parties on the growth of governments by looking at increased welfare effort or other measures of spending. But before turning to those efforts, I will examine the few studies that have produced findings related to the link between parties and specific tax policies.

Garrett (1995, 1998) argued that left governments can be expected to be more aggressive in taxing capital than right governments; in addition, they are likely to place greater emphasis on potentially progressive income taxes than on highly regressive consumption taxes.[7] In his effort to test the thesis of the structural dependence of the state on capital,[8] Swank (1992) produced findings that are consistent with the latter hypothesis, but not the former. He found that left and center parties can be expected to increase income taxes as a share of national income, but he also found that, other things being equal, an increase in left or center party participation in cabinets can be expected to lead to a reduction in taxes on corporate profits. Indeed, Swank concluded that left-wing governments are likely to be "particularly sensitive to trends in new capital investment when formulating corporate tax policy" (47). Hallerberg and Basinger (1998) lend partial support to these findings. Contrary to their expectations, their cross-sectional examination of the wave of tax reforms in the late 1980s suggested that left-wing governments tended to make sharper cuts in taxes on capital than right-wing parties, but they found no partisan effects on cuts in personal income tax.

Government Spending or Welfare Effort

The empirical literature examining the relationship between partisanship and government spending is large and full of conflicting evidence. Stephens (1979) and Castles and McKinley (1979) were among the first to argue that the expansion of the welfare state is slowest where right-wing parties are dominant. Castles (1982) found bivariate correlations between partisan indicators and a number of categories of spending. Specifically, he found that social democratic control at the cabinet level was associated with more total public spending as well as more spending on government consumption, public education, and health. Social democratic control of the legislature appeared to be less important, having an effect only on spending on public health. In contrast, right party control at both the cabinet and parliamentary levels seemed to matter: both measures of right party control were associated with reductions in total spending, total welfare spending, and spending on transfers and subsidies, public education, and public health.

Other cross-sectional studies seem to confirm these initial results. Hicks and Swank (1984) found that transfer payments grew more quickly during the 1960s in countries where the frequency and extent of left control was greatest. Similarly, Swank (1988) found cross-sectional evidence that parties of the right spent less than parties of the center or left during the 1960s and that center parties were more likely to increase expenditures than parties of the right or left in the mid- to late 1970s. Comiskey (1993) found a relationship between a broad partisanship measure (which captured the participation of left, center, and Christian Democratic parties) and changes in both total nondefense spending and health and welfare spending between 1950 and 1973. In the decade following 1973, left governance was correlated with changes in spending.[9]

Evidence from time-series and cross-sectional time-series data tends to be mixed, however. Using annual data from 1950 to 1980, Rice (1986) ran individual time-series tests for twelve different European nations and found a significant relationship between any form of left governance and government spending in only five (Denmark, Ireland, Italy, Norway, and the United Kingdom). In perhaps the first cross-sectional times-series study in this literature, Pampel and Williamson (1988) used seven observations from 1950 to 1980 from each of nineteen countries in a pooled cross-section and found little evidence that social welfare spending was related to the partisan orientation of government. They estimated five equations, four using GLS and one using OLS regression, and found evidence of partisan effects only in the latter—and that was contrary to the Hibbsian expectation. An increase in left participation in government was associated with less social welfare spending, and an increase in right governance was associated with more social welfare spending (the reference group was "other" as defined in Castles 1982—a category composed of centrist parties).

Hicks and Swank (1992) used pooled cross-sectional time-series data to examine a number of hypotheses about the importance of partisanship—both inside and outside of government—but their failure to give a conditional interpretation to their partisan variables (which enter into multiple multiplicative interactions) in their "final" model makes their results difficult to interpret beyond the assertion that "party matters." In addition, Beck and Katz's reanalysis (1995) of Hicks and Swank's data calls many of these results into question. When panel-corrected standard errors are used, none of the partisan-government variables are significantly related to government welfare effort—but since they are also entered into interactions with measures of partisan opposition, this does not necessarily negate the partisan argument.[10]

Hicks and Misra (1993) reported an association between left and Christian Democratic governance and welfare efforts. Blais, Blake, and Dion (1993) used time-series, cross-sectional, and time-series cross-sectional data to evaluate the hypothesis that left governments spend more than governments of the right. Their individual-country time-series and individual-time-period cross-sectional tests failed to detect a general tendency toward partisan difference in spending, but given the lack of variance in the independent variable of interest in the former test and the small sample size of the latter test, these results are inconclusive. Indeed, their pooled cross-sectional test does lend support to the hypothesis that an increase in left governance leads to an increase in spending.[11] Consistent with this result, Huber, Ragin, and Stephens (1993), using both OLS and GLS, found consistent evidence of a relationship between Christian Democratic and left party control of cabinets and two separate measures of social security transfers (the *OECD* and *ILO* measures).

Roubini and Sachs (1989b) found cross-sectional evidence of a positive association between left governance and their estimate of the long-run government spending target in thirteen OECD countries. This result is supported by de Haan and Sturm's cross-sectional time-series analysis (1994b) of members of the European Community during the 1980s. In sharp contrast, Ross (1997) found no relationship between budget cuts and left governance in the 1970s; and, echoing results in Alesina and Perotti 1995 (see next subsection), she found that left governments were *more* aggressive than parties of the right in cutting spending during the 1980s.[12] One explanation for this is the "Nixon in China" metaphor—left governments were able to use close contacts with labor unions to exact bigger sacrifices without producing a backlash. Another (but not mutually exclusive) explanation is that this is evidence of Downsian "position jumping." Perhaps left governments stood to gain market-oriented voters by demonstrating their willingness to get tough on budgets. Iversen (1997) found no evidence of a partisan difference in total government spending, but he found important party differences in the form of spending used. Right governments are more likely to use government transfers, while left governments are more likely to expand government consumption. This pattern emerges, he argued, because transfer payments do not directly involve the state in the provision of services, and they can be designed to preserve earnings and status differences.

Budget Deficits and Public Debt

The ongoing process of European integration has led to a number of attempts to explain cross-national and intertemporal differences in fiscal postures, and some of the most prominent studies control for the effect of partisanship. Using Blanchard's index of "fiscal impulse" (1993) to classify the fiscal stances of nineteen governments during the period between 1960 and 1992, Alesina and Perotti (1995) produced results that call into question a simple relationship between partisanship and fiscal policy. Bivariate cross-tabulations suggest that left governments are more likely than right governments—but not as likely as center governments—to implement "very loose" fiscal policies. What is more,

left governments are more likely than parties of the right and center to implement "very tight fiscal policies"—a result that is echoed in Ross's study (1997)
of cuts in public expenditures during the 1970s and 1980s. Finally, Alesina and
Perotti found that left governments are slightly more likely than right governments and *much* more likely than center governments to implement "successful" adjustment policies. Together, Alesina and Perotti's findings suggest that
left governments are most likely to adopt very tight policies, right governments
are least likely to adopt very loose policies, and center governments are most
likely to have unsuccessful adjustments.[13]

Boix (2000) examined whether the relationship between partisanship and
government debt changes over time. He found that increases in left participation in government were associated with increased public debt as a share of
GDP during the 1973–82 period but not during the 1962–72 or 1983–93 period.[14]
Curiously, many countries maintained floating exchange rates amid mobile
capital during this period (between the final collapse of Bretton Woods and the
"hardening" of the EMS)—which, according to the Mundell-Fleming model,
should have restricted fiscal policy autonomy.[15]

Finally, however, there is considerable evidence that once one controls for the
structure of fiscal policy institutions, party orientation has no effect on either
public debt or budget deficits (Clark and Hallerberg 2000; Hahm, Kamlet, and
Mowery 1996; Hallerberg and von Hagen 1998). Hahm's study (1996) of the interaction between parliamentarism and political cohesion also produces little
support for the partisan hypothesis.

In sum, the evidence from existing studies regarding the Hibbsian relationship between fiscal policy and the ideological orientation of government is
mixed at best. There is some support for the notion that smaller shares of national income are extracted as revenues when right parties are influential, but
the evidence related to specific tax policies does not support the partisan
model. Contrary to the partisan hypothesis, center and left parties are *more* reluctant to tax capital than parties of the right, and there is conflicting evidence
about the relationship between partisanship and personal income taxes. The
picture is similar with respect to studies on spending. The early cross-sectional
work tends to confirm the hypothesis that parties of the left have a tendency to
spend more than parties of the right, but for both technical reasons (limited
degrees of freedom) and conceptual reasons (lack of evidence for party differences *within* countries), these results are a slender reed on which to rest the
partisan model. Evidence from recent time-series cross-sectional tests is problematic as well. First, these tests produce conflicting results. Some studies suggest that social democratic and Christian Democratic parties spend more,

some suggest that parties of the left spend less, and still others suggest that there is no relationship at all between partisanship and spending. In addition, many of these studies have been criticized on technical grounds (Beck and Katz 1995), and revisions have been either not forthcoming or inconclusive. Finally, recent evidence suggests that there is no relationship between partisanship and either budget deficits or public debt.

The Social Democratic Corporatist Model

Because of the close ties that often exist between parties of the left and labor unions, partisan arguments have often been interwoven with and qualified by arguments about the effect of the strength and centralization of labor unions. Often, these "social democratic corporatist" arguments are contrasted with the pure partisan, or pluralist, argument attributed to Hibbs, but most analysts view them as interrelated. Hibbs himself argued (1978) that strike activity decreased in interwar Europe where newly ascendant leftist parties used public spending to achieve levels of redistribution that had previously been obtainable only through private-sector battles. If this is true, cross-national differences in strike activity driven by differences in labor-market structures could be expected to lead to cross-national differences in spending. Cameron (1978) argued that strong and centralized labor unions lead to both leftist-dominated governments and higher levels of spending along with the collection of revenues to support it.

Lange and Garrett (1985) found that the effects of left governance and "encompassing" labor unions on macroeconomic performance depended crucially on their combination.[16] For example, when labor unions were encompassing, an increase in left governance led to increased growth and stability, but when labor unions were not strong and centralized, an increase in left governance led to stagflation. Hicks, Swank, and Ambuhl (1989) extended this logic to particular macroeconomic policy variables. They argued that the tripartite bargaining that undergirds coordinated wage bargains (also made possible by centralized, inclusive, neocorporatist union confederations) would be successful only when governments were willing to underwrite union cooperation with higher spending meant to increase the "social wage." This, they stated, would be most easily accomplished when left parties ruled. Thus, like macroeconomic outcomes, fiscal policy is the product of an interaction between partisanship and labor-market structures.[17] In contrast, Garrett's more recent discussion (1998, chap. 2) seems to imply that while left governance and labor-market encompassment may both be expected to influence policy, the influence of each is *not* affected by the value of the other. In the absence of compelling theoretical arguments in support of either of these positions, it is reasonable to treat this as an empirical question; unfortunately, straightforward tests for an interaction have not been published.

Hicks, Swank, and Ambuhl (1989) divided a sample of OECD countries into four subsamples according to their scores on two hypothesized modifying variables—the strength and centralization of labor and the existence of economic expansion (1957–73) or crisis (1973–82)—and then analyzed the relationship between partisanship and welfare state expansion. They concluded that the influence of left government on welfare state expansion is strongest in the context of strong, highly centralized unions and expansionary macroeconomic climates and weakest where unions are weak and the macroeconomy is in crisis. Hicks and Swank (1992) used factor analysis to construct a single measure for "left corporatism" out of a number of indicators of labor-market structure and left rule. They found a positive association between this indicator and government welfare effort, but it is not possible to determine whether the effects of the individual variables are linearly related to welfare effort.[18]

In earlier cross-sectional studies, Hicks and Swank (1984) found a positive linear relationship between "union collective action capacities" and welfare spending. In contrast, the Pampel and Williamson study (1988) discussed earlier found that the scope of union activity was associated (in a linear fashion) with more social welfare spending in only one of five cross-sectional time-series equations. Pampel and Williamson also found an association between increased union scope on the one hand and more spending on public assistance and less on family allowances on the other; but this association was unrelated to any of eight other types of welfare spending.

Roubini and Sachs (1989a) also presented evidence related to arguments about corporatist bargaining institutions. They found a positive association between wage indexation (which they argued is a proxy for demands for social insurance) and their estimate of government spending targets. Since wage indexation is typically used in countries lacking corporatist bargaining institutions, this link could be interpreted as indirect evidence that government spending is lower where corporatist institutions are present.

Boix 2000 is one of the few studies to examine the interaction between left governance and corporatist labor institutions as they affect policy. Boix found no evidence that the relationship between left governance and public debt is moderated (in a statistically significant sense) by the structure of labor-market institutions.[19] Simmons and Clark (1997) presented little evidence that labor-market encompassment modifies the relationship between left governance and two dozen indicators of policy. In addition, they found that linear relationships between either left governance or labor-market encompassment and these policy indicators are more the exception than the rule. To summarize, there is little evidence that labor-market institutions have the same sort of modifying effects on the relationship between parties and macroeconomic policy choice that they have been argued to have on the relationship between parties and macroeconomic performance. The evidence regarding a linear relationship between the structure of labor-market institutions and government spending is mixed. Some studies find a relationship between the organizational capacities of unions and increased government spending, but others do not.

The Open-Economy Model

From the beginning, scholars examining the effects of social democratic corporatism have pointed to the importance of international economic conditions. Cameron (1978) and Castles (1982) both emphasized the importance of increased exposure to trade in explaining the growth of the public sector—in fact, Cameron concluded that it was the single most important factor in determining growth in revenues as a share of GDP. The explanation offered for this empirical finding was that increased exposure to trade was accompanied by a relatively small domestic market and high levels of industrial concentration. These factors, in turn, were said to encourage high levels of unionization, strong labor confederations, and, as a result, the growth of left parties, which would expand the public sector for the reasons discussed earlier. Katzenstein (1985) argued that neocorporatist arrangements were created in part as a response to economic openness and that the interventionist policies associated in the partisan literature with left governments played a vital role in sheltering citizens from the risks associated with trade dependence. Largely on the basis of Katzenstein's insightful analysis of the small, open European economies, a consensus arose that trade posed no threat to interventionist macroeconomic policies (which were thought to be made possible in part by stringent controls on capital movements). Thus, "embedded liberalism" became the standard way for scholars to think about the relationship between state and society in all advanced industrialized countries in the "golden age" under the Bretton Woods institutions.[20]

The rapid increase in cross-border capital flows and the secular decline in legal barriers to capital movements that began in the mid-1970s (but only later became fashioned in the public consciousness as globalization) were widely thought to be a challenge to "embedded liberalism." With barriers to capital

movements greatly reduced, the common wisdom went, firms and other holders of liquid assets could credibly threaten to roam the world in search of the
highest expected return for their investment. This new dynamic of "footloose
capital" was thought by many observers to have two profound implications for
what had until that point been accepted as the "postwar Keynesian consensus."[21] First, because capital mobility resulted in increased international competition, it made the welfare state no longer affordable. Second, rapid capital
movements could quickly counteract any policy choices of governments and
thus rendered Keynesian demand management almost completely ineffective.

The "common wisdom" about the effects of globalization circulated far and
wide without much attempt, until recently, to subject it to empirical test. Rodrik (1997) found that governments had so far been able to respond to increased capital-market integration in a manner similar to the way earlier studies said they had responded to the integration of goods markets. Cusack (1997)
found little evidence that what he interprets as strong support for the partisan
model has diminished over the time period commonly associated with the increase in capital-market integration. Similarly, Hallerberg and Basinger (1998)
found no statistical evidence of a link between a country's reduction in capital
controls and capital-friendly tax reforms. Huber and Stephens's close examination (1998) of the experiences of four countries where social democrats had
been most successful in obtaining and protecting full employment and institu-
tionalizing the welfare state lends some support, however, for the notion that
capital mobility could be responsible for the decline of the "golden age" of the
welfare state. While confirming the finding of early studies that trade has contributed little to what some see as the recent problems of social democracy,
they argue that financial liberalization and deregulation have undermined important features of the model of macroeconomic policy that was the backbone
of the welfare state. In addition, changes in the international and domestic
economies have weakened centralized bargaining.

In a pioneering effort, Garrett (1995) found that, contrary to the common
wisdom about the homogenizing effects of globalization, left government and
encompassing unions appear to have *more* effect on policy, not less, after
capital-market liberalization. These results were largely replicated in his book-
length treatment of the subject (1998). The implications of these results are
sufficiently provocative to warrant a detailed reanalysis, which will be under-
taken in the next section of this chapter.

What is interesting about these studies is that they attempt to gauge the effects of globalization on the politics of macroeconomic policy choice by examining the ways in which integration affects *partisan* control of the economy,

despite the fact that, as indicated by the extensive literature we have reviewed, there is little evidence that partisan effects are present before the onset of globalization. Garrett (1998) is quite clear that there is little evidence of partisan differences in macroeconomic policy indicators prior to the onset of global integration. Simmons and Clark (1997) found that there is little evidence of partisan differences in policy behavior after global integration as well. In contrast, Cusack (1997) claims to find support for the partisan model before, during, and after global integration, but his evidence actually suggests that changes in spending conform much more closely to the Downsian than the Hibbsian model. To understand why, it is necessary to consider his model in some detail.

For our purposes, Cusack's model of government spending decisions can be written as

$$G = \alpha + \gamma_1 P_1 + \gamma_2 (P_1 - E) + \varepsilon, \tag{1}$$

where G is the change in spending, P_1 is the government position on a left-to-right scale, E is the electorate's position on the left-to-right scale, and ε is the error term. If, as the partisan argument suggests, right governments prefer less spending than left governments, γ_1 will be less than zero. Cusack argues that governments may need to make trade-offs between the pursuit of their preferred policies and winning votes from an electorate that may have different preferences. To the extent that this is true, it will dampen the effects of the government's preferences on its spending behavior, causing it to set spending closer to the preferences of the electorate than it otherwise would. If this is the case, γ_2 will be greater than zero; and, as Cusack points out, when politicians are purely electoralist, $\gamma_1 = -\gamma_2$. Under such conditions, the ideology of the party in power has no net effect on its spending behavior.[22] Cusack's empirical test is a straightforward estimate of equation (1) after controlling for other influences on spending. He finds that in general, and in three successive time periods between 1955 and 1989, $\gamma_1 < 0$ and $\gamma_2 > 0$. Furthermore, these two parameters are consistently very close to each other in absolute value. While a Wald test would provide a rigorous test of the hypothesis that these coefficients have the same absolute value, an eyeballing of Cusack's results (table 6) is sufficient to suggest that there is little chance of rejecting such a hypothesis. The two estimates are consistently very close in absolute value—in no case is the gap between their absolute values larger than the smaller of their individual standard errors. Thus, if the ideological position of the government affects spending, it is probably only in the counterfactual sense captured by γ_1. If governments did not have to respond to the policy preferences of the electorate, right-wing parties would spend less than left-wing parties. In fact, however, Cusack's evidence shows that parties *are* responsive to the preferences of the electorate, so much so that there is no evidence of partisan differences in behavior. This is an exhilarating finding in that it simultaneously gives us a rare glimpse into the usually unobservable *preferences* of policymakers (γ_1) as well as strong evidence that their *actions* do not reflect those preferences in a straightforward way. All of this adds up to strong support for a subtle version of the Downsian hypothesis—one that says that while parties may differ in the preferences they hold over policy outcomes, the structural environment is such that they behave *as if* they agreed over policy issues.

In an important development in the literature on partisanship and macroeconomic policy, Oatley (1999) examined the effects of increased capital mobility on partisan differences in monetary and fiscal policy. Using the Mundell-Fleming model that I employed in chapter 2, Oatley argued that increased capital mobility induces a partisan convergence in fiscal policies only when the exchange rate is allowed to fluctuate. Clark, Hallerberg, and Kim (2000) raised several questions about the inferences drawn from Oatley's results, and Clark and Hallerberg's test (2000) of the same argument produced contradictory evidence.

In sum, existing research that attempts to analyze the effect of increased capital mobility on partisan differences in behavior has found little evidence that partisan differences exist before or after the onset of global integration. It is not surprising, therefore, that attempts to gauge the effects of capital mobility on

TABLE 6. **Relationship between Government Spending and Government Center of Gravity (γ_1) and the Difference between Government and the Electorate's Center of Gravity (γ_2)**

	Full Sample		Subsample	
	γ_1	γ_2	γ_1	γ_2
Entire period	−.65	.70	−.62	.60
	(.14)	(.17)	(.16)	(.17)
1955/1961–73	−.79	.89	−.72	.78
	(.15)	(.19)	(.16)	(.19)
1974–79	−.67	.71	−.60	.62
	(.15)	(.19)	(.16)	(.19)
1980–89	−.69	.74	−.64	.56
	(.15)	(.19)	(.16)	(.19)

Source: Cusack 1997.

Note: Full sample includes Australia, but excludes all observations prior to 1961. Numbers in parentheses are standard errors, deduced from the *t*-scores reported by Cusack (1997). All parameters are significantly different from zero at the .01 level or better.

the politics of macroeconomic policy-making within countries have produced conflicting results.

In the next section of this chapter, I will reexamine the evidence in an exemplary study utilizing the partisan approach and show that there is little evidence of partisan differences in monetary and fiscal policies. I will then extend the existing work on partisan differences to see if such differences are observable once we adopt a more sophisticated view of the context in which policy-making takes place.

The Effect of Capital Mobility: A Reappraisal

Geoffrey Garrett's *Partisan Politics in the Global Economy* (1998) is the most systematic examination of the effect of increased capital mobility on the politics of macroeconomic policy choice in OECD economies. In this study, and in a number of influential journal articles, Garrett argues that the literature on social democratic corporatism predicts partisan and institutional differences in macroeconomic policy. Left governments and governments confronting strong, centrally organized labor unions are more likely than right governments to use the instruments of the state to encourage growth and employment and redistribute income to low-income groups. Specifically, "increasing the power of the left and organized labor should be associated with higher public spending, bigger deficits, higher taxes on capital, and lower interest rates" (1995, 671).

Garrett tests competing claims about the effects of internationalization on the politics of macroeconomic policy choice. On the one hand, increased internationalization leads to heightened competition, which, in turn, increases the costs of interventionist policies. Thus, as internationalization proceeds, left governments and governments confronting strong, centralized unions will be less likely to pursue the interventionist policies traditionally associated with them. The alternative view is that internationalization increases market dislocations, creating an increased demand for interventionist policies—which left governments and governments confronting strong, centralized labor unions are happy to supply.[23] Consequently, left governments are *more*, not *less*, likely to provide interventionist policies as internationalization proceeds (Garrett 1995, 672).[24]

Garrett attempts to distinguish between these arguments using pooled cross-sectional time-series data covering fourteen OECD countries from the mid-1960s until the end of the 1980s. There are small differences in data and model specification between Garrett 1995 and Garrett 1998, but these differences are not important for the current discussion.[25] Since the 1998 work uses a wider array of policy indicators, I will use it as the basis for my reevaluation.[26] The consequences of internationalization for the hypothesized policy effects of left-labor power are estimated by interacting an indicator that combines left governance and labor-union encompassment with measures of capital mobility and trade openness. Specifically,

$$Pol_{it} = + b_1 Llp_{it} + b_2 Trade_{it} + b_3 Cm_{it} + b_4 (Llp \cdot Trade_{it}) + b_5 (Llp \cdot Cm_{it})$$

$$+ b_6 Pol_{it-1} + \Sigma(b_j Period_{it}) + \Sigma(b_k Country_{it}) + \Sigma(b_l X_{lit}) + \varepsilon_{it}, \quad (2)$$

where *Pol* is the policy indicator in question, *Cm* is a measure of capital mobility based on the number of government restrictions on cross-border capital movements, *Trade* is exports plus imports over GDP, and *Left-labor power* (*Llp*) is an index constructed by adding standardized scores for the partisan composition of government and labor-market encompassment. *Period* and *Country* are vectors of four period variables and fourteen country dummy variables, respectively, intended to capture temporal and country-fixed effects; and *X* is a vector of control variables that are presumed to influence fiscal and monetary policy.[27]

Following Garrett, I will estimate equation (2) using three sets of policy variables—those related to government spending, revenues, and overall macroeconomic policy position. There are five indicators related to government spending (total spending, spending on income transfers, civilian government consumption, subsidies to industry, and capital spending); five more related to government revenues and tax collection (total revenue, and revenues derived from personal income tax, consumption taxes, corporate taxes, and employer contributions to social security); and one indicator of overall fiscal policy stance (budget deficits).

It is well known that time-series cross-sectional data such as those used in this book may violate important assumptions of the standard ordinary least squares (OLS) regression model. Like Garrett, I will take the basic approach of following the advice of Beck and Katz (1995, 1996). Panel-corrected standard errors, country dummy variables, and lagged dependent variables are used to address the likely presence of contemporaneous correlation, panel-wise heteroskedasticity, and first-order serial correlation. Since it is possible, however, that substantial autocorrelation may exist despite the inclusion of a lagged dependent, I use the Durbin-Watson *m*-test to evaluate whether serial correlation is present in each model reported.[28] The presence of positive serial correlation raises concerns about valid statistical inference because, though parameter estimates are unbiased in its presence, the standard errors produced by OLS will be biased downward. As a result, the confidence interval around my estimate may be smaller than it should be, and I may incorrectly reject a null hypothesis that in fact should not be rejected (Pindyck and Rubinfeld 1991, 138). The primary danger to valid inference, therefore, comes when the coefficient has the hypothesized sign and is statistically significant. Under these conditions, it is possible to accept a hypothesized relation between variables that would be rejected in light of the true confidence interval, were it available. In contrast, the loss of efficiency created by serially correlated errors is unlikely to lead me to make inferential errors when my estimates lead me to embrace the null hypothesis.

Since the inferences drawn from data in chapters 4 and 6 that elections have a nonzero causal effect on macroeconomic policy and outcomes depend crucially on the size of the confidence intervals placed around my estimates, I will treat the presence of autocorrelation as cause for serious concern. When the evidence of serial correlation is sufficiently strong to raise questions about the inferences I draw from the data, I compare the results produced by OLS with those produced by Prais-Winsten regression—a technique that transforms the data so that serially correlated errors are replaced with errors that satisfy the "classical" assumptions of regression (Greene 1990; Kmenta 1986). In contrast, since the overwhelming tendency in chapters 3 and 5 is toward null findings, the presence of serial correlation poses a less serious threat to valid inference. Consequently, while I will report the results of Durbin-Watson statistics in order to alert readers when serial correlation is present, I will not use the Prais-Winsten transformation in chapters 3 and 5. This produces the additional benefit of easy comparison with Garrett 1998. Since valid inference from nonstationary time series is problematic, it is also important to establish that the time series being used as dependent variables do not suffer from a unit root. Information germane to this question is already present in any estimation of a model with a lagged dependent variable. Since the coefficient on the lagged dependent variable estimates the first-order dynamics of the dependent variable when the other variables in the model are held constant, we can be confident that a unit root is not present when this coefficient is several standard deviations less than one.[29]

In general, the partisan argument predicts that left governments will pursue more-expansionary macroeconomic policies and favor the aggressive expansion of the welfare state. Thus, it implies a positive association between left control of government and total government spending. Furthermore, while left governments may favor some forms of spending over others (Iversen 1997), the positive relationship between left control and spending is likely to show up in each of the spending categories examined here. As mentioned, the partisan model's implications for total revenues are not as straightforward as they are for spending, but most partisan studies view total revenues as a reflection of the government's involvement in the economy and so expect a positive association between left control and total revenues. Since the specific form of tax policy can have large distributional implications, the partisan approach predicts that left governments will have a greater propensity to rely on forms of taxation capable of redistributing wealth downward (such as personal income taxes and taxes on capital). In contrast, parties of the right are assumed to have a greater enthusiasm for flat taxes, such as those on consumption. Finally, the partisan approach predicts that governments of the left will be more likely to use deficit financing than parties of the right. Table 7 summarizes the partisan approach's predictions about the relationship between left governance and the eleven policy indicators examined here.

Spending

Table 8 reports the regressions related to five indicators of government spending. The first of each set of equations reproduces Garrett's results, and the second of each set is identical to the first except for the construction of the

TABLE 7.   **Predictions of the Partisan Model**

Indicator	Predicted Relationship with *Left-labor power*
Total spending	+
Spending on	
Income transfers	+
Civilian government consumption	+
Subsidies to industry	+
Capital expenditures	+
Total revenues	+
Revenues from	
Personal income tax	+
Consumption taxes	−
Corporate income taxes	+
Employer contributions to social security	+
Macroeconomic policy	
Budget deficits	+
Interest rates	−

TABLE 8. The Estimated Effect of *Left-labor power* on Government Spending Conditioned upon the Degree of Trade and Capital-Market Openness

	Total Spending (1)		Income Transfers (2)		Civilian Government Consumption (3)		Subsidies to Industry (4)		Capital Spending (5)	
	Cm = Cmg (a)	Cm = Cml (b)	Cm = Cmg (a)	Cm = Cml (b)	Cm = Cmg (a)	Cm = Cml (b)	Cm = Cmg (a)	Cm = Cml (b)	Cm = Cmg (a)	Cm = Cml (b)
Left-labor power (Llp)	0.082	−0.829***	0.068	−0.197**	0.134*	−0.168*	−0.096**	−0.156**	0.081	0.038
	(0.192)	(0.252)	(0.089)	(0.106)	(0.097)	(0.120)	(0.051)	(0.070)	(0.129)	(0.155)
Trade	−0.043*	−0.043*	−0.008	−0.008	−0.016*	−0.016*	−0.008	−0.008	−0.016	−0.016
	(0.024)	(0.024)	(0.011)	(0.011)	(0.009)	(0.009)	(0.007)	(0.007)	(0.012)	(0.012)
Capital mobility (Cm)	−0.885***	−0.885***	−0.193	−0.193	−0.382**	−0.382**	−0.067	−0.067	−0.044	−0.044
	(0.298)	(0.298)	(0.151)	(0.151)	(0.155)	(0.155)	(0.083)	(0.083)	(0.181)	(0.181)
Trade · Llp	0.008*	0.008*	0.001	0.001	0.001	0.001	0.003***	0.003***	0.000	0.000
	(0.004)	(0.004)	(0.002)	(0.002)	(0.001)	(0.001)	(0.001)	(0.001)	(0.002)	(0.002)
Cm · Llp	0.228***	0.228***	0.066***	0.066***	0.075***	0.075***	0.015	0.015	0.011	0.011
	(0.058)	(0.058)	(0.028)	(0.028)	(0.028)	(0.028)	(0.016)	(0.016)	(0.036)	(0.036)
Lagged dependent variable	0.806***	0.806***	0.859***	0.859***	0.860***	0.860***	0.785***	0.785***	0.709***	0.709***
	(0.025)	(0.025)	(0.030)	(0.030)	(0.026)	(0.026)	(0.040)	(0.040)	(0.052)	(0.052)

GDP growth	−0.399***	−0.399***	−0.168***	−0.168***	−0.138***	−0.138***	−0.014*	−0.014*	−0.052***	−0.052***
	(0.029)	(0.029)	(0.016)	(0.016)	(0.012)	(0.012)	(0.007)	(0.007)	(0.016)	(0.016)
Unemployment	0.086*	0.086*	0.068***	0.068***	0.008	0.008	−0.022*	−0.022*	−0.038*	−0.038*
	(0.045)	(0.045)	(0.019)	(0.019)	(0.019)	(0.019)	(0.012)	(0.012)	(0.022)	(0.022)
Old-age population	0.241**	0.241**	0.134**	0.134**	0.006	0.006	−0.017	−0.017	−0.064	−0.064
	(0.106)	(0.106)	(0.055)	(0.055)	(0.056)	(0.056)	(0.025)	(0.025)	(0.055)	(0.055)
Constant	5.291***	8.833**	−0.141	0.630	1.972***	3.502***	0.642*	0.909**	1.873**	2.047**
	(1.651)	(1.744)	(0.858)	(0.907)	(0.751)	(0.773)	(0.376)	(0.378)	(0.885)	(0.861)
F_{DW}	0.60	0.60	1.31	1.31	0.65	0.65	0.65	0.65	7.49	7.49
Prob. > F	0.661	0.661	0.267	0.267	0.629	0.629	0.629	0.629	0.112	0.112
Observations	350	350	350	350	350	350	350	350	350	350
Number of countries	14	14	14	14	14	14	14	14	14	14

Note: Columns 1a–5a use Garrett's coding for the capital-mobility measure; columns 1b–5b use transformed capital-mobility measure.

Panel-corrected standard errors are in parentheses.

The term F_{DW} is the test statistic for Durbin-Watson's m.

*p < .10, **p < .05, ***p < .01, one-tailed test for variables involving Llp, two-tailed otherwise.

capital-mobility measure. Garrett (1995, 1998) uses a standard measure of capital mobility (*Cmg* in table 8) based on the IMF's record of the capital controls in place in a given country during a given year. His indicator is the number of controls in place (out of a set of four controls) multiplied by -1, so that a higher score indicates greater capital mobility (a country employing none of the controls would be scored zero, indicating more capital mobility, while a country employing all four of the controls would be scored -4, indicating less capital mobility). This is a straightforward procedure and does no damage to the validity of any of the estimates in the model. Given the conditional nature of regression coefficients for variables involved in a multiplicative interaction model (Friedrich 1982; Jaccard, Turrisi, and Wan 1990), however, such a setup can and does create some interpretation problems. Since Garrett's indicator of capital mobility equals zero when capital is most mobile, the coefficient for *Left-labor power* describes the relationship between left-labor power and macroeconomic policy when the country is sheltered from trade (*Trade* $= 0$) and capital is highly mobile (*Cmg* $= 0$). Since we want to examine the effects of increasing capital mobility, this is not an intuitively appealing baseline case; indeed, Garrett makes several inferential errors that can probably be traced to this coding decision.

Consequently, for all the new analysis in this book, I have transformed the same capital-mobility measure by a simple additive transformation so that *Cml* (capital-market liberalization) is zero when all four capital controls are in place and 4 when all four have been removed. It should be emphasized that this rescaling does not change the substantive results at all (note that the coefficients and standard errors for all of the variables except *Cm* are the same) but allows us to now interpret the *Left-labor power* coefficients as the estimated causal effect of an increase in left-labor power on macroeconomic policy where goods markets and capital markets are fully closed.[30] Again, it should be stressed that results in column a and column b are mathematically equivalent, as long as one remembers that the *Left-labor power* coefficients are estimating the effects of left-labor power on government spending under two very different situations. In column a, the coefficient for *Left-labor power* estimates the effect of a one-unit rise in *Left-labor power* when trade is closed and capital markets are open, but in column b the coefficient for *Left-labor power* estimates the effect of a rise in *Left-labor power* when both trade and capital markets are closed.

Garrett suggests that his results lead to two broad conclusions. First, the standard argument that capital mobility has produced a fiscal "race to the bottom" either is a gross simplification of a much more complex reality or is just plain wrong. Second, the combination of left governance and encompassing labor unions continues to produce distinctive policies—specifically, higher levels of spending—in the post-capital-mobility world. In fact, he argues, there may be an increased incentive for left governments to engage in fiscal activism. If the first claim is correct, one would expect that an increase in capital mobility would result in either no change or an *increase* in coefficients on variables that are understood to be proxies for fiscal activism. If the second claim is correct, one would expect that an increase in *Left-labor power* would be associated with the predicted change in macroeconomic policy variables (see table 7); and the stronger claim that capital mobility creates incentives for increased fiscal activism predicts that the conditional coefficients for the *Left-labor power* variable would increase in magnitude when capital mobility is high.

The multiplicative interaction effect model that Garrett uses sheds some light on these theoretical expectations. As already mentioned, the coefficient on the *Left-labor power* variable in column a of table 8 estimates the causal effect of an increase in this variable on fiscal activism when trade is closed *and capital is fully mobile.* Thus, if Garrett's argument that capital mobility does not constrain—and may even reinforce—the effect of *Left-labor power* on fiscal activism is correct, we would expect this variable to be positive and statistically significant. Garrett's results (which I replicate in columns 1a–5a) show that this is not the case: in only one of these equations (civilian government consumption) is there any evidence that left-labor power encourages higher levels of spending.[31] Perhaps the extreme case of complete market opening is too strong a test of the argument that "traditional partisan politics . . . matter" (Garrett 1998, 82). When the capital-mobility variable is recoded, as I have recommended, so that a zero value represents the case of a closed capital market, the *Left-labor power* variable estimates the causal effect of an increase in this variable when both capital and goods markets are closed. Columns 1b–5b in table 8 show that "traditional partisan politics" did not matter in the expected fashion in the closed-economy case, either. There is some evidence of a link between *Left-labor power* and government spending when capital markets are closed, but the nature of the relationship is contrary to expectation. An increase in *Left-labor power* under these conditions is associated with a *decrease* in total spending, income transfers, and subsidies to industry (columns 1b, 2b, and 4b).

Of course, the above inferences hold only when *Trade* equals zero, and such complete autarky is not present in any of the countries in the sample during the observed time period. Consequently, I will calculate conditional coefficients and standard errors to determine if and when there is a statistically significant relationship between *Left-labor power* and government spending over observed values of the modifying variables.

The conditional coefficients are graphed in figure 5. Each line in these graphs plots the conditional coefficients for *Left-labor power* calculated from the regression results in columns 1a–5a in table 8 for various values of the two modifying variables—capital mobility and trade openness. The vertical axis on these graphs is the estimated causal effect of a one-unit increase in *Left-labor power*. Hence, points on lines above (below) zero on the vertical axis indicate that the estimated causal effect of an increase in *Left-labor power* is positive (negative). Points marked with an asterisk indicate that the associated conditional coefficient is statistically significant at the .10 level using a one-tailed test. Since trade openness is on the horizontal axis, movement to the right along this axis is an indication of the expected effect of an increase in trade openness on the size of the estimated causal effect of an increase in *Left-labor power*. The degree of capital-market liberalization is indicated by the thickness of the lines. The darkest line indicates that all capital controls have been removed, the medium-dark line indicates that one capital control is in place, and the lightest line indicates that two capital controls are in place.[32]

According to table 7, an increase in *Left-labor power* is expected to lead to an increase in overall government spending as well as in each of the spending categories examined. Positive and significant *Left-labor power* coefficients would support this prediction. If the convergence view of globalization related to trade is correct, we would expect these positive coefficients to converge toward zero as trade openness increases (the plots of these coefficients would slope downward). If, as some have argued (Katzenstein 1985; Cameron 1978), trade openness encourages social democratic activism because of the need to compensate those who are put at risk by trade, the positive *Left-labor power* coefficients should move away from zero as trade openness increases (the plots of these coefficients should slope upward). If the partisan argument is correct and the convergence view of globalization related to capital mobility is correct, we would expect darker lines to be below lighter lines. If Garrett's argument that capital mobility does not lead to convergence and may in fact encourage increased partisan difference in policy is correct, we would expect the lines in figures 6.1a and b to be very near each other or for darker lines to be above lower lines.

Figure 5 indicates considerable support for Garrett's claim that the convergence view of globalization is incorrect, but it also raises questions about the partisan basis of fiscal policy. Note first that there is evidence of a link between increases in *Left-labor power* and increased spending in relatively closed

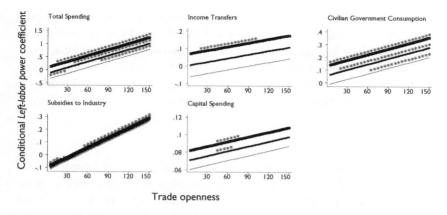

Fig. 5.   The estimated effect of *Left-labor power* on government spending at various lev-els of trade and capital-market openness. Darker lines denote increased capital-market liberalization. (*Note:* * indicates coefficient is significant at $p < .10$, one-tailed.)

economies (i.e., in the presence of two capital controls, denoted by the thinnest line) in three out of five tests. An increase in *Left-labor power* is expected to lead to increased total spending, civilian government consumption, and subsidies to industry when two capital controls are in place and when trade is relatively open. In contrast, there is no evidence of a link between *Left-labor power* and income transfers or capital spending when the capital account is relatively closed. Also note that when two capital controls are in place and trade is rela-tively closed, an increase in *Left-labor power* is associated with a *drop* in total spending—though the magnitude of this decline is modest.

In contrast to the expectations of the convergence hypothesis, what evidence there is for a link between *Left-labor power* and increased spending before cap-ital-market liberalization persists after the removal of capital controls. Note that the plots for the *Left-labor power* coefficients conditioned on the removal of all capital controls (the darkest lines) are further away from zero than the lighter lines are in the total spending, civilian government consumption, and subsidies to industry panels. In fact, when evaluated near the mean of the trade openness variable, the estimated causal effect of an increase in *Left-labor power* on total spending or civilian government consumption is estimated to be about twice as large when capital controls have been removed as it is when two capital controls are in place. This is more consistent with the compensatory hypothesis than the convergence hypothesis. The evidence for the compensatory hypothesis is even more dramatic when we examine income transfers and capital spending. In these cases, there is evidence of a positive association between *Left-labor power* and increased spending only when the capital market is relatively open. Across the board, there is evidence that, if anything, increased trade openness reinforces the positive association between *Left-labor power* and government spending.

Revenues

But are patterns in government revenue collection tied to *Left-labor power?* As in table 8, the *Left-labor power* coefficients in columns 1b–5b of table 9 are estimates of the causal effect of an increase in *Left-labor power* when trade and capital markets are both closed. There is evidence of the hypothesized association only between *Left-labor power* and a reliance on personal income tax under these circumstances. The coefficients in columns 1a–5a are estimates of the causal effect of an increase in *Left-labor power* when trade markets are closed but capital markets are fully open. There is evidence of the hypothesized link between *Left-labor power* and both total revenues and reliance on personal income taxes under these circumstances.

Thus, there is very little evidence of a link between fiscal policy and *Left-labor power* when trade markets are closed. But before rejecting the social democratic corporatist version of the partisan argument as it relates to revenues, it would be wise to examine the estimated causal effect of *Left-labor power* over historically relevant values of trade openness. These are plotted in figure 6. The evidence in support of the social democratic corporatist version of the partisan argument is mixed. First, there is evidence in support of the hypothesized link between fiscal policy and *Left-labor power* in the panels based on total revenues, personal income taxes, and employer social security contributions, but only under fairly specific conditions. The first two plots, for example, indicate that increased *Left-labor power* is expected to lead to an increase in revenues under all three levels of capital-market liberalization, but only when trade openness is relatively modest. These results would indicate that the convergence view of trade liberalization is accurate but that the convergence view of capital-market liberation is not accurate. Finally, there is no evidence of a link between *Left-labor power* and reliance on either consumption taxes or corporate income taxes at any level of trade or capital-market openness, and the hypothesized negative relationship between *Left-labor power* and reliance on employer contributions to social security is evidenced only when capital markets are relatively closed and trade openness is moderate.

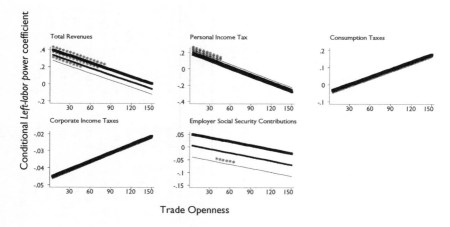

Fig. 6. The estimated effect of *Left-labor power* on government revenues at various levels of trade and capital-market openness. Darker lines denote increased capital-market liberalization. (*Note:* * indicates coefficient is significant at $p < .10$, one-tailed.)

Macroeconomic Policy

The above results suggest that there are many findings related to taxation and revenue collection that must be considered anomalies from the perspective of the open-economy social democratic model in either its convergence or its compensatory form. It is possible, however, that such tests are putting too fine a point on the social democratic corporatist argument. Perhaps there are national differences that lead left governments to find different ways to accomplish their expansionary goals in different times and places that are not being captured in the model used here (Garrett and Lange 1991; Boix 1998). If, however, these differences in the means used to effect policy are not manifested in the overall macroeconomic policy stance the government takes, then one might conclude that the social democratic corporatist model is, at the end of the day, not a model of the politics of macroeconomic policy. Many of its proponents believe that it is and, therefore, expect it to be related to overall fiscal and monetary policy indicators such as budget deficits and interest rates. Table 10 reports the OLS results for tests identical to Garrett's for budget deficits and interest rates. The model for budget deficits is identical to the other fiscal policy tests above except for the change in the dependent variable and the lagged dependent variable.

TABLE 9. The Estimated Effect of *Left-labor power* on Government Revenues Conditioned upon the Degree of Trade and Capital-Market Openness

	Total Revenues (1)		Personal Income Tax (2)		Consumption Taxes (3)		Corporate Income Taxes (4)		Employer Social Security Contributions (5)	
	Cm = Cmg (a)	Cm = Cml (b)	Cm = Cmg (a)	Cm = Cml (b)	Cm = Cmg (a)	Cm = Cml (b)	Cm = Cmg (a)	Cm = Cml (b)	Cm = Cmg (a)	Cm = Cml (b)
Left-labor power (Llp)	0.410**	0.164	0.199**	0.297**	-0.039	-0.075	-0.046	-0.049	0.053	-0.127*
	(0.182)	(0.236)	(0.097)	(0.146)	(0.084)	(0.097)	(0.076)	(0.098)	(0.072)	(0.097)
Trade	0.028	0.028	0.025*	0.025*	-0.015*	-0.015*	-0.004	-0.004	0.012	0.012
	(0.021)	(0.021)	(0.013)	(0.013)	(0.009)	(0.009)	(0.009)	(0.009)	(0.009)	(0.009)
Capital mobility (Cm)	-0.180	-0.180	-0.126	-0.126	-0.077	-0.077	-0.040	-0.040	-0.251*	-0.251*
	(0.295)	(0.295)	(0.177)	(0.177)	(0.123)	(0.123)	(0.138)	(0.138)	(0.144)	(0.144)
Trade · Llp	-0.003	-0.003	-0.003*	-0.003*	0.001	0.001	0.000	0.000	-0.001	-0.001
	(0.003)	(0.003)	(0.002)	(0.002)	(0.001)	(0.001)	(0.001)	(0.001)	(0.001)	(0.001)
Cm · Llp	-0.061	0.061	0.024	-0.024	-0.009	0.009	-0.001	0.001	-0.045*	0.045*
	(0.058)	(0.058)	(0.037)	(0.037)	(0.025)	(0.025)	(0.023)	(0.023)	(0.029)	(0.029)
Lagged dependent variable	0.784***	0.784***	0.878***	0.878***	0.723***	0.723***	0.841***	0.841***	0.875***	0.875***
	(0.035)	(0.035)	(0.031)	(0.031)	(0.047)	(0.047)	(0.060)	(0.060)	(0.054)	(0.054)

GDP growth	−0.125***	−0.125***	−0.066***	−0.066***	0.019	0.019	0.015	0.015	−0.029	−0.029
	(0.031)	(0.031)	(0.018)	(0.018)	(0.013)	(0.013)	(0.013)	(0.013)	(0.019)	(0.019)
Unemployment	−0.080*	−0.080*	−0.100***	−0.100***	0.026	0.026	−0.015	−0.015	−0.026	−0.026
	(0.044)	(0.044)	(0.026)	(0.026)	(0.018)	(0.018)	(0.014)	(0.014)	(0.027)	(0.027)
Old-age population	0.280**	0.280**	0.073	0.073	0.050	0.050	0.008	0.008	0.095	0.095
	(0.114)	(0.144)	(0.066)	(0.066)	(0.050)	(0.050)	(0.035)	(0.035)	(0.074)	(0.074)
Constant	3.150	3.869**	0.699	0.195	0.826	1.133	0.746	0.586	−0.699	0.306
	(1.720)	(1.658)	(0.894)	(0.928)	(0.804)	(0.735)	(0.573)	(0.583)	(1.041)	(0.892)
F_{DW}	0.46	0.46	1.47	1.47	17.88	17.88	0.30	0.30	3.92	3.92
Prob. > F	0.77	0.77	0.21	0.21	0.00	0.00	0.87	0.87	0.00	0.00
Observations	350	350	350	350	350	350	350	350	350	350
Number of countries	14	14	14	14	14	14	14	14	14	14

Note: Columns 1a–5a use Garrett's coding for the capital-mobility measure; columns 1b–5b use transformed capital-mobility measure.

Panel-corrected standard errors are in parentheses.

The term F_{DW} is the test statistic for Durbin-Watson's m.

$*p < .10$, $**p < .05$, $***p < .01$, one-tailed test for variables involving LIp, two-tailed otherwise.

Following Garrett, the interest-rate test includes additional control variables that are expected to influence monetary policy. As before, I present a test identical to Garrett's and then one with the recoding of the capital-market liberalization variable I have recommended. Recall that the social democratic corporatist

TABLE 10.   The Estimated Effect of *Left-labor power* on Macroeconomic Policy Conditioned upon the Degree of Trade and Capital-Market Openness

	Budget Deficits (1)		Interest Rates (2)	
	$Cm = Cmg$ (a)	$Cm = Cml$ (b)	$Cm = Cmg$ (a)	$Cm = Cml$ (b)
Left-labor power (Llp)	−0.361*	−1.162***	0.475***	0.242*
	(0.241)	(0.318)	(0.143)	(0.171)
Trade	−0.072**	−0.072**	0.014	0.014
	(0.029)	(0.029)	(0.016)	(0.016)
Capital mobility (Cm)	−0.834**	−0.834**	−0.529**	−0.529**
	(0.391)	(0.391)	(0.240)	(0.240)
Trade · Llp	0.012***	0.012***	−0.005*	−0.005*
	(0.004)	(0.004)	(0.002)	(0.002)
Cm · Llp	0.200***	0.200***	0.058	0.058
	(0.072)	(0.072)	(0.046)	(0.046)
Lagged dependent variable	0.739***	0.739***	0.610***	0.610***
	(0.043)	(0.043)	(0.036)	(0.036)
GDP growth	−0.264***	−0.264***	0.067**	0.067**
	(0.041)	(0.041)	(0.030)	(0.030)
Unemployment	0.200***	0.200***	−0.130***	−0.130**
	(0.054)	(0.054)	(0.041)	(0.041)
Old-age population	0.041	0.041		
	(0.149)	(0.149)		
Inflation			0.205***	0.205***
			(0.022)	(0.022)
USIR			0.485***	0.485***
			(0.090)	(0.090)
Cbi			6.462***	6.462***
			(2.226)	(2.226)
Constant	2.212	5.548**	−5.764***	−3.646***
	(2.280)	(2.344)	(1.932)	(1.974)
F_{DW}	1.54	1.54	1.23	1.23
Prob. $> F$	0.192	0.192	0.301	0.301
Observations	350	350	300	300
Number of countries	14	14	12	12

Note: Columns 1a–5a use Garrett's coding for the capital-mobility measure; columns 1b–5b use transformed capital-mobility measure.

Panel-corrected standard errors are in parentheses.

The term F_{DW} is the test statistic for Durbin-Watson's m.

*$p < .10$, **$p < .05$, ***$p < .01$, one-tailed test for variables involving *Llp*, two-tailed otherwise.

model predicts that budget deficits should increase and interest rates should decrease with increases in *Left-labor power*. The coefficients for *Left-labor power* indicate that where trade markets are closed, the opposite is more likely to be the case. Both when capital markets are fully open (columns 1a–2a) and when they are fully closed (columns 1b–2b), the estimated causal effect of an increase in *Left-labor power* is a *decrease* in budget deficits and an *increase* in interest rates!

Of course, at no time or place in our sample were trade markets fully closed, so it is important to look at the relationship between *Left-labor power* and deficits and interest rates over a more representative set of values for *Trade*. Conditional *Left-labor power* coefficients calculated from the budget-deficit and interest-rate equations are plotted in figure 7. The first plot indicates support for the hypothesized link between *Left-labor power* and deficits, but only at relatively high levels of trade openness. When trade is relatively closed, increased *Left-labor power* is associated with *smaller* deficits. This finding could be used to support a strong version of the convergence argument about trade: a relatively high degree of trade openness is a prerequisite for social democratic corporatist fiscal activism. In fact, in the absence of trade openness, right-wing governments tend to run bigger budget deficits than left-wing governments—a result that casts new light on the Reagan budget deficit, as well as the Clinton administration's reluctance—and George W. Bush's enthusiasm—to cut taxes in response to budget surpluses. Note also that increased capital mobility appears to have little effect on the relationship between budget deficits and *Left-labor power*.

The relationship between *Left-labor power* and interest rates also appears to be at odds with social democratic corporatist expectations. There is very little evidence that left governments and governments confronting encompassing labor-market institutions have a tendency to adopt loose monetary policies. In fact, when trade openness is moderate, *Left-labor power* is associated with higher interest rates. Garrett suggests (1998, 102) that this is probably the result of capital markets' charging left governments an interest-rate premium because they expect them to implement inflationary policies. It could also be the case, however, that left governments adopt tight monetary policies in an attempt to convince wary investors that they can be "responsible." This behavior is predicted by scholars emphasizing the "structural dependence of the state on capital," and is the exact opposite of the behavior predicted by the standard partisan model and its social democratic corporatist variant. It is important to note, however, that the observed positive relationship between interest rates and *Left-labor power* disappears when trade becomes more open. In fact, when

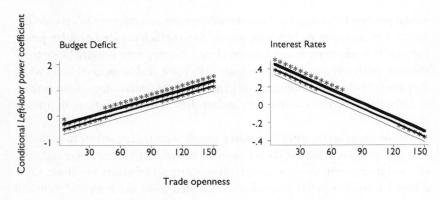

Fig. 7.   The estimated effect of *Left-labor power* on macroeconomic policy at various levels of trade and capital-market openness. Darker lines denote increased capital-market liberalization. (*Note:* * indicates coefficient is significant at $p < .10$, one-tailed.)

trade is extremely open but capital markets are relatively closed, there is some evidence that *Left-labor power* is associated with lower interest rates. This last result, curiously, simultaneously supports an extremely strong version of the compensation hypothesis as it relates to trade (very high levels of trade openness are necessary before left governments have a propensity to lower interest rates) and the convergence hypothesis as it relates to capital-market liberalization (having fewer than two capital controls is sufficient for left government to have no propensity to lower interest rates).

Thus, the evidence that *Left-labor power* is associated with overall monetary and fiscal policy indicators such as budget deficits and interest rates is, at best, mixed. While there is evidence that increases in *Left-labor power* are associated with increased deficits, this is the case only when trade is relatively open. Evidence of the hypothesized connection between *Left-labor power* and lower interest rates is restricted to when trade is extremely open. In fact, consistent with the "structural dependence of the state on capital" argument, there is broader evidence that increases in *Left-labor power* result in higher interest rates.

In summary, while there is evidence of a link between *Left-labor power* and various monetary and fiscal instruments, the observed influence of capital-market and trade liberalization on this relationship is consistent with neither the compensation nor the convergence view of globalization. For a number of indicators, there is no evidence of a link between *Left-labor power* and fiscal policy in relatively closed economies, and for those indicators where a relationship is found, the evidence is split between the compensation and the convergence views of the effects of trade liberalization.

But before discarding the partisan model, I will examine a number of respecifications of the tests reported in tables 8–10 in order to be certain that the lack of empirical evidence for partisan effects is because the partisan model is flawed, not because the model is misspecified. Specifically, I will examine the possibility that the dearth of evidence to support the partisan model is due to the failure to control for the modifying effects of the exchange rate regime and central bank independence discussed in chapter 2.

The Modifying Effect of the Exchange Rate

By ignoring the ways in which the choice of exchange rate regime and increased capital mobility interact to limit the effectiveness of fiscal instruments, the existing literature on the effects of globalization on partisan politics—with the exception of Oatley 1999 and Clark and Hallerberg 2000—has implicitly focused on only one of the common wisdom's proposed effects of globalization—that international competition makes the welfare state cost-prohibitive. As Huber and Stephens (1998) point out, the common wisdom about globalization also holds that the ease and rapidity of capital movements renders the tools of traditional demand management ineffective. The Mundell-Fleming approach to open-market macroeconomics, however, indicates quite clearly that the relationship between capital mobility and the effectiveness of fiscal policy instruments is crucially dependent upon the nature of the exchange rate regime. In line with the common wisdom about globalization, capital mobility is expected to erode the effectiveness of fiscal instruments when exchange rates are flexible but increase the effectiveness of fiscal instruments when exchange rates are fixed.[33] If the Mundell-Fleming model is correct (or, perhaps, even if policymakers merely believe it is correct), then a model that treats all increases in capital mobility as having the same effect on the relationship between left governance and fiscal policies is misspecified. Since according to the Mundell-Fleming framework an increase in capital mobility has exactly opposite implications for fiscal policy under different exchange rate regimes, the consequences of this misspecification could be substantial. With this in mind, I propose a test of a refinement of the common-wisdom hypothesis that capital mobility reduces the effectiveness of fiscal instruments that, prior to globalization, were (according to the partisan approach) used more vigorously by parties of the left than parties of the right. The refinement is that the common-wisdom argument should be expected to hold with respect to fiscal (monetary) policy only when exchange rates are flexible (fixed); in fact, since increased capital mobility increases the effectiveness of fiscal (monetary) policy when the exchange rate is fixed (flexible), it is possible for partisan differences in fiscal (monetary) policy to actually *increase* as capital becomes more mobile.

To test this argument, it is necessary to introduce the exchange rate as a modifying variable and examine its interaction with both the degree of capital mobility and the ideological orientation of government. This can be easily accomplished by use of a triple interaction term in a model that is otherwise quite similar to equation (2):

$$Pol_{it} = + b_1 Llp_{it} + b_2 Cm_{it} + b_3 Flex_{it} + b_4(Llp \cdot Cm_{it}) + b_5(Llp \cdot Flex_{it})$$

$$+ b_6(Cm_{it} \cdot Flex_{it}) + b_7(Llp \cdot Cm_{it} \cdot Flex_{it}) + b_8 Pol_{it-1}$$

$$+ \Sigma(b_j Period_{it}) + \Sigma(b_k Country_{it}) + \Sigma(b_l X_{lit}) + \mu_{it}. \tag{3}$$

Because of the increased complexity introduced by the triple interaction, trade openness has been dropped as a modifying variable. It will be retained, however, as a linear control variable.

According to such a model, the effect of *Left-labor power* on policy is given by

$$\frac{\partial Pol_{it}}{\partial Llp} = b_1 + b_4(Cm_{it}) + b_5(Flex_{it}) + b_7(Cm_{it} \cdot Flex_{it}); \tag{4}$$

that is, b_1 is the estimated causal effect of an increase in *Left-labor power* on fiscal policy when capital is immobile and the exchange rate is fixed. For most of the fiscal indicators, this is expected to be positive (recall from table 7). The effects of an increase in capital mobility on the relationship between *Left-labor power* and policy are captured by b_4 for the case of fixed exchange rates and by $b_4 + b_7$ for the case of flexible exchange rates. Since most convergence theorists maintain that the effects of capital mobility on partisan differences do not depend on the exchange rate regime, they would expect both b_4 and $b_4 + b_7$ to have a different sign than the hypothesized sign for b_1. If, however, the model in chapter 2 is correct, an increase in capital mobility should lead to a convergence in fiscal policy when the exchange rate is flexible, but not when it is fixed. In this case, $b_4 + b_7$ would have the opposite sign from b_1, but b_4 would not. More generally, partisan differences in fiscal policy should be in evidence except when capital is mobile and the exchange rate is flexible.

The results for equation (3) related to spending are reported in table 11.

The most noticeable result is that, contrary to the expectations of the game-theoretic model in chapter 2, there is no evidence that increases in *Left-labor power* are associated with increases in spending when the exchange rate is fixed and capital is immobile (i.e., the coefficient for *Left-labor power* is never positive and significant).

TABLE 11. The Estimated Effect of *Left-labor power* on Government Spending Conditioned upon the Degree of Capital-Market Liberalization and the Exchange Rate Regime

	Total Spending (1)	Income Transfers (2)	Civilian Government Consumption (3)	Subsidies to Industry (4)	Capital spending (5)
Left-labor power (Llp)	−0.385**	−0.196**	−0.101	−0.026	0.152
	(0.223)	(0.107)	(0.104)	(0.061)	(0.132)
Cml	−0.713**	−0.266	−0.384**	−0.062	0.155
	(0.344)	(0.162)	(0.171)	(0.087)	(0.186)
Flexible (Flex)	0.463	−0.384	−0.056	−0.024	1.801
	(2.449)	(1.210)	(1.352)	(0.633)	(1.507)
Llp · Cml	0.205***	0.084***	0.071**	0.015	−0.028
	(0.064)	(0.030)	(0.031)	(0.016)	(0.037)
Llp · Flex	0.134	0.143	−0.215	−0.012	−0.287
	(0.530)	(0.260)	(0.284)	(0.127)	(0.315)
Cml · Flex	−0.235	0.181	−0.047	0.002	−0.585
	(0.711)	(0.351)	(0.355)	(0.182)	(0.411)
Llp · Cml · Flex	−0.039	−0.051	0.072	0.001	0.083
	(0.152)	(0.075)	(0.076)	(0.036)	(0.086)
Lagged dependent variable	0.800***	0.856***	0.863***	0.801***	0.699***
	(0.026)	(0.032)	(0.026)	(0.040)	(0.051)
Trade	0.000	−0.004	−0.006	0.007**	−0.017***
	(0.013)	(0.006)	(0.004)	(0.003)	(0.005)
GDP growth	−0.386***	−0.168***	−0.139***	−0.013*	−0.047***
	(0.030)	(0.016)	(0.012)	(0.008)	(0.016)
Unemployment	0.063	0.070***	−0.007	−0.032***	−0.039*
	(0.042)	(0.019)	(0.018)	(0.011)	(0.022)
Old-age population	0.305***	0.143***	0.006	−0.007	−0.063
	(0.107)	(0.053)	(0.056)	(0.024)	(0.054)
Constant	6.861***	0.462	3.360***	0.362	1.762**
	(1.612)	(0.851)	(0.808)	(0.348)	(0.829)
F_{DW}	1.15	1.61	1.09	0.73	2.30
Prob. > F	0.331	0.172	0.362	0.572	0.059
Observations	350	350	350	350	350
Number of countries	14	14	14	14	14

Note: Panel-corrected standard errors are in parentheses.

The term F_{DW} is the test statistic for Durbin-Watson's *m*.

*p < .10, **p < .05, ***p < .01, one-tailed test for variables involving *Llp*, two-tailed otherwise.

Similarly, we can see from table 12 that government revenues are also un-correlated with *Left-labor power* when capital mobility is severely limited and the exchange rate is fixed (the coefficient for *Left-labor power* is, once again, never significant and positive). These results suggest that in the Bretton Woods period, when capital controls were common and fixed exchange rates were

TABLE 12. The Estimated Effect of *Left-labor power* on Government Revenues Conditioned upon the Degree of Capital-Market Liberalization and the Exchange Rate Regime

	Total Revenues (1)	Personal Income Tax (2)	Consumption Taxes (3)	Corporate Income Taxes (4)	Employer Social Security Contributions (5)
Left-labor power (Llp)	0.090	0.133	−0.008	−0.006	−0.305***
	(0.221)	(0.154)	(0.092)	(0.085)	(0.102)
Cml	−0.067	0.095	−0.078	0.127	−0.492***
	(0.312)	(0.202)	(0.134)	(0.128)	(0.171)
Flexible (Flex)	−0.898	−0.901	−0.204	0.598	−2.017
	(2.442)	(1.272)	(1.104)	(1.143)	(2.004)
Llp · Cml	0.025	−0.026	0.007	−0.017	0.103***
	(0.061)	(0.043)	(0.026)	(0.021)	(0.032)
Llp · Flex	−0.361	−0.021	−0.076	−0.159	0.711
	(0.593)	(0.281)	(0.253)	(0.209)	(0.621)
Cml · Flex	0.059	0.229	0.014	−0.245	0.635
	(0.702)	(0.387)	(0.316)	(0.326)	(0.555)
Llp · Cml · Flex	0.114	0.007	0.028	0.058	−0.175
	(0.165)	(0.084)	(0.071)	(0.059)	(0.165)
Lagged dependent variable	0.769***	0.868***	0.728***	0.832***	0.865***
	(0.035)	(0.032)	(0.047)	(0.060)	(0.049)
Trade	0.017*	0.009	−0.006	−0.004	0.008
	(0.009)	(0.007)	(0.004)	(0.004)	(0.005)
GDP growth	−0.131***	−0.072***	0.019	0.017	−0.033*
	(0.030)	(0.018)	(0.013)	(0.013)	(0.017)
Unemployment	−0.084**	−0.091***	0.016	−0.019	−0.011
	(0.041)	(0.024)	(0.017)	(0.013)	(0.024)
Old-age population	0.287**	0.066	0.056	0.007	0.100
	(0.116)	(0.068)	(0.049)	(0.034)	(0.065)
Constant	4.761***	0.995	0.911	0.547	0.641
	(1.608)	(0.942)	(0.735)	(0.556)	(0.814)
F_{DW}	0.62	3.50	27.86	0.10	4.23
Prob. > F	0.646	0.008	0.000	0.982	0.002
Observations	350	350	350	350	350
Number of countries	14	14	14	14	14

Note: Panel-corrected standard errors are in parentheses.

The term F_{DW} is the test statistic for Durbin-Watson's *m*.

*p < .10, **p < .05, ***p < .01, one-tailed test for variables involving *Llp*, two-tailed otherwise.

nearly universal, government spending was unrelated to the combination of partisan orientation and labor-market encompassment.

Finally, let us examine the effect of *Left-labor power* on budget deficits and interest rates. Table 13 indicates that when the exchange rate is fixed and capital is immobile (again, as was the case during the Bretton Woods period), the estimated causal effect of an increase in *Left-labor power* is a decrease in the size of the budget deficit and no statistically significant change in interest rates. Both of these results are contrary to the social democratic corporatist hypothesis. So the evidence suggests that under the conditions in which the social democratic corporatist hypothesis is most expected to apply, an increase in *Left-labor power* has no discernible effect on interest rates and exactly the opposite of the expected effect on budget deficits. While these results alone suggest that the social democratic corporatist model needs serious reconsideration, it is worth asking whether *Left-labor power* is related to fiscal policy under other structural conditions.

Recall that the primary expectation of the model in chapter 3 is that when the exchange rate is fixed, partisan differences should be at least as pronounced after capital mobility as before, but when the exchange rate is flexible, increased capital mobility should discourage the use of fiscal policy for partisan purposes. Consequently, if we plot conditional *Left-labor power* coefficients for various degrees of capital mobility under alternative exchange rate regimes and this open-economy version of the partisan argument is correct, we would expect to observe conditional coefficients that are positive and significant when capital controls exist whether the exchange rate is fixed or flexible. As capital controls are removed, however, we should expect the coefficients for the flexible exchange rate case to converge toward zero and the coefficients for the fixed exchange rate case to either stay the same or increase in magnitude.

This, however, is not the pattern that emerges from the plots presented in figures 8, 9, and 10. Note first that positive and significant coefficients are very much the exception. When all capital controls are removed ($Cml = 4$), increases in *Left-labor power* are associated with an increase in total spending, income transfers, and civilian government consumption (fig. 8). There is also a positive association between *Left-labor power* and total spending and civilian government consumption when one capital control is in place. These results are contrary to expectations in a number of ways.

First, there is little evidence of a connection between *Left-labor power* and government spending in economies where capital markets are relatively closed. Second, there is no evidence that capital mobility is any greater a restriction on fiscal policy when the exchange rate is flexible than when it is fixed. In fact, the

TABLE 13. The Estimated Effect of _Left-labor power_ on Macroeconomic Policy Conditioned upon the Degree of Capital-Market Liberalization and the Exchange Rate Regime

	Budget Deficits (1)	Interest Rates (2)
Left-labor power (Llp)	−0.601**	0.241
	(0.269)	(1.26)
Cml	−0.755*	−0.058
	(0.428)	(0.19)
Flex	0.878	0.467
	(3.334)	(0.22)
Llp · Cml	0.218***	−0.045
	(0.078)	(0.74)
Llp · Flex	0.759	0.099
	(0.753)	(0.20)
Cml · Flex	−0.194	−0.330
	(0.966)	(0.51)
Llp · Cml · Flex	−0.223	−0.024
	(0.215)	(0.16)
Lagged dependent variable	0.721***	0.599
	(0.044)	(16.68)**
Trade	−0.013	0.067
	(0.014)	(2.31)*
GDP growth	−0.241***	−0.112
	(0.041)	(2.78)**
Unemployment	0.187***	0.204
	(0.049)	(8.91)**
Old-age population	0.132	
	(0.152)	
Inflation		0.498
		(5.68)**
U.S. interest rate		4.240
		(1.98)*
Cbi		−0.017
		(2.62)**
Constant	2.394	−2.158
	(2.271)	(1.42)
F_{DW}	2.33	1.96
Prob. > F	0.0563	0.1022
Observations	350	300
Number of countries	14	12

Note: Panel-corrected standard errors are in parentheses.
The term F_{DW} is the test statistic for Durbin-Watson's m.
*$p < .10$, **$p < .05$, ***$p < .01$, one-tailed test for variables involving Llp, two-tailed otherwise.

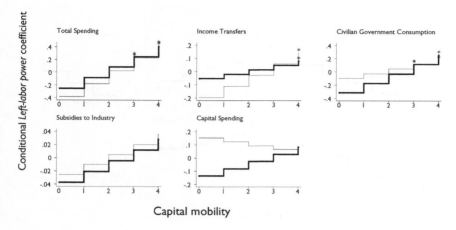

Fig. 8.   The estimated effect of *Left-labor power* on government spending under various degrees of capital-market openness and alternative exchange rate regimes. Darker lines denote flexible exchange rate. (*Note:* * indicates coefficent is significant at $p < .10$, one-tailed.)

difference in conditional coefficients tends to be greater before capital mobility than after.

The results for the revenue equations (fig. 9) are also filled with anomalies. There is evidence of a positive association between *Left-labor power* and total revenues only when capital controls have been entirely removed. There is evidence of a positive association between *Left-labor power* and employer contributions to social security, but only when the exchange rate is flexible. As was the case with the spending equations, these results are surprising in that evidence of a link between partisan politics and fiscal policy is rare when capital controls are relatively numerous. If anything, the removal of capital controls seems to encourage partisan differences in fiscal policy. This could be understood to be evidence for the convergence argument, except that rather than *reinforcing* partisan differences in fiscal policy, capital mobility appears to *create* partisan differences in fiscal policy. Garrett (1998) argues that left politicians may use increased activism to shelter groups most imperiled by the risks of globalization, but he does not argue that capital mobility is a necessary condition for such left activism. One could argue that the left may have always wanted be more activist, but it is only with the increase in the effectiveness of

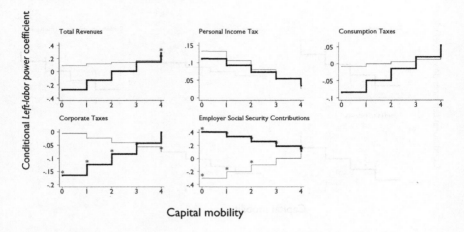

Fig. 9.   The estimated effect of *Left-labor power* on government revenues under various degrees of capital-market openness and alternative exchange rate regimes. Darker lines denote flexible exchange rate. (*Note:* * indicates coefficent is significant at $p < .10$, one-tailed.)

fiscal policy and the decline in monetary policy autonomy associated with increased capital mobility under fixed exchange rates that the left has the power to act on this desire. If this were true, however, *Left-labor power* would be associated with increased fiscal activism in the after-capital-mobility world only where exchange rates were fixed. No such pattern is exhibited in the plots related to the effect of left governance on the ways governments tax and spend (figures 8 and 9).

The evidence for the partisan model is also mixed when we turn to what Garrett refers to as broader indicators of the macroeconomic policy position of governments—budget deficits and interest rates. Under the partisan model, one would expect that increases in *Left-labor power* will lead to lower interest rates and higher deficits. The plots in figure 10 indicate that *Left-labor power* is associated with higher, not lower, interest rates. Garrett (1998) interprets a similar result to be an indication of an "interest-rate premium" that capital markets exact from left governments. This interest-rate premium appears to get smaller as capital becomes more mobile, perhaps because investors are, under such circumstances, able to "vote with their feet."[34] Finally, there is an observed

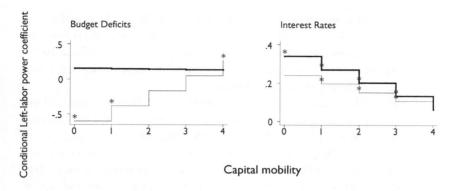

Fig. 10.   The estimated effect of *Left-labor power* on macroeconomic policy under various degrees of capital-market openness and alternative exchange rate regimes. Darker lines denote flexible exchange rate. (*Note:* * indicates coefficent is significant at $p < .10$, one-tailed.)

association between increased *Left-labor power* and increased budget deficits when no capital controls are in place, but only when the exchange rate is fixed.

Conclusion

In this chapter I have engaged in a critical reevaluation of the literature on the relationship between partisanship and macroeconomic policy. A review of this literature reveals many contradictory findings and few authoritative empirical tests. Virtually all prior empirical tests have suffered from at least one serious threat to valid inference. Despite limited degrees of freedom, early cross-sectional studies found that countries that frequently elected left governments tended to implement more expansionary policies. While interesting, this result is not directly relevant to the causal claim that expansionary policies were the result of electing left-wing governments. Many of the early time-series cross-sectional tests of the social democratic corporatist hypothesis have been challenged on econometric grounds (Beck and Katz 1995). More recent times-series cross-sectional tests that have been sensitive to these criticisms are frequently flawed in the way they handle interaction effects. Inferential errors are frequent in these studies because the authors commit at least one of the following errors.

First, some fail to model the modifying effects explicitly called for in the theoretical literature. Second, those that do model these modifying effects either fail to calculate the conditional coefficients necessary to directly evaluate conditional hypotheses or fail to include all the "additive" or "lower-order" terms necessary for straightforward, unbiased inference.

In light of these weaknesses in existing works, I reevaluate the results of one of the strongest existing tests of the social democratic corporatist hypothesis in an open-economy setting (Garrett 1998). After making minor changes to his model and calculating conditional coefficients, I argue that Garrett's results suggest that there is little evidence of a systematic relationship between *Left-labor power* and fiscal and monetary policy in the absence of trade and capital-market liberalization. I argue that the results after trade and capital-market liberalization are not easily understood in terms of existing theory.

In light of the theoretical models in chapter 2, I have tried to determine whether these contradictory findings are the result of a failure to control for the modifying effects of the exchange rate regime, and I conclude that this is not the case. While theory tells us that the modifying effects of capital mobility on partisan influences on fiscal policy should be more pronounced when the exchange rate is flexible, there is little evidence that this is the case.

Since every attempt to bring the relationship between partisanship and macroeconomic policy into focus produces contradictory findings, it is not unreasonable to conclude that the partisan model of macroeconomic policy choice may be fundamentally flawed. One could reasonably conclude from the findings presented in this chapter that the recent increase in international capital mobility did not lead to convergence in monetary and fiscal policies because this convergence occurred some time ago. More than four decades ago, Samuel Beer referred to "the startlingly close agreement among the [two major British] parties on social and economic issues" (Beer and Ulam 1958, 157–58). At the time, Beer attributed the consensus on policy in part to the ability of the Tories to "trim their program to any prevailing wind of doctrine" (158). The "prevailing wind of doctrine" at the time was the benefits of the postwar Keynesian welfare state. In the 1980s and 1990s, consensus appears to depend on the left's ability to bend to the prevailing neoliberal winds.

When temporally local changes are viewed in isolation, one is tempted to attribute causality to them. It was prewar economic crisis or the wartime destruction of productive capacities that led parties of the right to embrace state-centered policies. Similarly, the need to compete in a "globalized" economy compelled left-wing leaders to abandon their program and accept a dismantling of the welfare state. When these two periods of change are viewed together, however, a different picture emerges. Interparty policy consensus appears to be the norm; what changes is the content of the consensus. When conditions change (be they "objective" or "epistemic"), so does policy orientation—but it changes for both the right and the left.

These changes are not necessarily frictionless, but they can be swift. The ideological orientation of government probably influences the speed of policy change, but not the direction. It was easier for Labour to propose changes to the welfare state, but the Tories were not far behind. The tendency of one party to feel more at home in the new environment can lead to temporary partisan differences—often accompanied by pronounced electoral defeat for the party that is slow to adapt. This may be one reason that Garrett found some evidence that partisan differences increase as capital mobility increases. The first part of his sample is taken from the height of the Keynesian consensus and is filled with observations of severe restrictions on capital mobility. Virtually all incidents of capital-market liberalization occur in the latter part of the sample, during the transition to a new consensus around neoliberal policies. The observation that left governments may have been more expansionary than right governments under mobile capital, but not when capital was immobile, may not be evidence of left-wing governments responding to new demands for intervention from voters displaced by international economic upheaval. Rather, it may be evidence that right-wing parties shifted away from interventionist policies more quickly than left-wing parties did.

From this perspective, increased capital mobility may have more of an influence on the content than the existence of partisan consensus. Indeed, the foregoing suggests that partisan convergence is the ordinary state of affairs and that, with the possible exception of periods of transition between macroeconomic paradigms, the ideological orientation of government has little effect on the policies chosen.[35] But if the ideological orientation of government does not drive macroeconomic policy, what does? In the next chapter, I examine the evidence for the partisan model's main political economic competitor—the electoralist model.

CHAPTER 4

Elections and Fiscal and Monetary Policy

President Johnson has found in modern economic policy an instrument that serves him well in giving form and substance to the stuff of which his dreams for America are made, in molding and holding a democratic consensus, and in giving that consensus a capital "D" in national elections.
      —Walter Heller, chairman of the Council of Economic Advisers,
                                         1961–64

In the previous chapter, evidence was presented that called into question the partisan perspective on macroeconomic policy. The extant empirical literature is full of contradictory findings. An attempt to control for the modifying effects of institutional context deduced from the theoretical models in chapter 2 failed to clarify this web of tangled results. One conclusion that can be drawn from the exercise in chapter 3 is that systematic partisan differences in monetary and fiscal policy simply did not exist before, during, or after the recent increase in international capital mobility because partisan convergence occurred a long time ago. Does this mean that monetary and fiscal policies have been, and remain, *apolitical?* Perhaps, but another alternative is that it was electoral pressures that induced partisan convergence and also induced the politically motivated policy choices predicted by the political business cycle literature. This chapter asks whether monetary and fiscal policies are tied to the electoral calendar. As was the case with the partisan model, the existing literature on electoral cycles in monetary and fiscal policies is fraught with contradictory findings. Can sense be made of the empirical results if we pay adequate attention to the institutional context in which policy choices take place?

85

This chapter examines how the interaction of the international environment with domestic political institutions constrains a government's ability to use monetary and fiscal policy to engineer preelectoral macroeconomic expansions. It has long been argued that incumbent politicians who want to win the next election may manipulate economic tools at their disposal in an attempt to satisfy the electorate enough so that they are reelected (Nordhaus 1975; MacRae 1977; Tufte 1978; Keech 1995, chap. 3). Clark and Nair Reichert (1998) find that such cycles are almost entirely absent in states with independent central banks. They also find that opportunistic cycles are not likely to occur when capital is mobile and the exchange rate is fixed.

Clark and Nair Reichert's evidence is consistent with the decision-theoretic model in chapter 2, but it is not consistent with the game-theoretic model in that same chapter. Specifically, one aspect of their findings is curious. While there are good reasons to expect the identified constraints to make it difficult to use monetary policy for electoral purposes, there is no a priori reason to expect fiscal policy to be constrained under such circumstances. Even when a central bank has complete control over monetary policy, the government can still attempt to affect macroeconomic outcomes through cuts in taxes or increases in expenditures. Similarly, while monetary policy may be constrained when exchange rates are fixed and capital is mobile, incumbents are free to use fiscal policy to create preelectoral expansions. The temptation to use these instruments before upcoming elections to win over undecided voters may be especially high; in particular, discussions of taxes and attempts to reduce them often seem to dominate election campaigns. Clark and Nair Reichert's results regarding the conditions under which electoral cycles in output and unemployment occur will be examined more fully in chapter 6. This chapter will focus on the electorally motivated manipulation of monetary and fiscal instruments thought to produce such cycles.

While open-economy models have often privileged monetary policy over fiscal policy, the literature on the domestic determinants of fiscal policy tends to ignore the international environment in which policy is made. This may be one reason that these studies have produced inconclusive results: while Burdekin and Laney (1988) and Franzese (1996) find that independent central banks do reduce the size of deficits, several others have not confirmed the relationship (Grilli, Masciandaro, and Tabellini 1991; Pollard 1993; de Haan and Sturm 1994a [the latter two works as quoted in Eijffinger and de Haan 1996].) The Mundell-Fleming model indicates that governments can, at best, pursue only two of the following three goals: capital mobility, fixed exchange rates, and independent monetary policy.[1] The absence or presence of each of these conditions affects the nature of the game between a government, which we assume wants to use fiscal and monetary instruments to stimulate the economy shortly before elections, and a central banker, who, if independent from the government, is immune from such electoral pressures. In particular, an independent central bank may be able to prevent opportunistic business cycles when it has autonomy over monetary policy, which will be the case so long as capital is immobile, as it generally was in the industrialized world in the 1960s, or so long as flexible exchange rates are present, as has been the case in several countries after the collapse of the Bretton Woods system. When capital is mobile and exchange rates are fixed, however, monetary policy is ineffective, and a central bank, independent or not, cannot deter fiscal expansions. These different expectations based on the Mundell-Fleming conditions may explain why the empirical evidence so far has been mixed.

This chapter begins with a summary of the implications from the game-theoretic model in chapter 2 for the electoral manipulation of monetary and fiscal instruments. The next section examines the predictions of the model with quarterly data from OECD countries from 1973 to 1989 for monetary policy and annual data from OECD and European Union sources from 1981 to 1992 for fiscal policy. These results—which both replicate and elaborate the results of Clark and Hallerberg (2000)—largely confirm the game-theoretic model. There is evidence that preelectoral monetary expansions occur only when the exchange rate is flexible and the degree of central bank independence is low; and that preelectoral fiscal expansions occur when the exchange rate is fixed.

Context-Dependent Electoral Cycles

According to both the game-theoretic and decision-theoretic models in chapter 2, the incentives to manipulate monetary and fiscal instruments for electoral purposes depend on the context in which policymakers find themselves. Both models assume that the choice of exchange rate regime and the degree of central bank independence and capital mobility are relevant, but there are important differences in the precise predictions yielded by the two models. The decision-theoretic model, for example, downplays the use of fiscal policy for electoral purposes and focuses instead on the ways in which these institutional choices influence the use of monetary policy for electoral purposes. Since the game-theoretic model makes predictions similar to those of the decision-theoretic model with respect to monetary policy but also yields clear predictions about fiscal policy, it is clearly the more fruitful model for examining the possibility of context-dependent electoral cycles in policy instruments.[2] Consequently, the predictions derived from the game-theoretic model in chapter 2 will be the focus of attention in this chapter.

The standard method for testing opportunistic political business cycle arguments has been to examine the relationship between various macroeconomic outcomes (such as growth, unemployment, and inflation) and the occurrence of elections. Given the focus here on the strategic interaction between fiscal and monetary policymakers, the instruments that the respective agents are presumed to control are examined. In the theoretical discussion in chapter 2, the fiction was maintained that the central bank controls the rate of inflation directly; here we will make the more realistic assumption that the central bank controls the money supply. The government is assumed to control the size of the government surplus (or deficit).

The model put forth in chapter 2 suggests that the relationship between elections and policy instruments depends upon the degree of capital mobility, the exchange rate regime, and the degree of independence enjoyed by the central bank. Following Clark and Nair Reichert (1998), it was presumed that capital was highly mobile at the time of the collapse of Bretton Woods. Consequently, we will concentrate our empirical examination on observations during the period 1973–95. This allows us to treat capital mobility as essentially constant and to examine the effects of exchange rate regimes and central bank independence on the existence of monetary and fiscal cycles. This coding has limitations, but it does follow a tradition in the measurement of capital mobility that treats the existence of mobility as a systemwide rather than a country-by-country variable (Andrews 1994; Frieden 1991b; Kurzer 1993; Webb 1995; Hallerberg and Clark 1997; McNamara 1998). To be sure that this assumption is not what is driving our results, we also report regressions that consider the effects of country-specific restrictions on capital movements.

Again following Clark and Nair Reichert (1998), we use a dummy variable interaction model to examine the modifying effects of fixed exchange rates and central banking institutions. We use Clark and Nair Reichert's coding of participation in fixed exchange rate regimes as well as their dummy variable for central bank independence, updating where necessary.[3] The standard test for political business cycles employs a multivariate regression model aimed at isolating the relationship between elections and macroeconomic variables. We will examine two sets of models to evaluate hypotheses related to budgetary and monetary cycles. Table 14 summarizes the predictions of the game-theoretic model in chapter 2 for the presence of electorally induced monetary and fiscal cycles under full capital mobility.

Monetary Cycles

The theoretical discussion in chapter 2 suggests that the existence of monetary cycles is likely to be sensitive to the environment in which policymakers find themselves. We will test this argument using a pooled cross-sectional time-series model that extends the empirical work of Alesina and Roubini (1997). They test for monetary cycles using the following equation:

$$m_{it} = \beta_0 + \beta_1 m_{it-1} + \beta_2 m_{it-2} + \cdots + \beta_n m_{it-n} + \beta_{n+1} PBCN_{it} + \varepsilon_t, \quad (1)$$

where m_{it} is the rate of growth of money for country i at time t, and $PBCN$ is an electoral dummy variable that equals 1 during electoral quarters and in either the three or five quarters (depending on the specific test) before the election. With dummy variables and interaction terms added to capture context-specific effects, equation (1) becomes

$$m_t = \beta_0 + \beta_1 E_t + \beta_2 Cbi + \beta_3 Fixed_t + \beta_4 E \cdot Cbi_t + \beta_5 E \cdot Fixed_t$$

$$+ \beta_6 Cbi \cdot Fixed_t + \beta_7 E \cdot Cbi \cdot Fixed_t + \Sigma(\beta_j m_{t-j}) + e_t. \quad (2)$$

Table 15 reports the pooled cross-sectional time-series results for four specifications. Following Alesina and Roubini (1997), all of these models use the annual rate of change in M-1 as an indicator of change in the money supply. Models 1 and 3 use qualitative indicators of the hypothesized constraints on monetary policy. These specifications implicitly assume that capital was uniformly mobile during the time period examined and that central banks were either independent or not. The models in columns 2 and 4 retain the assumption that capital is mobile during this period but use Cukierman, Webb, and Neyapti's (1992) continuous indicator of legal central bank independence. All models include country dummies to control for country-specific fixed effects, but these are not reported here. Models 1 and 2 use a lagged dependent variable

TABLE 14.   Electorally Induced Cycles in Macroeconomic Policy Instruments under Various Structural Conditions

	No Central Bank Independence	Central Bank Independence
Capital mobility and fixed exchange rates	Fiscal cycles; no monetary cycles	Fiscal cycles; no monetary cycles
Capital mobility and flexible exchange rates	Monetary cycles; no fiscal cycles	No fiscal or monetary cycles

and panel-corrected standard errors. While Beck and Katz (1996, 9) argue that serial correlated errors are unlikely in such a model, Durbin-Watson's m suggests that autocorrelation may be present in both these models.[4] Consequently, it is possible that the standard errors reported here may understate the uncertainty of our estimates of their corresponding coefficients. To allow for comparison with earlier work (Clark and Hallerberg 2000) and similar models that show no evidence of serially correlated errors elsewhere in this book, these OLS results will be tentatively discussed, but these models will also be reestimated

TABLE 15.   The Conditional Effects of Elections on the Money Supply in the Post–Bretton Woods Era

	Qualitative Modifiers (1)	Continuous Modifiers (2)	Qualitative Modifiers (3)	Continuous Modifiers (4)
Election	1.070**	0.964*	1.558**	2.274**
	(0.499)	(0.704)	(0.725)	(0.984)
Cbi	1.698**	3.916*	6.466**	13.230**
	(0.777)	(2.087)	(3.221)	(8.179)
Fixed	−1.650	−1.774*	−0.746	−0.837
	(1.056)	(1.056)	(2.251)	(2.242)
Election · Cbi	−1.189**	−1.611	−1.760**	−4.802**
	(0.665)	(1.734)	(0.909)	(2.325)
Election · Fixed	−0.211	0.249	−1.025	−0.703
	(0.641)	(0.581)	(0.905)	(0.795)
Cbi · Fixed	−0.419	0.209	−7.674*	−5.547
	(1.341)	(1.236)	(4.294)	(3.633)
Election · Cbi · Fixed	1.195	0.488	1.386	1.082
	(0.999)	(0.905)	(1.373)	(1.246)
M_{t-1}	0.797***	0.800***		
	(0.027)	(0.027)		
Intercept	2.322***	1.718**	13.450***	11.926***
	(0.488)	(0.670)	(1.206)	(2.227)
F_{DW}	38.21	34.71		
Prob. $> F$	0.000	0.000		
ρ			0.785	0.786
Observations	928	928	933	933
Number of countries	16	16	16	16

Note: Coefficients and panel-corrected standard errors. Columns 1 and 2 use ordinary least squares regression with a lagged dependent variable. The term F_{DW} is the test statistic for Durbin-Watson's m. Columns 3 and 4 use the Prais-Winsten transformation to remove first-order serial correlation. Columns 2 and 4 use Cukierman, Webb, and Neyapti's (1992) measure of legal central bank independence and a continuous measure of eroding monetary policy autonomy. Columns 1 and 3 use a categorical variable that equals one if the country's score is above the sample median and zero otherwise; and a categorical measure of eroding monetary policy that equals one if the exchange rate is fixed and zero otherwise.

*$p < .10$, **$p < .05$, ***$p < .01$, one-tailed test for coefficients involving *Election*, two-tailed otherwise.

using a method designed to remove first-order serial correlation. These Prais-Winsten regression results are reported in columns 3 and 4 of table 15.

Note first that the results are qualitatively stable across specifications and estimation techniques. Recall that both the decision-theoretic and game-theoretic models predicted that electorally induced monetary expansions should occur if and only if the central bank is not independent and the exchange rate is allowed to fluctuate. Because the electoral coefficient in table 15 describes the relationship between elections and the money supply when both modifying variables equal zero, it describes the situation when central banks are dependent and exchange rates are flexible. The statistically significant positive coefficient for *Election* in all four specifications in table 15 is evidence that monetary expansions do occur when these conditions prevail, as expected.

Furthermore, specifications of equation (2) that use qualitative modifying variables (models 1 and 3) make it easy to test all four of the implications of the game-theoretic model in chapter 2 related to monetary policy by calculating the conditional coefficients for each relevant institutional combination (see table 14).[5] The conditional coefficient for the effect of elections on the money supply when exchange rates are fixed and central bank independence is high can be determined by substituting the appropriate values of the institutional variables into equation (2),

$$m_t = \beta_0 + \beta_1 E_t + \beta_2(1) + \beta_3(1) + \beta_4(E \cdot (1)) + \beta_5(E \cdot (1)) + \beta_6(1)$$

$$+ \beta_7(E \cdot (1) \cdot (1)) + \Sigma(\beta_j m_{t-j}) + e_t, \tag{3}$$

which simplifies to

$$m_t = \beta_0 + \beta_1 E_t + \beta_2 + \beta_3 + \beta_4 E + \beta_5 E + \beta_6 + \beta_7 E$$

$$+ \Sigma(\beta_j m_{t-j}) + e_t, \tag{4}$$

and then comparing the electoral ($E = 1$) and nonelectoral periods ($E = 0$) periods given the presence of both constraints. Were a monetary cycle to occur under such conditions, the change in the money supply should be greater during electoral periods (left side of equation (5)) than during nonelectoral periods (right side of equation (5)):

$$\beta_1(1) + \beta_2 + \beta_3 + \beta_4(1) + \beta_5(1) + \beta_6 + \beta_7(1) > \beta_1(0) + \beta_2 + \beta_3$$

$$+ \beta_4(0) + \beta_5(0) + \beta_6 + \beta_7(0), \tag{5}$$

which simplifies to $\beta_1 + \beta_4 + \beta_5 + \beta_7 > 0$. By analogous reasoning, a finding that $\beta_1 + \beta_4 > 0$ or $\beta_1 + \beta_5 > 0$ would be evidence of electorally induced monetary expansions under dependent central banks with fixed exchange rates or under independent central banks with floating exchange rates, respectively. Hypothesis 2M (from chap. 2), however, predicts that monetary cycles will not occur under such circumstances, so we expect that $\beta_1 + \beta_4 + \beta_5 + \beta_7, \beta_1 + \beta_4$, and $\beta_1 + \beta_5$ will each be indistinguishable from zero. In contrast, hypothesis 2M predicts that electorally induced monetary expansions *will* occur when the exchange rate is flexible and the central bank is dependent. As noted, the test for this last proposition is simply $\beta_1 > 0$.

The conditional coefficients and their associated standard errors based on the results in column 1 of table 15 are reported in the upper portion of table 16. Note that the coefficients in table 16 are estimates of the relationship between elections and monetary policy under the various open-economy conditions presented in table 2. As hypothesis 2M predicts, when capital is mobile there is evidence of electorally induced monetary expansions if the exchange rate is allowed to fluctuate, but only when central bank independence is low. Also consistent with hypothesis 2M, there is no evidence of electorally induced monetary expansions when the exchange rate is fixed and the central bank is independent. Contrary to expectation, however, there is evidence of electorally

TABLE 16. Conditional Effects of Elections on Monetary Policy

Central Bank Independence	Exchange Rates	
	Flexible	Fixed
	Calculated from column 1 in table 15	
High	−0.118	0.866
	(.429)	(.655)
Low	1.071**	0.859**
	(0.499)	(0.413)
	Calculated from column 3 in table 15	
High	−0.202	0.159
	(0.540)	(0.922)
	1.56**	0.533
Low	(0.725)	(0.553)

Note: The coefficients are conditional coefficients with conditional standard errors in parentheses.

*$p < .10$, **$p < .05$, one-tailed test.

induced monetary expansions when the exchange rate is fixed and the central bank is not independent.

Because tests reveal that serial correlation may be present, the conclusion that monetary expansions occur when the exchange rate is fixed and the central bank is not independent is open to question. Specifically, the presence of positive serial correlation may have biased the estimate of the relevant standard error downward. It is therefore possible that in the absence of this bias, we might conclude that the estimated causal effect of elections on the money supply is not statistically distinguishable from zero. To check to see if this is the case, conditional coefficients based on the Prais-Winsten estimates in column 3 are displayed in the lower portion of table 16.[6] These results are quite similar to the OLS results, except that the anomalous finding for the fixed exchange rate, dependent central bank case has vanished. As hypothesis 2M predicts, elections are associated with an increase in the money supply if and only if the exchange rate is flexible and the central bank is not independent.

The evidence based on the specifications in columns 1 and 3 supports the main implications of the model for monetary policy. The existence of opportunistic monetary cycles is conditioned by the level of central bank independence and the choice of exchange rate regime. Furthermore, there is evidence of monetary expansions when the government retains both national monetary policy autonomy and influence over the central bank. There is no evidence of such cycles when the central bank is independent or the exchange rate is allowed to float, once auto correlation is controlled for.[7]

The evidence derived from the specifications in columns 2 and 4 is also consistent with many of our theoretical expectations. As noted, the coefficient for *Election* is in both cases positive and statistically significant. This suggests that the money supply tends to expand in preelectoral periods when the exchange rate is fixed and the central bank is maximally dependent on the government, and this result holds even after the data have been transformed to remove serial correlation (column 4). But what about when the exchange rate is flexible or the central bank is independent? Figure 11 plots the conditional electoral coefficients based on columns 2 and 4 of table 15. Note first that in both cases, the estimated causal effect of an election on the money supply is a decreasing function of the degree of central bank independence. As expected, central bank independence constrains the electoral use of monetary policy. The evidence related to the effect of the exchange rate regime, however, is more mixed. As expected, when central bank independence is high, electorally induced monetary cycles do not occur under either exchange rate regime. But contrary to expectations, when central bank independence is low, the evidence for electoral

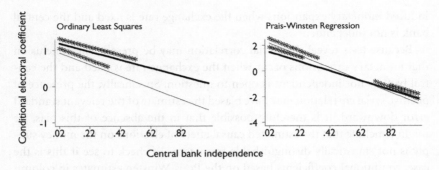

Fig. 11.   The estimated effect of an election on the money supply under fixed and flexible exchange rates and various degrees of central bank independence. Darker lines denote fixed exchange rate. (*Note:* * indicates coefficent is significant at $p < .10$, one-tailed.)

cycles under fixed exchange rates is about as strong as it is under flexible exchange rates.

Fiscal Cycles

In contrast to our expectations and results for monetary policy, hypotheses 1F and 2F indicate that electorally induced fiscal cycles are likely when exchange rates are fixed both when capital is mobile and when it is not.[8] In contrast, because fiscal policy is ineffective when exchange rates are flexible and capital is mobile, there should be no electorally induced fiscal cycles under these conditions (hypothesis 2F).

Previous research generally asks whether deficits are likely to increase in electoral years, and, unlike the empirical work on monetary cycles, the data are coded on a yearly, instead of quarterly, basis.[9] The evidence has been decidedly mixed, with some authors indicating support for opportunistic fiscal cycles in some subset of industrialized countries (Alesina and Roubini 1997; Hallerberg and von Hagen 1999; Franzese 1996 finds such cycles when the replacement risk to a sitting government is high), while others find no support for such cycles (de Haan and Sturm 1994b). One reason for these differences in findings may be that the studies do not differentiate between the effects of fixed and flexible exchange rates or of capital mobility or immobility. Much of the data used in this section of the chapter is borrowed from de Haan and Sturm 1997. We restrict the data to the period 1982–92 for two reasons, both of which concern policy in Europe. In fall 1992, the Exchange Rate Mechanism of the European Monetary System (EMS) suffered a severe crisis in the markets, which put in doubt the credibility of fixed exchange rates; and after 1992, European states that wished to join the Economic and Monetary Union faced restrictions on their debt levels, and these restrictions presumably affected decisions on fiscal policy in a direct way. This period is also theoretically interesting. Several European Community countries reestablished credible fixed exchange rates with the Exchange Rate Mechanism in 1979, so the period examined here represents a strong test of the effects of a given country's exchange rate regime on the likelihood of fiscal expansions before an election.

The model that has become a standard in the field comes from Roubini and Sachs 1989b. Roubini and Sachs's regression equation is

$$db_{it} = \beta_0 + \beta_1 db_{it-1} + \beta_2 dU_{it} + \beta_3 dy_{it} + \beta_4 b_{it-1} d(r_{it} - y_{it}) + \beta_5 pv_{it}, \quad (6)$$

where the dependent variable, db_{it}, is the change in the gross debt-to-GDP ratio. The authors break down the equation into a set of economic variables and a set of political variables (represented as pv_{it}). The set of economic variables included in all regressions is as follows: db_{it-1} represents the lagged debt ratio, dU_i the change in the unemployment rate, and $b_{it-1}d(r - y)$ the change in debt-servicing costs, which is computed as the change in the real interest rate minus the change in the growth rate times the gross deficit in the previous year.[10] These economic variables are expected to impact the budget in a given year, with higher levels of unemployment and debt-servicing costs increasing government debt levels and higher levels of economic growth decreasing debt levels.[11]

The standard political variables generally include codings for institutional differences or the partisanship orientation of the government. Roubini and Sachs 1989b received much attention when it was first published because the authors found that the type of government affected the size of budget deficits. One-party majority governments maintained the tightest fiscal discipline; two- and three-party majority governments were less disciplined; four- and five-party governments were even more problematic; and minority governments, regardless of the number of parties in the coalition, were the worst of all. Many other scholars have followed Roubini and Sachs in their examination of government type and other political variables. So that the value added in this book is clear, we include the political variables found in de Haan and Sturm 1997 as control variables. De Haan and Sturm find that Roubini and Sachs made several coding errors, and they argue, based on Roubini and Sachs's original coding procedures, that the type of government does not affect deficit levels. Hallerberg and von Hagen 1998, following Edin and Ohlsson 1991, break the government-type variable into three separate dummy variables, and they include a variable for the percentage of cabinet portfolios that left parties occupy—in order to control for partisan effects—and one for election years. They also add a variable for two fiscal institutions: a strong finance minister and negotiated targets. They find that there is a connection between government type and a fiscal institution meant to reduce the size of deficits, but that government type per se has no effect on the size of deficits. In particular, delegation to a strong finance minister who can monitor spending and punish ministers who "defect" is feasible in states with one-party majority governments. In multiparty and minority governments, coalition members are not willing to delegate to one actor the ability to monitor and punish the others. Commitment to numerical targets negotiated among the coalition partners for each ministry provides an alternative in multiparty governments.[12]

In order to test our contention that political business cycles are most likely to occur when exchange rates are fixed, we structure the regression equations to include the economic and political variables that Roubini and Sachs (1989b) and de Haan and Sturm (1997) found important, but we add variables to consider the effects of the exchange rate regime and elections. Our equations are as follows:

$$db_{it} = \alpha + \beta_1 Election + \beta_2 Flexible + \beta_3 Election \cdot Flexible + \beta_4 db_{it-1}$$

$$+ \beta_5 dU_{it} + \beta_6 b_{it-1} d(r_{it} - y_{it}) + \beta_7 Government\ type \qquad (7)$$

and

$$db_{it} = \alpha + \beta_1 Election + \beta_2 Capital\ mobility + \beta_3 Flexible + \beta_4 Election$$

$$\cdot Capital\ mobility + \beta_5 Election \cdot Flexible + \beta_6 Capital\ mobility$$

$$\cdot Flexible + \beta_7 Election \cdot Capital\ mobility \cdot Flexible + \beta_8 db_{it-1}$$

$$+ \beta_9 dU_{it} + \beta_{10} b_{it-1} d(r_{it} - y_{it}) + \beta_{11} Government\ type. \qquad (8)$$

These specifications follow closely the model provided in the previous section on monetary policy. Equation (7) is appropriate if we are prepared to assume that capital was mobile during the entire period. Equation (8), in contrast, allows us to treat capital mobility as a modifying variable. Expectations about the effects of these variables differ, however. Based on hypothesis 2F, we expect *fiscal* expansions to occur only when exchange rates are fixed (i.e., when the variable *Flexible* is equal to zero). We expect that when exchange rates are flexible, fiscal policy will be ineffective, and a government will not initiate a preelectoral fiscal expansion.

Based on our interest in the effects of elections under different exchange rate regimes, we also consider two alternative methods to code elections. Standard models calculate the election variable as a dummy variable for years in which an election is held. This coding is at best inexact and at worst inaccurate. Some countries hold elections in early spring, while others wait until late autumn. The same country may even hold elections at different times of the year over different electoral cycles. For example, in 1974 the United Kingdom held elections in February and October, while just five years later it conducted elections in May. A variable that makes no differentiation among these three elections will presumably understate the effects of elections, as well as increase the standard error of the variable.

We therefore supplement the standard measurement of elections with Franzese's more exact definition (1996). He calculates *Election* as the proportion of a preelectoral year that falls within a given year, so that, for example, a February 1 election would be coded as 1/12 in that year and 11/12 in the previous year.[13] We apply both codings in order to determine whether the different coding rules affect the results. The game-theoretic model predicts that fiscal cycles should exist when exchange rates are fixed. The sign of *Election* should therefore be positive. The model also predicts that the coefficient for the interaction term *Election* × *Flexible* will be negative, and indeed one would expect, since governments have no incentive to use fiscal cycles when exchange rates are flexible, that the coefficients for *Election* and *Election* × *Flexible* will sum to zero. To test directly for the effect of flexible exchange rates on fiscal cycles, we also calculate the conditional coefficient for elections when flexible exchange rates are present and when they are absent.

Table 17 shows strong evidence that countries with fixed exchange rates experience fiscal cycles and that flexible exchange rates eliminate these fiscal cycles. In both of the equations with the more precise measure for elections, there is evidence of preelectoral fiscal expansions when the exchange rate is fixed, but not when it is flexible. In column 2, for example, the coefficient for *Election* indicates that there is an increase in the gross debt level of roughly one and a half points during electoral periods when the exchange rate is fixed, compared to no increase during electoral periods when the exchange rate is flexible—that is, the

TABLE 17. The Conditional Effects of Elections on Changes in Gross Debt in the Period 1982–92

	Coding of Elections		
	Standard (1)	Franzese (2)	Franzese (3)
Election	0.49	1.52**	4.239
	(0.60)	(0.75)	(3.341)
Capital mobility			0.549*
			(0.292)
Flexible	−0.20	0.14	−0.420
	(0.60)	(0.64)	(3.839)
Election · Flexible	−0.26	−1.42	−0.742
	(1.18)	(1.25)	(0.855)
Election · Capital mobility			11.320
			(8.681)*
Capital mobility · Flexible			0.000
			(0.972)
Election · Capital mobility · Flexible			−3.342*
			(2.253)
d Debt$_{t-1}$	0.47***	0.48***	0.442**
	(0.10)	(0.10)	(0.109)
d Unemployment	1.27***	1.27***	1.212**
	(0.22)	(0.22)	(0.216)
d GDP			
d Debt costs	0.38**	0.39***	0.389**
	(0.15)	(0.14)	(0.142)
Government type	−0.17	−0.16	−0.257
	(0.24)	(0.25)	(0.256)
Intercept	0.67	0.35	−1.098
	(0.59)	(0.63)	(1.302)
Conditional coefficients			
Election | Flexible = 0	0.49	1.52*	
	(0.60)	(0.75)	
Election | Flexible = 1	0.22	0.10	
	(0.85)	(0.98)	
F_{DW}	0.57	0.57	0.06
Prob. $> F$	0.66	0.69	0.99
Observations	206	206	206
Number of countries	19	19	19

Note: The dependent variable is the change in the gross-debt-to-GDP ratio. Following de Haan and Sturm, I do not include country dummy variables, although their inclusion does not affect the qualitative results. Note that the political variables (election, the three variables for the type of government, strong finance ministers, and negotiated targets) are evaluated according to a one-tailed test.

The term F_{DW} is the test statistic for Durbin-Watson's m.

*$p < .10$, **$p < .05$, ***$p < .01$.

sum of the coefficients for *Election* and *Elections* × *Flexible* is close to zero (for convenience, we present the conditional coefficients for each exchange rate regime and their associated standard errors at the bottom of table 17). Clark and Hallerberg (2000) find even stronger evidence of the effect of exchange rate regime on the relationship between budgets and elections when using a data set composed of the fifteen current members of the European Union. They find that states with fixed exchange rates tend to increase their gross debt level–GDP ratios almost three percentage points in the year before an election.

There are additional nuances in the results. As column 1 of table 17 indicates, the coefficient on the standard *Election* variable has the correct sign but is not significant. The coefficient on *Election* almost doubles, and the standard deviation decreases, when one replaces the standard *Election* variable with Franzese's more exact measure in column 2. Once again, fiscal electoral cycles are completely absent when exchange rates are flexible.

The model in column 3 allows us to test the robustness of our results by relaxing the assumption that capital was fully mobile in every country during the entire observation period. By using the same capital-market liberalization variable employed in chapter 3, we can examine the combinations of capital mobility and exchange rate regime under which preelectoral fiscal expansions take place. The findings are qualitatively similar to those in column 2: elections are associated with an increase in government debt when fiscal policy autonomy is retained (i.e., the *Election* coefficient (which is the estimated causal effect of an election when capital is immobile and the exchange rate is fixed) is large and approaches statistical significance.)[14]

To determine the effects of increased capital mobility and a shift to a flexible exchange rate, it is necessary to examine conditional coefficients under various values of the modifying variables. The results plotted in figure 12 fit the expectations from our model. As already noted, there is evidence of preelectoral fiscal expansions when the exchange rate is fixed and capital is immobile. In addition, the plot for the fixed exchange rate case is relatively flat, indicating that an increase in capital mobility has little constraining effect on electorally induced fiscal cycles when the exchange rate is fixed. In fact, the conditional electoral coefficient is statistically significant and positive even when all capital controls have been removed (when $Cml = 4$). In contrast, when the exchange rate is flexible, capital-market liberalization leads to a reduction in the size of the estimated causal effect of an election on the size of the government debt. In fact, when all capital controls have been removed and the exchange rate is flexible, the conditional coefficient for *Election* is indistinguishable from zero.

The evidence in this section strongly suggests that electorally induced fiscal

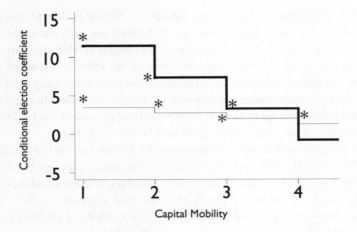

Fig. 12.   The estimated effect of an election on government debt under
fixed and flexible exchange rates and various degrees of capital-market
openness. Darker line denotes flexible exchange rate. (*Note:* * indicates
coefficent is significant at $p < .10$, one-tailed.)

cycles are context-dependent in a manner that is consistent with the game-
theoretic model in chapter 2. Electorally induced cycles in monetary policy do
not occur when the central bank is highly independent. In addition, there is
evidence that when the central bank is not independent, electorally induced
cycles in monetary policy are more likely to occur when the exchange rate is
flexible than when it is fixed. There is evidence that electorally induced cycles
in fiscal policy occur except when capital is highly mobile and the exchange
rate is flexible.

Implications for European Economic and Monetary Union

This evidence from OECD countries in the 1980s and early 1990s indicates that
opportunistic fiscal cycles are especially prevalent when capital is mobile and
exchange rates are fixed. This result has an important implication for the likely
conduct of fiscal policy under Economic and Monetary Union (EMU) in Europe. Fixed exchange rates and mobile capital will be the norm in all European
Union countries that adopted the common currency in the first wave on January 1, 1999, or that will do so in future waves.[15]

Although preparations for EMU may have reduced fiscal electoral cycles in the 1990s, it is by no means clear that EMU will restrict fiscal cycles. More generally, there has been some concern that governments, once they have been accepted into EMU, will have an incentive to renege on their commitment to low deficits. Excessively high deficits can cause both increased inflation and a depreciation of the euro, and states can hope to gain the political benefits of high deficits under a common currency without suffering the ill effects as long as the others maintain their budget discipline. Another concern is that the deficits could become so large that a state could not hope to pay back its debt without a bailout from the European Union. Since the bailout would be paid for by all European Union citizens but would reduce directly just the deficit of the country threatening default, states in this moral-hazard situation may have an incentive to run larger deficits than if the European Union did not exist.

The member governments have not been ignorant of this situation. The Treaty of Maastricht explicitly bans any European Union bailout of its member states, and the states have established a procedure to monitor the participants and punish any defectors under the Stability and Growth Pact that the European Council agreed to in Amsterdam in June 1997.[16] The European Commission will monitor the fiscal health of the member states and will report to the Council of Ministers whether, in its opinion, a deficit over 3 percent is "excessive." The Council of Ministers will then decide whether to accept the Commission's assessment, and, if it decides that a given country's deficits are indeed excessive, it will begin a procedure to sanction the transgressor. The country in question must make a non-interest-bearing deposit with the Commission equal to 0.2 percent of GDP plus an additional 0.1 percent per percentage point over the 3 percent limit. The entire process should take ten months, and if the country has not reformed its budget to the council's satisfaction, its deposit becomes a fine.[17]

Whether this pact will deter states from running chronic deficits is debatable. What is clear is that the pact will have no effect on the incentives for governments to promote opportunistic political business cycles, because of the timing of the pact's different procedures. Consider a country such as Germany, which traditionally holds elections in the fall. A government could promote a large fiscal expansion in the spring and summer that leads to large deficits. In principle, the European Commission could immediately inform the Council and begin proceedings against the government, but in practice it is most likely that the Commission would wait until the final yearly budget figures are published in March of the following year before making any recommendation, for fear that it would lose credibility if the preliminary figures turned out to be incorrect.[18] It then would take an additional ten months before fines could be imposed, and even then the fines would not be imposed if the government was taking corrective measures. The implication is that any government can push up the deficit shortly before elections so long as it cuts it back again after the elections are over.[19]

An alternative is for the states themselves to provide additional institutional constraints at the domestic level on their spending behavior. Consistent with Hallerberg and von Hagen (1999), our empirical results indicate that either a commitment to negotiated budget targets or delegation to a strong finance minister reduces preelectoral fiscal cycles. A move to one of these institutions might be in order. More generally, given that the temptation to use fiscal policy for short-term electoral gain will be greater under EMU while the domestic institutional structures will remain the same, states may have the incentive to develop such institutions only if they are sure that the European Union will not bail them out. Indeed, based on an analysis of federal systems, Eichengreen and von Hagen (1996) argue that a formal bailout rule from the European Union is not even needed as long as states maintain their ability to raise revenues. The European Union could simply say "no," much as the state of California did to Orange County in the mid-1990s when the county's creditworthiness plummeted. States may then learn, through a process of trial and error, to introduce greater restrictions on fiscal policy management at the national level. Another possible precedent comes from the United States, where fiscal mismanagement eventually led forty-seven of the fifty states to pass some form of fiscal policy restriction (Eichengreen and von Hagen 1996). It should be noted that these changes were not driven by a fear of what the states' budgets could do to the value of the dollar, but rather by more "domestic" concerns about the effects of the excessive budgets on home populations. These institutional rules seem to have some effect; states with tighter antideficit rules, as well as more restrictive rules on the fiscal authority of the legislature, pay lower interest rates on their bonds (Poterba and Rueben 1999).[20]

Conclusions

Our game-theoretic model makes fairly weak assumptions about the preferences of monetary and fiscal agents, but very strong assumptions about the institutional constraints under which they operate. The strong assumptions about the Mundell-Fleming conditions are made in part to make the analysis tractable, but they have the added benefit of stacking the deck in favor of falsification: if the predictions based on such a stark model withstand provisional tests, there are good reasons to believe that further refinement will be fruitful. Indeed, the empirical results support the insights of the model we have developed. Preelectoral monetary expansions are likely in states with mobile capital, a flexible exchange rate, and a dependent central bank, and they are absent otherwise; and preelectoral fiscal expansions are likely under mobile capital and fixed exchange rates.

These results have several interesting implications for the relationship between institutions and the international environment. In the presence of mobile capital, the exchange rate regime constrains the ability of policymakers to use one of the two macroeconomic instruments before elections. As states change their exchange rate regime, one should also expect a change in incumbents' behavior before an election. If an open-capital state fixes its currency to the dollar, for example, one would expect a shift from monetary to fiscal policy instruments. One could argue that such a shift is already under way in Britain. Under Stage III of EMU, which began January 1, 1999, the European Union members anticipate the eventual creation of an Exchange Rate Mechanism II for countries that do not join the common currency. The expectation is that the band around the euro for these currencies will progressively narrow so that these countries will also experience more or less fixed exchange rates. Preelectoral monetary expansions will become less effective than fiscal expansions.

This change also has an important effect on the selection of institutions by governments. With respect to the trade-offs involved in enhancing central bank independence, a government may consider what it gives up in terms of survival in the next election if it relinquishes monetary policy autonomy in exchange for greater general price stability with a more independent central bank. A government in a flexible exchange rate economy will lose its ability to influence outcomes with macroeconomic policy before an election if it makes the bank more independent. If the government moves the country to a fixed exchange rate regime, however, it can gain some price stability while maintaining the ability to manipulate the economy before an election. Our results suggest, for example, that British Chancellor of the Exchequer Gordon Brown would have given up little in terms of the maneuverability of his government before the next election by granting the Bank of England greater independence in May 1997. The government would be able to initiate a fiscal expansion before the next election so long as Britain has joined the Exchange Rate Mechanism II by then.

These results also suggest why previous empirical results for fiscal cycles have been so ambiguous. Few studies consider the effects of different exchange rate regimes on the likelihood of fiscal cycles. States engineered fiscal expansions when exchange rates were fixed but not when they were flexible, and studies that do not include the exchange rate regime are missing this critical variable. One of the articles that does consider the importance of exchange rate regimes, Clark and Nair Reichert 1998, appears to contradict the results here. The authors find that states with either fixed exchange rates or independent central banks are less likely to experience opportunistic political business cycles. Yet these authors concentrate their attention on outcomes, such as the unemployment rate and economic output, rather than on policy instruments, such as the money supply or budget balances. Our research here produces an interesting puzzle: why, if fiscal cycles exist when monetary policy is constrained by fixed exchange rates or a highly independent central bank, do Clark and Nair Reichert find no evidence of cycles in unemployment or growth under precisely these conditions? One possible explanation is that politicians use monetary policy before elections to affect the general economy, while they manipulate fiscal policy to sway specific constituencies. Indeed, while an increase in the money supply may help certain groups, such as home buyers, more than others, it is a blunt instrument for cultivating specific clienteles. Fiscal policy, on the other hand, is more suited to targeted use, through greater spending or tax cuts or both. The implication is that these different strategies have markedly different macroeconomic consequences.

Finally, it is clear that the choice of exchange rate regime and the degree of capital mobility have complex effects on the ability of politicians to influence the economy for electoral purposes. While the current study does not necessarily contradict the growing literature (cited in the introduction) on the effects of increased capital mobility on national policy autonomy, these effects vary a great deal across cases, both because they are refracted by the institutions through which they are transmitted, such as central banks, and because exchange rate regimes interact with capital mobility in important ways. A full consideration of both institutional and international constraints on government behavior in issue areas besides political business cycles is needed.

The context-dependent empirical analysis in this chapter suggests that the electoralist model does a better job of explaining monetary and fiscal policy choices than the partisan model does. The next two chapters will determine whether this is also the case for macroeconomic outcomes. Chapter 5 asks whether partisan differences in unemployment, economic growth, and inflation exist. Chapter 6 will examine the link between the electoral calendar and unemployment and economic growth.

CHAPTER 5

Partisan Differences and
Macroeconomic Outcomes

The whole art of Conservative politics in the 20th century is being deployed to enable wealth to persuade poverty to use its political freedom to keep wealth in power.

—Aneurin Bevan

In this chapter, I examine arguments about the effect of the partisan composition of government on macroeconomic performance. I examine propositions, including those drawn from the game-theoretic model in chapter 2, regarding the effects of central bank independence, capital mobility, and eroding national policy autonomy on partisan differences in macroeconomic performance. I begin with a reexamination of an exemplary study that tests propositions about the effect of increased capital mobility on the relationship among left governance, labor-market institutions, and macroeconomic performance (Garrett 1998). I use a data base composed of annual observations in fourteen OECD countries from 1966 to 1990 to examine the evidence that, in addition to the constraints I identified in chapter 2, the relationship between the ideological composition of government and macroeconomic performance is modified by the structure of labor-market institutions. I find that there is little evidence for the social democratic corporatist model of macroeconomic performance before, during, or after the recent increase in international capital mobility. I then examine whether there is more evidence in support of the social democratic corporatist model after controlling for the modifying effects of the international or domestic constraints identified by the decision-theoretic model in chapter 2. Finally, using a separate times-series cross-sectional data base consisting of quarterly observations in eighteen OECD countries from 1960 to 1989, I examine whether these international and domestic constraints interact in the manner described by the game-theoretic model in chapter 2. In both cases, I find little evidence of partisan differences in macroeconomic performance.

A Test of the Decision-Theoretic Model

The Hibbsian model discussed in chapter 3 has received considerable criticism. In a series of articles published between 1985 and 1991, Peter Lange and Geoffrey Garrett found that the effect of the partisan composition of government depends on the structure of labor-market institutions—left governance, for example, only has "a positive impact on economic growth when labor is highly and centrally organized" (Lange and Garrett 1985, 792). This result has proven to be quite robust against alternative specifications and small changes in sample.[1] In addition, it has been coupled with a coherent explanation that focuses on the strategic interaction between government and workers that is consistent with a large literature on democratic corporatism. Left governments can better pursue their preferred growth-oriented policies if the structure of labor-market institutions encourages wage restraint, and such wage restraint is most likely forthcoming when labor bargaining institutions are sufficiently large and centralized that they internalize the costs of inflationary real-wage demands and possess instruments to deter individual unions from defecting from industry-wide agreements.[2] Such cooperation between left governments and encompassing unions may also favorably influence the expectations of investors, leading to higher and less volatile levels of investments in human and physical capital. The implication of this literature is that it is not left governance per se but rather a broader sociopolitical regime of social democratic corporatism that produces distinct macroeconomic outcomes. Indeed, it has been argued (Alvarez, Garrett, and Lange 1991) that when encompassing labor-market institutions are not present, parties of the right outperform parties of the left. I will refer to this group of propositions as the social democratic corporatist (SDC) hypothesis and will return to the Hibbsian version of the partisan argument when evaluating the game-theoretic model later in this chapter.

The chapter begins with a reexamination of the baseline SDC model, followed by a consideration of the ways in which the relationships posited by this model may depend on the structural environment in which policymakers find themselves. Katzenstein (1985) has argued that the distinctiveness of social democratic corporatism is reinforced by, rather than threatened by, increased trade openness. This, he argues, is because social democratic governments act to compensate vulnerable constituents for the risks associated with increased competition from imports and dependence on exports. Garrett (1995) examines whether increased capital-market integration creates competitive pressures for convergence; he finds that the compensatory hypothesis that, Katzenstein argues, explains responses to trade openness outperforms the convergence hypothesis with regard to capital-market openness as well. In a parallel series of articles, Way (2000) and Hall and Franzese (1998) examine whether the purported advantages of central bank independence are mediated in important ways by the structure of labor-market institutions.

The Social Democratic Corporatist Model

Garrett (1998) reports results for a baseline model similar to that of Alvarez, Garrett, and Lange (1991) intended to examine the interaction between left governance and labor-market institutions in the absence of a consideration of the potentially perturbing effects of global integration. The model to be tested is as follows:

$$Perf_{it} = b_1 Left_{it} + b_2 Lmi_{it} + b_3(Left_{it} \cdot Lm_{it}) + b_4 Perf_{it-1} + \Sigma(b_j Period_{it})$$

$$+ \Sigma(b_k Country_{it}) + \Sigma(b_1 X_{lit}) + \varepsilon_{it}, \tag{1}$$

where *Perf* is a macroeconomic performance indicator such as *Unemployment*, *GDP growth*, or *Inflation*, *Left* is Garrett's political center of gravity measure (capturing the representation of left parties in both the cabinet and the legislature), and *Lmi* is Garrett's measures of labor encompassment (a higher score means more-encompassing labor-market institutions). As elsewhere in this volume, a lagged dependent variable and country dummies are included. Finally, *X* is a vector of control variables expected to influence macroeconomic performance (*Oecdd* captures OECD demand for a country's exports, and *Oild* captures the country's dependence on oil imports).

Since the SDC hypothesis predicts that left governance is associated with increased growth and decreased unemployment and inflation when labor markets are encompassing, but with decreased growth and increased unemployment and inflation when they are not, one would expect to find a positive and significant coefficient on *Left* (since it describes the relationship between growth and left governance when labor-market institutions are not encompassing [*Lmi* = 0]) in the unemployment and inflation equations, but a negative and significant coefficient for *Left* in the growth equation. In addition, one would expect the sign on the coefficient for the interaction term to be negative for the unemployment and inflation equations and positive for the growth equation, and large enough in magnitude to have a substantive effect on the coefficient for *Left*.

Table 18 presents the OLS results for equation (1). At first glance, the results appear to lend support to the SDC hypothesis, but a closer look raises serious questions about the empirical support for the SDC hypothesis. As predicted, the *Left* coefficients are positive in the unemployment and inflation models and negative in the growth model. Furthermore, the coefficients on the interaction terms in two of the three models have the opposite sign as the *Left* coefficient. This pattern suggests that left governance is associated with relatively poor macroeconomic performance when unions are weak and decentralized, but that these deleterious effects are diminished by increases in labor-market encompassment. Indeed, as the SDC hypothesis suggests, left governance may even be associated with better performance at high levels of encompassment.

Looking at the OLS results alone, it is difficult to tell what effect left gover-

TABLE 18.   The Effect of Left Governance on Macroeconomic Performance as Conditioned by Labor-Market Encompassment

	GDP Growth (1)	Unemployment (2)	Inflation (3)
Left	−0.592**	0.233**	0.060
	(0.266)	(0.127)	(0.309)
Lmi	−0.122	0.189	1.246*
	(0.559)	(0.251)	(0.692)
Left · Lmi	0.226**	−0.086*	0.002
	(0.124)	(0.060)	(0.134)
Lagged *GDP growth*	0.125*	0.880***	0.566***
	(0.072)	(0.034)	(0.079)
Openlag · Oecdgdp	0.006**	−0.002***	−0.006***
	(0.002)	(0.001)	(0.002)
Oild	−6.591	−0.210	5.931
	(6.424)	(1.801)	(7.189)
Constant	2.310*	0.323	−0.028
	(1.192)	(0.556)	(1.777)
F_{DW}	2.98	5.69	2.36
Prob. > *F*	0.0195	0.0002	0.0542
Observations	350	350	350
Number of countries	14	14	14

Note: Panel-corrected standard errors are in parentheses.
Coefficients for country and period dummy variables are not reported.
The term F_{DW} is the test statistic for Durbin-Watson's *m*.
*$p < .10$, **$p < .05$, ***$p < .01$, one-tailed test for variables involving *Left*, two-tailed otherwise.

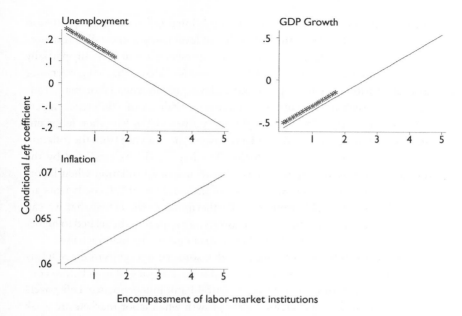

Fig. 13.   The estimated causal effect of *Left-labor power* on macroeconomic performance at various levels of labor-market encompassment. (*Note:* * indicates coefficent is
significant at $p < .10$ level, one-tailed.)

nance has on macroeconomic performance for any given degree of labor-
market encompassment. To do so requires the calculation of conditional
coefficients. Figure 13 plots the conditional *Left* coefficients for a range of
plausible values of the hypothesized modifying variable (labor-market encompassment). Thus, the downward-sloping solid line suggests that when
labor-market institutions are encompassing, the model estimates that an increase in left governance will be associated with an increase in unemployment, but that the estimated effect of left governance converges toward zero
as labor-market institutions become more encompassing. Indeed, when
labor-market institutions are sufficiently encompassing, the estimated effect
of left governance on unemployment becomes *negative*. All of this is perfectly
consistent with the SDC hypothesis. But, as King, Keohane, and Verba (1994)
remind us, in addition to estimating causal effects, empirical researches
should provide the reader with an indication of the degree of confidence with
which we can make inferences from such estimates. For this reason, I have

indicated with an asterisk which of the conditional *Left* coefficients plotted in figure 13 are statistically significant at the .10 level using a one-tailed test.[3]

An examination of figure 13 suggests that the evidence is at best only partially consistent with the SDC hypothesis. While there is evidence that left governance is associated with more unemployment and less growth when labor-market institutions are weak and decentralized, there is no evidence of a difference in performance between parties of the right and parties of the left when labor encompassment meets or exceeds moderate levels. The evidence from the inflation model is even less consistent with the SDC hypothesis. As predicted by the hypothesis, left governance is associated with increased inflation when labor-market encompassment is low, but none of the conditional *Left* coefficients are statistically distinguishable from zero. Furthermore, to the extent that we can have confidence in these estimates, left governance appears to be related to higher inflation, not price stability, when labor-market encompassment increases.

The evidence presented here suggests that some components of the SDC argument are supported by the evidence, and some are not—at least before considering the effects of capital flows or central bank independence. Left governance is associated with decreased GDP growth when labor markets are weak and decentralized, but not otherwise. Similarly, there is some evidence that left governance leads to higher rates of unemployment if and only if labor unions are weak and decentralized. There is, in contrast to earlier studies (Alvarez, Garrett, and Lange 1991), no evidence that governments dominated by left parties are associated with higher growth rates or lower unemployment rates when labor-market institutions are encompassing. Unhappily for supporters of left-wing parties, these results suggest that right parties perform as well as left parties under some labor-market conditions and better than left parties under other conditions.

Finally, there is no evidence that inflation is related to the ideological orientation of the government. The absence of statistically significant support for the SDC hypothesis as it relates to inflation is particularly troubling, since the achievement of price stability through wage restraint under left governance and encompassing labor-market institutions plays a big role in the explanation for the model's predictions related to growth.[4]

If the findings presented here are correct, prior results indicating that left governments achieve better macroeconomic performance than right governments when labor-market institutions are encompassing need to be reevaluated. There are at least two possible explanations for the presence of partisan differences when labor-market institutions are weak and decentralized, but not when they are encompassing.

Since stable growth under social democratic corporatist institutions requires successful bargaining between business, government, and labor, left-wing governments have no particular advantage over parties of the right in securing such agreements. The reverse, however, is not true—where labor-market institutions are not encompassing, stable growth occurs only in the presence of investor confidence, which depends on expectations about labor quiescence in the face of market-oriented policies. Poor macroeconomic performance may result if investor confidence is lower when left-wing governments are in power.

Another, and perhaps related, explanation is that left parties may be less ideologically mobile than parties of the right. If this turns out to be true, then a Hibbsian framework may predict behavior under weak and decentralizing institutions, and a Downsian model might do better when labor-market institutions are encompassing.

These two explanations could, in a sense, be combined. If, as the SDC model suggests, the interventionist policies associated with left parties outperform laissez-faire policies when encompassing labor-market institutions are present, would not right-wing parties ape the policies of the left under these conditions? Similarly, if market-oriented policies are more effective than interventionist policies when labor markets are encompassing, would not left-wing governments adopt policies of the right when they ruled in such circumstances? The results presented above suggest that left-wing parties have more difficulty adapting to their environment than parties of the right, which suggests that it is harder for left-wing parties to make commitments that investors will deem credible than it is for right-wing parties to make commitments that are credible to workers.

The Social Democratic Corporatist Model in the Open Economy

One explanation for the relative lack of evidence supporting the SDC hypothesis is that conditional effects of left governance are themselves sensitive to other contextual factors. In the remainder of this chapter, I will examine whether evidence consistent with the SDC hypothesis is brought into sharper focus when we develop a more refined institutional setting for the making of macroeconomic policy. Recently, for example, many analysts have argued that increased capital mobility has led to fundamental changes in the politics of macroeconomic policy. If this is true, the test in the preceding section would be misspecified, because the proposed relationship may be in effect only in the before-capital-mobility period.

The Modifying Effects of Capital Mobility

The most straightforward way to examine the effect of increasing capital mobility on the behaviors posited by the SDC hypothesis is to see if the empirical regularities outlined above are modified in important ways by changes in capital mobility. Garrett (1998) does just that, but, as I argued in chapter 3, small changes in method can lead to different conclusions about the effects of globalization on the domestic politics of macroeconomic policy. The basic model is an extension of equation (1):

$$Perf_{it} = b_1 Left_{it} + b_2 Lmi_{it} + b_3 Cm_{it} + b_4(Left_{it} \cdot Lmi_{it}) + b_5(Left_{it} \cdot Cm_{it})$$

$$+ b_6(Lmi_{it} \cdot Cm_{it}) + b_7(Left_{it} \cdot Lmi_{it} \cdot Cm_{it}) + b_8 Perf_{it-1}$$

$$+ \Sigma(b_j Period_{it}) + \Sigma(b_k Country_{it}) + \Sigma(b_l X_{lit}) + \varepsilon_{it}, \tag{2}$$

where all terms are as before and *Cm* is a measure of capital mobility. Table 19 reports the OLS results for six equations—two each for the unemployment, growth, and inflation equations. The first of each set of equations reproduces Garrett's results, and the second of each set is identical to the first except for the construction of the capital-mobility measure. Garrett (1998) uses a standard measure of capital mobility based on the IMF's record of the capital controls in place in a given country during a given year. His indicator is the number of controls in place (out of a set of four controls) multiplied by -1, so that a higher score indicates greater capital mobility (a country employing none of the controls would be scored zero, indicating more capital mobility, while a country employing all four of the controls would be scored -4, indicating less capital mobility). This is a straightforward procedure and does no damage to the validity of any of the estimates in the model or inferences drawn from them. It can, however, create some minor interpretation problems, which can descend rather quickly into major inferential errors. Since Garrett's indicator of capital mobility equals zero when capital is most mobile, the conditional co-efficient for *Left* (in columns 1a–3a) describes the relationship between left governance and macroeconomic performance when labor-market institutions are not encompassing ($Lmi = 0$) and capital is highly mobile ($Cmg = 0$). Since we want to examine the effects of increasing capital mobility, this does not strike me as an intuitively appealing baseline case, so I have transformed the Garrett capital-mobility measure by a simple additive transformation so that *Cml* (or capital-market liberalization) is zero when all four capital controls are in place and 4 when all four have been removed. It should be emphasized that this rescaling does not change the substantive results at all (note that the co-efficients and standard errors for eleven of the fourteen reported variables are identical across each pair of equations)[5] but allows us to now interpret the *Left* coefficients as describing the relationship between macroeconomic outcomes and left governance where labor-market institutions are not encompassing and capital markets are not liberalized. Only the coefficients that are conditioned upon the value of the capital-mobility variable are affected by the rescaling,

TABLE 19.   The Effect of Left Governance on Macroeconomic Performance in 14 OECD Countries, under Various Degrees of Capital Mobility and Labor-Market Encompassment

	Unemployment (1)		GDP Growth (2)		Inflation (3)	
	(a) Cmg	(b) Cml	(a) Cmg	(b) Cml	(a) Cmg	(b) Cml
Left	0.629***	−1.127*	0.325	−5.138***	0.335	−2.149
	(0.229)	(0.689)	(0.564)	(1.743)	(0.466)	(1.861)
Lmi	0.431	−1.340**	0.135	−2.349	1.502**	−0.765
	(0.285)	(0.636)	(0.614)	(1.432)	(0.697)	(1.525)
Cml	−0.849**	−0.849**	−2.450***	−2.450***	−2.324**	−2.324**
	(0.382)	(0.382)	(0.950)	(0.950)	(1.103)	(1.103)
Left · Lmi	−0.287***	0.523**	0.074	1.254***	−0.093	0.733*
	(0.094)	(0.240)	(0.192)	(0.534)	(0.179)	(0.547)
Cml · Left	0.439**	0.439**	1.366**	1.366***	0.621	0.621
	(0.216)	(0.216)	(0.551)	(0.551)	(0.545)	(0.545)
Cml · Lmi	0.443**	0.443**	0.621	0.621	0.567	0.567
	(0.180)	(0.180)	(0.392)	(0.392)	(0.373)	(0.373)
Cml · Left · Lmi	−0.203***	−0.203***	−0.295**	−0.295**	−0.206	−0.206
	(0.076)	(0.076)	(0.165)	(0.165)	(0.162)	(0.162)
Lagged dependent variable	0.852***	0.852***	0.110	0.110	0.524***	0.524***
	(0.037)	(0.037)	(0.071)	(0.071)	(0.083)	(0.083)
Openlag · Oecdgdp	−0.002*	−0.002*	0.007***	0.007***	−0.006***	−0.006***
	(0.001)	(0.001)	(0.002)	(0.002)	(0.002)	(0.002)
Oild	0.638	0.638	−5.828	−5.828	5.880	5.881
	(1.814)	(1.814)	(6.413)	(6.413)	(7.122)	(7.122)
Constant	0.101	3.499**	1.440	11.239***	0.016	9.312**
	(0.581)	(1.552)	(1.281)	(3.662)	(1.789)	(4.610)
F_{DW}	4.27	4.27	4.25	4.27	0.50	4.27
Prob. > F	0.0023	0.0023	0.0024	0.0023	0.733	0.0023
Observations	350	350	350	350	350	350
Number of countries	14	14	14	14	14	14

Note: Panel-corrected standard errors are in parentheses.
Coefficients for country and period dummy variables are not reported.
The term F_{DW} is the test statistic for Durbin-Watson's *m*.
*p < .10, **p < .05, ***p < .01, one-tailed test for variables involving *Left*, two-tailed otherwise.

and this change is easily handled by (indeed, it was done to facilitate) a careful conditional interpretation of the coefficients.

If the SDC hypothesis is the appropriate description of the domestic politics of macroeconomic policy choice in the before-capital-mobility world, then we should expect to find evidence of increased unemployment and inflation and decreased growth under left rule when labor-market institutions are not encompassing ($Lmi = 0$) and capital flows are highly regulated ($Cml = 0$). This, of course, is the situation described by the *Left* parameter estimate in columns 1b–3b in table 19. Is there evidence for this implication of the SDC hypothesis under the conditions of highly regulated capital flows? The results are mixed. The *Left* coefficient has the hypothesized sign and is statistically significant in the growth equation, but it is not significant or has the wrong sign in the unemployment and inflation equations. In the case where capital markets have not been liberalized and labor markets are not encompassing, left governance is associated with decreased growth but with neither increased unemployment nor increased inflation.

A quick and dirty way of gauging the effects of increased capital mobility on this baseline situation is available in the comparison between the *Left* coefficients in each of the pairs of equations in table 19. As noted, since Garrett's measure of capital mobility equals zero when all four controls have been removed, the *Left* coefficient indicates the relationship between left governance and macroeconomic outcomes when labor encompassment is low and capital mobility is high. If an increase in capital mobility does not constrain the behavior of the SDC hypothesis, then the predictions discussed above about the conditional *Left* coefficient for the case where capital controls are in place ought to continue to hold where capital controls have been removed. This turns out not to be the case. A comparison of the two equations for each of the three indicators of macroeconomic performance reveals that the sign on the *Left* coefficient always changes when going from the hypothetically closed capital market to the completely open capital market. While there is no evidence that SDC relationships have persisted in the face of, or have been reinforced by, increased capital mobility, there is surprising evidence in the unemployment equation (column 1a). The positive and significant *Left* coefficient suggests that one of the hypothesized effects of left governance (that it leads to increased unemployment when labor-market encompassment is low) occurs after capital mobility, but not before. From the standpoint of the SDC hypothesis, this is not terribly surprising, since capital mobility can be expected to intensify the problems of macroeconomic management when there is a high degree of incoherence between the orientation of government and labor-market institutions. What is surprising is that the SDC hypothesis about the relationship between left governance and unemployment in the absence of encompassing unions does not appear to be supported in the *absence* of capital mobility (column 1b). Under such conditions, according to the SDC hypothesis, left governance should produce stagflation, but according to the evidence presented here, it *reduces* unemployment.

Inexplicably, an increase in capital mobility appears to have the opposite effect on the relationship between left governance and growth when labor markets are not encompassing. As predicted by the SDC hypothesis, left governance leads to a loss in output when labor markets are not encompassing if capital is strictly controlled (column 2b), but the advantages held by right-led governments amid market-oriented labor institutions appear to dissipate in the face of capital mobility (the coefficient for *Left* goes from negative in column 2b to indistinguishable from zero in 2a). This is puzzling; if the reason right governments produce higher rates than left governments when labor markets are weak and decentralized is that the latter cannot commit to market-based policies in a way that is credible to investors, would we not expect this effect to be *more* pronounced when capital is mobile?

Finally (according to the *Left* coefficient in column 3a), there is no more evidence of a link between inflation and partisanship when labor-market institutions are weak and decentralized and capital is fully mobile than when capital was completely constrained.

While interesting and provocative, such comparisons are ultimately limited because they only tell us about the effects of extreme changes in capital mobility, and then only under one specific situation—the case of zero labor encompassment. To get a more comprehensive look at the effects of capital mobility on SDC behavior, we need to calculate conditional coefficients for a range of values for both of the modifying variables. Figure 14 displays the conditional *Left* coefficients calculated from the equations in columns 1b–3b in table 19 for three discrete levels of capital mobility and all observed levels of labor encompassment.[6] Recall from the discussion of figure 13 that the closed-economy SDC argument implies that the conditional *Left* coefficient in the unemployment and inflation equations should be decreasing in labor encompassment and significantly above the horizontal axis when labor encompassment is low and significantly below the horizontal axis when labor encompassment is high (note that the opposite is expected for the coefficients derived from the growth equation). If, as some have argued, the SDC hypothesis is an accurate description of the domestic politics of macroeconomic policy-making only when national economies are not highly integrated, we would expect to observe this

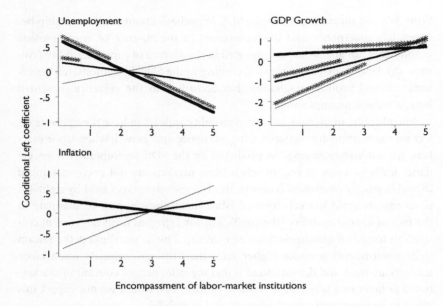

Fig. 14.   The estimated causal effect of *Left-labor power* on macroeconomic performance at various levels of labor-market encompassment and capital mobility. Darker lines denote increased capital-market liberalization. (*Note:* * indicates coefficient is significant at $p < .10$, one-tailed.)

pattern when capital-market liberalization is modest (e.g., *Cml* = 2) but not where it is advanced (e.g., *Cml* = 4). If, as others have argued, the SDC hypothesis continues to be an apt description of the domestic politics of macroeconomic policy-making even in a world of integrated capital markets, we would observe no change in the aforementioned downwardly sloping conditional *Left* coefficient. Finally, if, as Garrett argues, the recent increase in international capital mobility may have reinvigorated the relationships outlined by the SDC framework, we would expect the downward slope in the conditional *Left* coefficient to steepen as capital controls are removed.

A careful examination of the unemployment and inflation panels of figure 14 seems to belie both the convergence and the compensation arguments. The upward-sloping solid line in the unemployment panel—which plots the estimated conditional coefficients for the case where two capital controls are in place—suggests that there is no discernable partisan difference in unemployment rates at any level of labor-market encompassment when capital markets are relatively closed. While the upward slope is consistent with the expected effect of labor-market institutions, none of the estimated conditional effects it plots are statistically significant. (The conditional coefficients that are statistically significant at the .10 level [one-tailed test] are indicated by asterisks.) These results—representative of the before-capital-mobility world—run contrary to expectations informed by the SDC hypothesis. It seems that in the "good old days" of insulated capital markets, unemployment was independent from the ideological orientation of the government, and the degree of encompassment of labor-market institutions made very little difference. Perhaps even more surprising is that the pattern of conditional *Left* coefficients predicted by the SDC hypothesis *is* displayed in the unemployment panel of figure 14 for the case where capital controls are entirely absent! The thickest downward-sloping line (it meets the y-axis above .50) suggests that left governance is associated with increased unemployment when labor unions are weak and decentralized. Also consistent with the SDC hypothesis is the finding that when labor-market institutions are encompassing, an increase in left governance is associated with a decrease in unemployment. Not surprisingly, the case of one capital control falls between these two cases. The plot of the conditional coefficients slopes downward, but only a few of the conditional coefficients are statistically significant.

The inflation panel of figure 14 shows that a similarly anomalous set of results is produced by the inflation equation. Once again, the line plotting the effect of changes in labor-market encompassment on the conditional effect of left governance on inflation in closed economies slopes upward rather than downward (as the SDC hypothesis predicts). Too much should not be made of this result, however, since none of the conditional coefficients are statistically significant. Once again, if a pattern of conditional *Left* coefficients consistent with the SDC hypothesis is to be found, it is when capital controls are entirely absent; but again, none of these conditional coefficients are statistically significant.[7] This result is surprising, since, as noted, the ability of left governments and encompassing labor unions to enforce wage restraint is a crucial element of the causal arguments underlying the SDC hypothesis (Bruno and Sachs 1985; Golden 1993).

With respect to unemployment and inflation, therefore, the evidence in support of the SDC hypothesis is at best mixed. While there is evidence that left governance is associated with increased unemployment when labor-market encompassment is low and lower unemployment when it is high, this is the case only when capital markets are highly open. In contrast, the implications of the SDC hypothesis for inflation are not supported under any degree of capital-market openness commonly experienced in the postwar period. There is no evidence that left governance combines with labor-market encompassment to produce price stability. In fact, when two capital controls are in place, an increase in left governance is associated with a decrease in inflation *only if labor-market institutions are weak and decentralized.*

The evidence produced by the growth equation is, however, more consistent with the SDC hypothesis. Recall that the closed-economy SDC argument implies that the conditional *Left* coefficient in the GDP growth equation should be increasing in labor encompassment and significantly below the horizontal axis when labor encompassment is low and significantly above the horizontal axis when labor encompassment is high. This turns out to be largely the case. The estimated causal effect of an increase in left governance is negative when labor-market institutions are weak and decentralized but positive when labor-market encompassment is very high. If an increase in capital mobility reinforced these relationships, we would expect the line that plots these conditional coefficients to steepen. If capital mobility constrained the conditional effect of left governance on economic growth that is posited by the SDC hypothesis, however, we would observe a flattening of the line plotting the conditional *Left* coefficients to the point where they were, for the most part, statistically indistinguishable from zero. While some flattening is observed (indicating that an increase in international capital mobility does *not* reinforce the patterns posited by the SDC hypothesis), it is not so pronounced as to reduce to zero the estimated causal effect of left governance on growth. Specifically, the estimated causal effect of an increase in left governance on growth when one capital control is in place is completely consistent with the SDC hypothesis: left governance leads to output losses when labor-market institutions are weak and decentralized but to gains in output when labor-market institutions are encompassing. Indeed, the latter portion of this story appears to be true even when capital markets are completely open. In the absence of capital controls, an increase in left governance is associated with an increase in growth when labor encompassment is high.

Thus, broadly speaking, the evidence seems to suggest that Alvarez, Garrett, and Lange's findings (1991) regarding growth hold up in the face of increasing capital mobility.[8] That said, the effect of capital-market liberalization on partisan differences, for any given level of labor-market encompassment, can be seen in figure 14 by vertical movements from one line to another. Such a comparison suggests that when labor-market institutions are not encompassing, an increase in capital mobility lessens the deleterious effects of left governance. Put differently, under such conditions, capital mobility weakens the benefits of right governance. This result is consistent with the argument that left governments have a greater need for devices that will lend the kind of credibility to their policies that will instill market confidence.

The results here suggest that encompassing labor-market institutions may be one such device. Central bank independence and commitments to fixed exchange rates are obvious alternatives. Since encompassing labor unions are the products of long-term historical developments, left governments that confront weak and decentralized unions should be eager to enhance the independence of the central bank and/or the credibility of commitments to fixed exchange rates. Such a result is consistent with the Wilson government's reluctance to devalue the pound in Britain in the 1960s, the Blair government's enthusiasm for transferring control over interest rates to the Bank of England in the 1990s, and the enthusiasm of the Socialists in France for schemes that pegged the franc to the deutschemark. Finally, it should be noted that the magnitude of the effects of capital mobility on partisan differences is smaller when labor encompassment is high.

Overall, the results presented up to this point fail to add up to strong evidence that the SDC hypothesis is an accurate description of the politics of macroeconomic performance before capital mobility. While there is some support for the SDC hypothesis as it pertains to GDP growth, there is little evidence consistent with the SDC hypothesis as it concerns either inflation or unemployment.

The Modifying Effect of Exchange Rates

The previous section suggests there are some good reasons for a fundamental reconsideration of the social democratic corporatist model. There seems to be little evidence of a systematic relationship between partisanship and macroeconomic outcomes—before, during, or after the recent increase in capital mobility. That said, there are also reasons to believe that the preceding tests relied upon a misspecified model. As argued in chapter 2, the Mundell-Fleming model tells us that an increase in international capital will lead to a decrease in monetary policy effectiveness when the exchange rate is fixed but not when it is flexible. Indeed, monetary policy may be particularly effective when the exchange rate is flexible. Similarly, an increase in capital mobility is expected to lead to a decrease in fiscal policy effectiveness when the exchange rate is flexible, but an increase in capital mobility can actually enhance the effectiveness of fiscal policy when the exchange rate is fixed. If the ability of policymakers to produce the types of macroeconomic outcomes predicted by the SDC model is related to their ability to control these instruments, then the effect of capital mobility on partisan differences in outcomes is likely to be mediated by the nature of the exchange rate commitment. We can model this modifying effect by entering an interaction term for flexible exchange rates and interact it with capital mobility in the preceding model:

$$Perf_{it} = b_1 Left_{it} + b_2 Lmi_{it} + b_3 Cm_{it} + b_4(Left_{it} \cdot Lmi_{it}) + b_5(Left_{it} \cdot Cm_{it})$$

$$+ b_6(Lmi_{it} \cdot Cm_{it}) + b_7(Left_{it} \cdot Lmi_{it} \cdot Cm_{it}) + b_9(Cm_{it} \cdot Flex)$$

$$+ b_{10}(Left_{it} \cdot Cm_{it} \cdot Flex) + b_{11}(Lmi_{it} \cdot Cm_{it} \cdot Flex)$$

$$+ b_{12}(Left_{it} \cdot Lmi_{it} \cdot Cm_{it} \cdot Flex) + b_8 Perf_{it-1} + \Sigma(b_j Period_{it})$$

$$+ \Sigma(b_k Country_{it}) + \Sigma(b_l X_{lit}) + \varepsilon_{it}. \tag{3}$$

Now we can calculate conditional coefficients for the case where the exchange rate is flexible as well as for the case when it is fixed. In the latter case, when *Flex* = 0, the conditional coefficients and standard errors are the same as they would have been in the previous section:

$$\frac{\partial Perf_{it}}{\partial Left} = b_1 Left_{it} + b_4 Lmi_{it} + b_5 Cm_{it} + b_7(Lmi_{it} \cdot Cm_{it}), \tag{4}$$

When the exchange rate is flexible, the conditional coefficient would be

$$\frac{\partial Perf_{it}}{\partial Left} = b_1 Left_{it} + b_4 Lmi_{it} + b_5 Cm_{it} + b_7(Lmi_{it} \cdot Cm_{it}) + b_{10}(Cm_{it} \cdot Flex)$$

$$+ b_{11}(Cm_{it} \cdot Flex) + b_{12}(Lmi_{it} \cdot Cm_{it} \cdot Flex)_{it}, \tag{5}$$

which, especially when calculating the associated conditional standard errors, can be rather cumbersome, but the logic is identical to that in the simpler models above. Indeed, since the third modifying variable is dichotomous, the relevant conditional coefficients can be easily calculated by defining the modifying variable as *Fixed* and calculating the conditional coefficient for the case where *Fixed* = 0.

The OLS results from model 3 are reported in table 20 (columns 1a–3a), as well as a model that defines the exchange rate regime as *Fixed* (columns 1b–3b). Note that in columns 1a–3a, the coefficients for the first seven variables describe

TABLE 20. The Effects of Left Governance on Macroeconomic Performance as Conditioned by the Degree of Labor-Market Encompassment, Capital Mobility, and the Exchange Rate Regime

	Unemployment (1) ERR = 1 if		GDP Growth (2) ERR = 1 if		Inflation (3) ERR = 1 if	
	Flexible = 1 (a)	Fixed = 1 (b)	Flexible = 1 (a)	Fixed = 1 (b)	Flexible = 1 (a)	Fixed = 1 (b)
Left	−0.862	−0.499	−8.123***	4.517	−2.054	9.653
	(0.815)	(5.372)	(1.764)	(12.531)	(2.221)	(16.900)
Lmi	−1.304*	−2.699	−3.642**	−4.232	−1.122	13.451
	(0.699)	(2.671)	(1.516)	(7.128)	(1.639)	(9.737)
Cml	−0.675	−1.120	−4.206***	0.045	−2.557**	2.537
	(0.472)	(1.540)	(1.004)	(3.938)	(1.267)	(4.801)
Left · Lmi	0.462**	0.631	1.857***	−0.554	0.858*	−5.556
	(0.267)	(1.986)	(0.559)	(4.871)	(0.627)	(6.781)
Left · Cml	0.331	0.305	2.420***	−1.404	0.586	−2.144
	(0.261)	(1.387)	(0.559)	(3.240)	(0.688)	(4.292)
Cml · Lmi	0.397*	0.798	0.936**	1.093	0.837*	−3.080
	(0.209)	(0.691)	(0.426)	(1.830)	(0.434)	(2.459)
Left · Lmi · Cml	−0.180**	−0.231	−0.503***	0.224	−0.256*	1.347
	(0.086)	(0.511)	(0.175)	(1.243)	(0.196)	(1.720)
Exchange rate regime (ERR)	1.017	−1.017	−14.187	14.187	−18.625	18.625
	(6.261)	(6.261)	(15.380)	(15.380)	(19.098)	(19.098)
Left · ERR	0.363	−0.363	12.640	−12.640	11.707	−11.707
	(5.523)	(5.523)	(12.744)	(12.744)	(17.249)	(17.249)
Lmi · ERR	−1.395	1.395	−0.590	0.590	14.574	−14.574
	(2.794)	(2.794)	(7.100)	(7.100)	(9.850)	(9.850)
Cml · ERR	−0.445	0.445	4.251	−4.251	5.094	−5.094
	(1.688)	(1.688)	(4.178)	(4.178)	(5.029)	(5.029)
Left · Lmi · ERR	0.169	−0.169	−2.412	2.412	−6.414	6.414
	(2.030)	(2.030)	(4.904)	(4.904)	(6.902)	(6.902)
Left · Cml · ERR	−0.026	0.026	−3.824	3.824	−2.730	2.730
	(1.446)	(1.446)	(3.330)	(3.330)	(4.421)	(4.421)
Lmi · Cml · ERR	0.401	−0.401	0.157	−0.157	−3.917	3.917
	(0.748)	(0.748)	(1.878)	(1.878)	(2.570)	(2.570)
Left · Lmi · Cml · ERR	−0.051	0.051	0.727	−0.727	1.603	−1.603
	(0.530)	(0.530)	(1.262)	(1.262)	(1.768)	(1.768)
Lagged dependent variable	0.852***	0.852***	0.082	0.082	0.480***	0.480***
	(0.038)	(0.038)	(0.069)	(0.069)	(0.082)	(0.082)
Openlag · Oecdgdp	−0.002**	−0.002**	0.006***	0.006***	−0.007***	−0.007***
	(0.001)	(0.001)	(0.002)	(0.002)	(0.002)	(0.002)
Oild	0.624	0.624	−4.039	−4.039	4.992	4.992
	(1.864)	(1.864)	(6.281)	(6.281)	(7.570)	(7.570)
Constant	3.351**	4.368	16.289***	2.103	9.234*	−9.391
	(1.701)	(6.002)	(3.589)	(15.292)	(4.838)	(18.967)
F_{DW}	2.59	2.59	4.51	4.51	0.61	0.61
Prob. > F	0.038	0.038	0.002	0.002	0.656	0.656
Observations	350	350	350	350	350	350
Number of countries	14	14	14	14	14	14

Note: Panel-corrected standard errors are in parentheses.
Coefficients for country and period dummy variables are not reported.
The term F_{DW} is the test statistic for Durbin-Watson's m.
*$p < .10$, **$p < .05$, ***$p < .01$, one-tailed test for variables involving Left, two-tailed otherwise.

the estimated causal effects of a change in that variable in the case where the exchange rate is fixed (*Flex* = 0). In columns 1b–3b, however, these same coefficients describe the estimated causal effect of a change in those variables in the case where the exchange rate is allowed to fluctuate (*Fixed* = 0). The negative and significant sign on the *Left* coefficient in column 2a, for example, indicates that an increase in left governance is estimated to have a large negative effect on GDP growth when the exchange rate is fixed, capital is immobile, and labor-market institutions are weak and decentralized. Note that the *Left* coefficient is significant in only one column out of six. This suggests that with the exception of the fixed exchange rate case and growth, left governance is not linked to macroeconomic performance when labor-market encompassment is low in the period prior to capital-market liberalization—whether the exchange rate is fixed or flexible.

A more general picture of the ways in which capital mobility and the exchange rate regime may interact to modify SDC relationships can be seen by examining conditional *Left* coefficients. Figure 15, for example, plots the conditional *Left* coefficients for various degrees of labor-market encompassment and capital-market liberalization for the case where the exchange rate is fixed. Under such circumstances, according to the Mundell-Fleming model, an increase in capital mobility reduces national monetary policy autonomy but potentially makes fiscal policy more effective. Clark and Nair Reichert (1998) argue that an increase in capital mobility that occurs in the context of fixed exchange rates erodes national monetary policy autonomy in a way that makes it more difficult for survival-maximizing incumbents to engineer preelectoral macroeconomic expansions (see chap. 6). If it similarly constrained the ability of incumbents to use monetary policy for partisan reasons—without enhancing their ability to use fiscal policy for partisan purposes in a completely offsetting fashion—then we would expect to find patterns consistent with the SDC hypothesis when the exchange rate is fixed and capital mobility is low, but not when it is high.

Recall that the SDC hypothesis implies that the plot of conditional *Left* coefficients would slope downward for the unemployment and inflation equations and upward for the growth equations. The convergence hypothesis implies that these lines would be flatter after capital-market liberalization than before, and the compensation hypothesis implies that these lines would become steeper. Note that the conditional coefficients in figure 15 suggest that the pattern implied by the SDC holds under fixed exchange rates and high barriers to capital mobility in the growth equation; the lightest line in the growth plot slopes upward, and many of the coefficients for the low labor-market en-

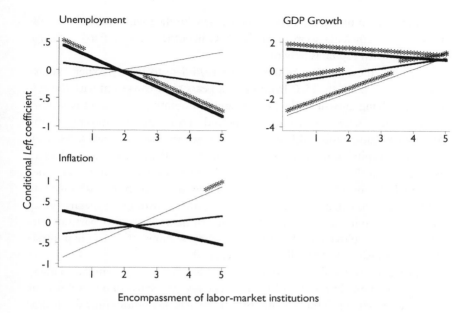

Fig. 15.   The estimated causal effect of *Left-labor power* on macroeconomic perform-ance at various levels of labor-market encompassment and capital mobility when the exchange rate is fixed. Darker lines denote increased capital-market liberalization. (*Note:* * indicates coefficient is significant at $p < .10$, one-tailed.)

compassment range are statistically significant. As predicted by the conver-gence hypothesis, the slope of this line flattens as barriers to capital mobility are removed—so much so that when no barriers to capital mobility exist, left governments are associated with increased growth irrespective of the degree of labor-market encompassment.

The plots of the conditional coefficients for the unemployment and inflation equations given high barriers to capital mobility move in the opposite direction than predicted by the SDC hypothesis—in fact, there is some evidence that when the exchange rate is fixed and capital is mobile, an increase in left gover-nance leads to higher inflation when labor-market encompassment is high. Sur-prisingly, when barriers to capital mobility are removed, the slope of the condi-tional coefficients' plot becomes more in line with SDC expectations, though the conditional *Left* coefficient is never statistically significant with the correct sign in the inflation equation. As was the case with the total sample, the conditional *Left* coefficients seem to fit the SDC hypothesis under fixed exchange rates only when capital is fully mobile.

Together, these results are difficult to assimilate to theory. When the exchange rate is fixed, the SDC hypothesis appears to be consistent with the evidence involving growth in the before-capital-mobility period and unemployment in the after-capital-mobility period. From the standpoint of the Mundell-Fleming model, this suggests that when the exchange rate is fixed, an increase in capital mobility constrains monetary policy more than it enhances fiscal policy as they relate to incumbents' ability to produce partisan outcomes in growth. In contrast, an increase in capital mobility when the exchange rate is fixed seems to enhance fiscal policy more than it constrains monetary policy as they relate to incumbents' use of these instruments to produce partisan outcomes in unemployment. As in the preceding sections, the SDC hypothesis does not appear to fit the inflation model at all.

The results for the flexible exchange rate case (figure 16) are similar in many respects, with one important difference. The results related to unemployment are largely unchanged: there is support for the SDC hypothesis only when capital markets are fully open. The results for the growth equation are also rather similar under flexible exchange rates to the results under fixed exchange rates, though none of the conditional coefficients are statistically significant. The biggest change under flexible exchange rates comes in the inflation equation, where the pattern is now consistent with the SDC hypothesis coupled with the convergence hypothesis. When capital is immobile, the exchange rate is flexible, and labor-market encompassment is low, an increase in left governance is associated with increased inflation. In addition, when labor-market institutions become more encompassing, left governments have the effect on price stability predicted by the SDC hypothesis. The downward-sloping plot of conditional *Left* coefficients that produces this pattern, however, flattens considerably as barriers to capital mobility are removed. Interestingly, none of the coefficients for the closed-economy case are statistically significant, but there is evidence that left governments produce more inflation than right governments when capital markets are open, unless labor-market institutions are highly encompassing.

Our examination of the possible interaction between capital mobility and the exchange rate regime reinforces a pattern that has existed throughout this section. Evidence consistent with the SDC hypothesis appears to be more difficult to come by than evidence that contradicts the SDC hypothesis. Both the convergence and the compensatory hypotheses lead us to expect evidence con-

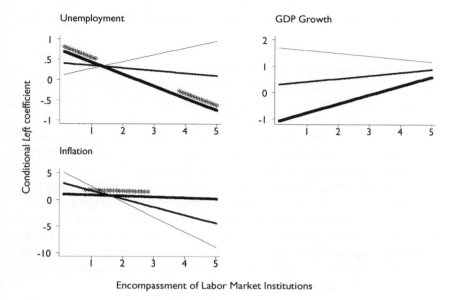

Fig. 16.   The estimated causal effect of *Left-labor power* on macroeconomic performance at various levels of labor-market encompassment and capital mobility when the exchange rate is flexible. Darker lines denote increased capital-market liberalization. (*Note:* * indicates coefficient is significant at $p < .10$, one-tailed.)

sistent with the SDC hypothesis when capital markets are highly restricted. Of the six lines in figures 15 and 16 that capture the conditions before capital-market liberalization, only one contains evidence consistent with the SDC hypothesis. In the before-capital-mobility period, there is evidence of SDC-type behavior as it relates to growth when the exchange rate is fixed. Interestingly, in the sole case where there is evidence of SDC behavior in the before-capital-mobility period, there is considerable evidence that the effects of an increase in capital mobility are more consistent with the convergence hypothesis than the compensatory hypothesis. Thus, one seems forced to conclude one of two things—either the SDC framework is not the appropriate framework for analyzing the politics of macroeconomic policy in OECD countries, or it is, under certain conditions, appropriate for the before-capital-mobility period but not the after-capital-mobility period. That is, either the SDC hypothesis is wrong, or it is correct and the convergence version of the capital-mobility hypothesis is also correct.

The Modifying Effect of Central Bank Independence

Clark and Nair Reichert (1998) presented evidence that central bank independence constrains opportunistic behavior, and the decision-theoretic model in chapter 2 suggests that such constraints should apply to partisan behavior as well. In addition, while Iversen (1998) and Hall and Franzese (1998) make competing claims about the consequences of central bank independence for macroeconomic performance, they both argue that it modifies the influence of labor-market institutions on macroeconomic performance. It is reasonable, therefore, to ask whether the labor-market-contingent partisan behavior predicted by the SDC hypothesis is influenced by the level of central bank independence, particularly because our discussion of the effects of central bank independence highlighted the need for parties of the left to be able to credibly commit to market-oriented policies when labor-market institutions are not encompassing.

To examine the hypothesis that the SDC politics of macroeconomic performance are influenced by the degree of central bank independence, I will estimate an equation identical to the one presented in equation (2), except that central bank independence will take the place of capital mobility as the second modifying variable. The OLS results for such a model are presented in table 21. Note first that with the exception of the $Lmi \cdot Cbi$ term in the unemployment equation, none of the interaction effects are statistically significant. Second, the coefficient for *Left* is not significant in any of the equations. Thus, where the central bank is utterly dependent and labor-market institutions weak and decentralized ($Cbi = 0$, $Lmi = 0$), there is no evidence of partisan differences in macroeconomic outcomes.

This is surprising, since theory suggests that this is a set of conditions in which left governance should have its biggest influence on macroeconomic outcomes. Is it possible, however, that left governance makes a difference under less extreme institutional conditions? To answer this question, it is once again necessary to calculate conditional *Left* coefficients over a broader range of values for labor-market encompassment and central bank independence. These are presented in figure 17. Note that none of the conditional *Left* coefficients derived from the unemployment and inflation equations are statistically significant, suggesting that even after controlling for the potential modifying effects of central bank independence, there is no difference in macroeconomic performance between parties of the left and right under any level of labor-market encompassment. There is, however, evidence that when labor-market encompassment is low, an increase in left governance is associated with a decrease in growth.[9]

I think it is fair to say that these results provide little evidence that the SDC hypothesis is empirically relevant for the before-capital-mobility period, and there is scant evidence consistent with it for the after-capital-mobility period. Furthermore, attempts to control for the potential constraining effects of eroding policy autonomy and central bank independence do not provide any assistance in finding evidence in support of the SDC hypothesis. Before dismissing

TABLE 21. The Effect of Left Governance on Macroeconomic Performance as Conditioned by Labor-Market Encompassment and the Degree of Central Bank Independence

	Unemployment (1)	GDP Growth (2)	Inflation (3)
Left	−0.230	−0.351	−0.418
	(0.382)	(1.037)	(1.123)
Lmi	−0.716*	0.229	1.323
	(0.435)	(1.066)	(1.515)
Cbi	−6.718**	0.867	−9.321
	(2.705)	(6.695)	(8.728)
Left · Lmi	0.096	0.177	0.178
	(0.139)	(0.377)	(0.414)
Left · Cbi	1.131	−0.716	1.357
	(1.238)	(3.503)	(3.380)
Lmi · Cbi	2.423**	−1.238	−1.155
	(1.028)	(2.644)	(3.343)
Left · Lmi · Cbi	−0.429	0.157	−0.428
	(0.393)	(1.087)	(1.070)
Lagged dependent variable	0.874**	0.125*	0.558***
	(0.035)	(0.072)	(0.079)
Openlag · Oecdgdp	−0.002***	0.006***	−0.006***
	(0.001)	(0.002)	(0.002)
Oild	0.303	−6.935	5.557
	(1.914)	(6.498)	(7.587)
Constant	3.167**	2.307	5.134
	(1.335)	(3.070)	(4.396)
F_{DW}	0.62	1.05	0.07
Prob. $> F$	0.647	0.383	0.990
Observations	350	350	350
Number of countries	14	14	14

Note: Panel-corrected standard errors are in parentheses.
Coefficients for country and period dummy variables are not reported.
The term F_{DW} is the test statistic for Durbin-Watson's m.
*$p < .10$, **$p < .05$, ***$p < .01$, one-tailed test for variables involving Left, two-tailed otherwise.

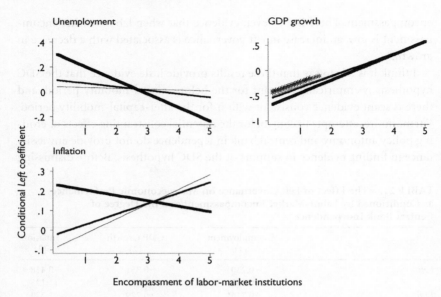

Fig. 17.   The estimated causal effect of *Left-labor power* on macroeconomic performance at various levels of labor-market encompassment and central bank independence.
Darker lines denote higher levels of central bank independence: high *Cbi* = .48 on
Cukierman, Webb, and Neyapti index (1992); moderate *Cbi* = .29; low *Cbi* = .24. (*Note:*
* indicates coefficient is significant at $p < .10$ level, one-tailed.)

the partisan model, however, it is worth asking whether more evidence for partisan differences would be found if we considered the nonadditive interaction
between domestic and international constraints on partisan behavior as implied by the game-theoretic model in chapter 2.

A Test of the Game-Theoretic Model

Partisan effects are captured in the game-theoretic model in chapter 2 by assuming that, all other things being equal, left governments have a greater tendency to attempt to push national income above the natural rate than parties
of the right.[10] Attention to the context in which policy is made, however, suggests that all other things are not always equal. This general propensity of left

governments does not, therefore, *necessarily* lead to observable differences in macroeconomic outcomes. For instance, when the exchange rate is fixed, an increase in left governance is expected to lead to an increase in national income, but this increase is likely to be less pronounced when capital is mobile and the central bank is independent than when capital is mobile or the central bank is not independent (hypothesis 1P from chap. 2). Similarly, when the exchange rate is allowed to fluctuate, an increase in left governance is expected to lead to an increase in national income, except when the central bank is independent and capital is mobile. Under such circumstances, the model in chapter 2 predicts that an increase in left governance will have *no* effect on national income (hypothesis 2P).

We see, therefore, that the existence of partisan differences is deeply context-dependent. Their occurrence depends on a complex interaction between the exchange rate regime, the degree of capital mobility, and the degree of central bank independence. Some scholars have responded to such complexity by limiting the scope of their analysis to subsamples of cases where particular causal mechanisms are thought to operate: if there is a peculiar logic to the political control of the economy when the exchange rate is fixed, capital is mobile, and the central bank is independent, then why not study such cases in isolation? While there may be benefits to restricting the domain of one's analysis in such a way, there are also two clear costs. First, if one selects a subsample on the basis of a theoretical supposition that those cases are "different," one has decided not to test that supposition. Second, such sample splitting can eventually lead to the familiar problem of "too many variables and too few cases."

An alternative is to use a multiplicative interaction model to capture the conditional nature of our hypotheses. Since the exchange rate regime, capital mobility, and central bank independence all interact in modifying partisan differences in the macroeconomy, such a model can get fairly complicated very quickly. Consequently, I will proceed in steps. First, I will discuss the strategy that might be used if we were to split our sample in half, between observations where the exchange rate is fixed and cases where it is allowed to fluctuate. Then I will introduce a model that allows for the testing of these conditional hypotheses on a broader sample that combines observations from both exchange rate regimes.

Expected Partisan Differences under Fixed Exchange Rates

The implications of the game-theoretic model in chapter 2 for the existence and magnitude of partisan differences in national income under fixed exchange rates are summarized in table 22. When the exchange rate is fixed, an increase in left governance is expected to lead to an increase in national income both when capital is mobile and when it is not, and whether the central bank is independent or not. These potential modifiers matter only in the sense that the magnitude of partisan differences in growth may be smaller when the central bank is independent and capital is immobile (see the lower-right cell of table 22). We can test arguments about the modifying effects of capital mobility and central bank independence in the subsample of cases where the exchange rate is fixed by using an interaction model with two modifying variables that interact with each other:

$$Growth_{it} = a + b_1 Left_{it} + b_2 Cbi_{it} + b_3 Cml_{it} + b_4(Left_{it} \cdot Cbi_{it})$$

$$+ b_5(Left_{it} \cdot Cml_{it}) + b_6(Left_{it} \cdot Cml_{it}) + b_7(Left_{it} \cdot Cbi_{it} \cdot Cml_{it})$$

$$+ b_9 Perf_{it-1} + \Sigma(b_k Country_{it}) + \varepsilon_{it}. \tag{6}$$

The effect of a change in left governance implied by such a model can be determined by taking the partial derivative of equation (6) with respect to *Left*. This yields

$$\frac{\partial Growth_{it}}{\partial Left} = b_1 + b_4 Cbi + b_5 Cml + b_7 Cbi \cdot Cm. \tag{7}$$

We can then use this general "conditional *Left* coefficient" to determine what the model in chapter 2 predicts about the parameters in equation (6). For example, when central bank independence and capital-market liberalization equal zero, the estimated causal effect of an increase in left government on growth is simply b_1. Since the model expects politically induced changes in growth under these circumstances, we would expect b_1 to be positive if the partisan model is correct. The effect of an increase in central bank independence on the estimated causal effect of left governance on growth *when capital mo-*

TABLE 22.   **The Predicted Magnitude of Partisan Differences in Growth under Fixed Exchange Rates (based on game-theoretic model)**

	No Central Bank Independence	Central Bank Independence
Capital mobility	$y''(k-1)$	$y''(k-1)$
No capital mobility	$y''(k-1)$	$\dfrac{\mu(\mu+\alpha)}{\mu^2+\alpha}y''(k-1)$

bility is absent is captured by b_4. Since this is a move from the bottom-left cell to the bottom-right cell in table 22, and since $0 < \frac{\mu(\mu-\alpha)}{\mu^2+\alpha} < 1$, we expect $b_4 < 0$. In addition, the effect of an increase in capital mobility on the estimated causal effect of left governance on growth *when central bank independence is absent* is captured by b_5. Since this is a move from the bottom-left cell to the top-left cell of table 22, we expect b_5 to equal zero.

Expected Partisan Differences under Flexible Exchange Rates

The implications of the game-theoretic model for the existence of partisan differences in macroeconomic performance for the flexible exchange rate case are summarized in table 23. An increase in left governance is expected to lead to an increase in national income except when capital is mobile and the central bank is independent. While, given flexible exchange rates, partisan differences are expected as long as either capital is immobile or the central bank is not independent, such differences are likely to be largest when capital is immobile and the central bank is not independent. The model predicts that the two other contexts (the upper-left and lower-right cells of table 23) are intermediate cases: partisan differences are likely to exist when capital is immobile and the central bank is independent and when capital is mobile and the bank is not independent, but these differences will not be as great as when capital is immobile and the central bank is not independent. Finally, the relative size of partisan differences in these two intermediate cases depends on the relative emphasis that policymakers place on price stability. Assuming that monetary policy and fiscal policy are equally effective in the before-capital-mobility period ($\mu = \phi = .5$), then central bank independence is slightly more effective than capital mobility as a constraint for suppressing partisan differences in macroeconomic outcomes as long as policymakers place more than twice as much weight on hitting their growth target as on hitting their price target ($\alpha < .5$) (see fig. 18). Otherwise, capital mobility is more constraining than central bank independence.

TABLE 23.   The Predicted Magnitude of Partisan Differences in Growth under Flexible Exchange Rates (based on game-theoretic model)

	No Central Bank Independence	Central Bank Independence
Capital mobility	$\frac{1}{1+\alpha}y''(k-1)$	0
No capital mobility	$y''(k-1)$	$\frac{\mu(\mu+\alpha)}{\mu^2+\alpha}y''(k-1)$

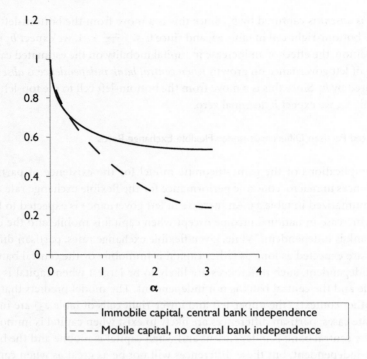

Fig. 18.   The size of partisan differences in income growth as a function of the emphasis policymakers place on price stability in two contexts

Arguments such as those laid out in the preceding paragraphs can be captured with a model similar to (6):

$$Growth_{it} = a + c_1 Left_{it} + c_2 Cbi_{it} + c_3 Cml_{it} + c_4(Left_{it} \cdot Cbi_{it})$$

$$+ c_5(Left_{it} \cdot Cml_{it}) + c_6(Left_{it} \cdot Cml_{it}) + c_7(Left_{it} \cdot Cbi_{it} \cdot Cml_{it})$$

$$+ c_9 Perf_{it-1} + \Sigma(c_k Country_{it}) + \varepsilon_{it}. \tag{8}$$

The conditional *Left* coefficients for the set of ideal typical contexts are strictly analogous to those in the previous example:

$$\frac{\partial Growth_{it}}{\partial Left} = c_1 + c_4 Cbi + c_5 Cml + c_7 Cbi \cdot Cm. \tag{9}$$

And, as above, c_1 is the estimated causal effect of an increase in left governance when the central bank is dependent and the capital market is closed. If the partisan model is correct, we would expect to observe partisan differences in macroeconomic performance under these circumstances ($c_1 > 0$). In addition, c_4 is the expected change in the estimated causal effect of left governance when central bank independence increases and the capital market remains closed. Since this constitutes a shift from the lower-left cell to the lower-right cell of table 23, we expect $c_4 < 0$. Similarly, c_5 is the expected change in the estimated causal effect of left governance when the capital market is liberalized but the central bank remains dependent, which is a move from the lower-left cell to the upper-right cell in table 23, and therefore c_5 is expected to be less than zero. Finally, since we do not expect to find partisan differences in macroeconomic performance when capital is highly mobile and the central bank is highly independent, we expect equation (9) to be equal to zero when Cbi and Cml are both large.

Evidence of Partisan Differences under Fixed and Flexible Exchange Rates

The preceding discussion allows us to examine the way in which central bank independence and capital mobility interact to influence the occurrence of partisan differences in macroeconomic policy while holding the exchange rate regime constant. One might pursue either of two strategies in testing these arguments. First, one could divide the sample into cases of fixed and floating exchange rates and specify the double interaction models as in equations (6) and (8). Alternatively, one could specify a triple interaction model that includes the exchange rate as the third modifying variable. While in many ways these strategies are equivalent, the latter makes better use of the degrees of freedom available in the data and allows for a more direct test of the effects of the third modifying variable. Unfortunately, these benefits come at the cost of a considerable increase in algebraic complexity. When the third modifying variable is added to equation (6), the result model looks like

$$Perf_{it} = b_1 Left_{it} + b_2 Cbi_{it} + b_3 Cml_{it} + b_4(Left_{it} \cdot Cbi_{it}) + b_5(Left_{it} \cdot Cml_{it})$$

$$+ b_6(Cbi_{it} \cdot Cml_{it}) + b_7(Left_{it} \cdot Cbi_{it} \cdot Cml_{it}) + b_8 Flex$$

$$+ \Sigma b_j Flex \cdot (Left_{it} + Cbi_{it} + b_3 Cml_{it} + (Left_{it} \cdot Cbi_{it})$$

$$+ (Left_{it} \cdot Cml_{it}) + (Cbi_{it} \cdot Cml_{it})$$

$$+ (Left_{it} \cdot Cbi_{it} \cdot Cml_{it})) \, b_9 Perf_{it-1} + \Sigma(b_k Country_{it}) + \varepsilon_{it}, \qquad (10)$$

the conditional *Left* coefficient becomes

$$\frac{\partial Perf}{\partial Left} = b_1 Left_{it} + b_4(Cbi_{it}) + b_5(Cml_{it}) + b_7(Cbi_{it} \cdot Cml_{it}) + b_9 Flex$$
$$+ b_{12}(Flex \cdot Cbi_{it}) + b_{13}(Flex \cdot Cml_{it}) + b_{15}(Flex \cdot Cbi_{it} \cdot Cml_{it}), \quad (11)$$

and the associated conditional standard error is far more unsightly. We can, however, use the fact that the first seven coefficients in equation (10) are conditional coefficients that are the estimates describing the interaction between these values when the third modifying variable, *Flex,* equals zero. So when *Flex* equals zero, (10) simplifies to (6). One can then respecify the equation so that the third modifying variable is *Fixed;* in that case, when *Fixed* equals zero, the equation simplifies to (8). Note that all of the hypotheses stated here refer to a model in which, according to the discussion of the game-theoretic model in chapter 2, growth is the dependent variable. Since Okun's law holds that unemployment is inversely related to growth, each of these hypotheses also has implications for the rate of unemployment; we need only change the hypothesized sign on the coefficient in question.

The results of both of these triple interaction models are presented in table 24. Columns 1 and 2 report the results from models that define the exchange rate regime so that *Regime* = 1 when the exchange rate is flexible. Columns 3 and 4 report the results from models that define the exchange rate regime so that *Regime* = 1 when the exchange rate is fixed. Consequently, the *Left* coefficient in columns 1 and 2 captures the relationship between an increase in left governance and macroeconomic performance when capital is immobile, the central bank is independent, and the exchange rate is flexible. In contrast, the *Left* coefficient in columns 3 and 4 estimates the causal effect of an increase in left governance on macroeconomic performance when capital is immobile, the central bank is independent, and the exchange rate is fixed. Note that none of the *Left* coefficients are statistically distinguishable from zero, suggesting that when capital is immobile and the central bank is independent (i.e., when there is no barrier to the political manipulation of the economy), there is no evidence of partisan differences in macroeconomic outcomes—whether the exchange rate is fixed or not.

While the complexity of the individual interaction terms is fascinating, most relevant for our purposes is how these structural factors affect partisan differences in macroeconomic performance. Note that the coefficient on *Left* in table 24 estimates the causal effect of an increase in left governance in a very specific circumstance: the case where all of the modifying variables are simultaneously

TABLE 24. The Estimated Effect of Left Governance on Macroeconomic Performance Conditioned upon Central Bank Independence, Capital-Market Liberalization, and the Exchange Rate Regime

		Growth (1)	Unemployment (2)		Growth (3)	Unemployment (4)
		Regime = Flex	Regime = Flex		Regime = Fixed	Regime = Fixed
Left	b_1	1.080	−0.036	c_1	2.483	55.907
		(1.283)	(0.054)		(12.778)	(62.917)
Central bank independence (Cbi)	b_2	7.119*	−0.068	c_2	32.540**	−44.070
		(4.230)	(0.154)		(14.242)	(62.323)
Capital market liberalization (Cml)	b_3	0.545	−0.020	c_3	1.699	−3.460
		(0.361)	(0.018)		(1.048)	(4.140)
Left · Cbi	b_4	−2.246	0.078	c_4	−16.189	−162.816
		(3.289)	(0.147)		(37.436)	(181.798)
Left · Cml	b_5	−0.230	0.010	c_5	0.349	−16.092
		(0.397)	(0.017)		(3.669)	(19.017)
Cbi · Cml	b_6	−1.749*	0.037	c_6	−7.676**	13.183
		(0.947)	(0.048)		(3.569)	(15.871)
Left · Cbi · Cml	b_7	0.501	−0.019	c_7	2.108	45.583
		(0.980)	(0.046)		(10.333)	(51.390)
Regime		−6.413	0.063		6.413	−6.313
		(4.089)	(0.166)		(4.089)	(16.591)
Left · Regime		1.403	0.595		−1.403	−59.495
		(12.825)	(0.632)		(12.825)	(63.177)
Regime · Cbi		25.421*	−0.373		−25.421*	37.288
		(13.521)	(0.631)		(13.521)	(63.143)
Regime · Cml		1.154	−0.014		−1.154	1.445
		(1.068)	(0.042)		(1.068)	(4.202)
Left · Cbi · Regime		−13.943	−1.707		13.943	170.659
		(37.656)	(1.828)		(37.656)	(182.76)
Left · Cml · Regime		0.579	−0.171		−0.579	17.052
		(3.696)	(0.191)		(3.696)	(19.139)
Cbi · Cml · Regime		−5.927*	0.094		5.927*	−9.447
		(3.452)	(0.158)		(3.452)	(15.776)
Left · Cbi · Cml · Regime		1.607	0.475		−1.607	−47.529
		(10.412)	(0.517)		(10.412)	(51.655)
Lagged dependent variable		−0.125***	0.004***		−0.125***	0.421***
		(0.036)	(0.000)		(0.036)	(0.047)
Constant		−1.142	0.037		−7.555	9.988
		(2.721)	(0.061)		(4.694)	(15.989)
F_{DW}		10.23	0.09		10.23	0.09
Prob. > F		0.00	0.98		0.00	0.98
Observations		1,451	1,672		1,451	1,672
Number of countries		14	16		14	16

Note: Panel-corrected standard errors are in parentheses.
Coefficients for country dummy variables are not reported.
The term F_{DW} is the test statistic for Durbin-Watson's m.
*p < .10, **p < .05, ***p < .01, one-tailed test for variables involving *Left*, two-tailed otherwise.

zero, that is, where the exchange rate is fixed, the maximum number of capital controls are in place, and central bank independence is entirely absent. Note also that the hypothesized sign appears on the *Left* coefficients in both the unemployment and growth equations but that neither is statistically significant; and none of the coefficients on the interaction terms are statistically significant. Contrary to expectations, b_4 and b_7 are not statistically significant with the opposite sign as b_1; nor are c_4, c_5, and c_7.

For our present purposes, however, we are most interested in examining the implications of the game-theoretic model regarding the conditions under which we should observe partisan differences in macroeconomic performance if the partisan model is the appropriate model of the political control of the economy. For these purposes, it is useful to restate the model's two main hypotheses related to performance.

HYPOTHESIS 1P. *When the exchange rate is fixed, politically induced increases in growth are expected to occur both when capital is mobile and when it is not, and when the central bank is independent and when it is not (though the size of such increases will be smallest when capital is immobile and the central bank is independent).*

HYPOTHESIS 2P. *When the exchange rate is allowed to fluctuate, politically induced changes in growth are expected unless capital is mobile and the central bank is independent (though when the central bank is not independent, the magnitude of politically induced changes in growth may be smaller when capital is mobile than when it is not).*

Hypothesis 1P suggests that partisan differences in macroeconomic performance variables should abound when the exchange rate is fixed. Thus, we should be able to calculate conditional *Left* coefficients for various degrees of central bank independence and capital-market openness, given that the exchange rate should be fixed, and these should all be greater than zero in the case of the growth equations and less than zero in the case of the unemployment equations. Hypothesis 2P predicts that politically induced differences in macroeconomic performance variables should also occur under flexible exchange rates, except when capital is mobile and the central bank is independent, in which case the conditional *Left* coefficients should be indistinguishable from zero. An examination of figure 19, however, shows that statistically significant partisan differences in macroeconomic performance do not occur under fixed exchange rates. Note also that the observed difference is the opposite of what the

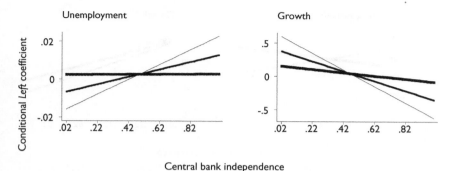

Fig. 19.   The estimated effect of left governance on macroeconomic performance under various degrees of central bank independence and capital mobility when the exchange rate is fixed. Darker lines denote increased capital-market liberalization. (*Note:* * indicates coefficient is significant at $p < .10$, one-tailed.)

partisan model anticipates—left governments under these circumstances are associated with higher, not lower, unemployment rates. The evidence with respect to partisan differences under flexible exchange rates is equally puzzling (see fig. 20). There is no evidence of statistically significant differences in unemployment, and differences in growth are seen only when all restrictions on capital have been removed and the degree of central bank independence is low. This last result is consistent with the decision-theoretic model's implications regarding the constraining effects of central bank independence, but it is inconsistent with the standard intuition about the constraining effects of capital mobility.

The evidence presented up to this point suggests that there are no systematic partisan differences in unemployment rates in the OECD economies but that, consistent with the partisan hypothesis, left governments do appear to produce higher rates of growth than right-wing parties. In addition, there is no evidence that these results are sensitive to either the degree of national policy autonomy or the independence of the central bank.

Conclusions

There is very little evidence of Hibbsian partisan differences in macroeconomic performance. Left governments are associated with increased growth,

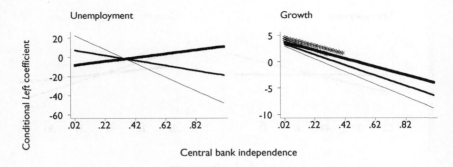

Fig. 20.   The estimated effect of left governance on macroeconomic performance under various degrees of central bank independence and capital mobility when the exchange rate is flexible. Darker lines denote increased capital-market liberalization. (*Note:* * indicates coefficient is significant at $p < .10$, one-tailed.)

but only under special circumstances—when the central bank is independent and capital is mobile. There is no evidence of a linear relationship between left governance and either unemployment or inflation in any of the many specifications used here—which suggests that there is no robust evidence of Hibbsian partisan differences at any level of central bank independence or any degree of capital-market integration or national policy autonomy observed in the current sample.[11]

The evidence that partisan differences in macroeconomic outcomes are conditioned by labor-market institutions is mixed. Before controlling for central bank independence, capital mobility, or the loss of national policy autonomy, there is evidence that left governments preside over less growth than right governments when labor unions are not encompassing (table 18). While this result is consistent with the social democratic corporatist argument, there is no evidence from these tests that left governments produce more growth when labor-market institutions *are* encompassing. In addition, there is no evidence related to unemployment and inflation to support the SDC hypothesis. In fact, there is some evidence that encompassing unions are, if anything, associated with inflation, not price stability (figure 16).

The evidence for the SDC argument is stronger, but still mixed, when the analysis allows for the potentially perturbing effects of capital-market liberalization. There is evidence that when all capital controls have been removed, an increase in left governance leads to more growth and less unemployment when labor encompassment is high, but more unemployment when labor encompassment is low. This result is entirely consistent with the SDC hypothesis; but, contrary to the hypothesis, there is no evidence that left governance leads to slowed growth when labor-market institutions are weak and decentralized. There is also no evidence that left governance is related to inflation when both the degree of labor-union encompassment and the degree of capital-market liberalization are included in the model. In addition, when capital-market liberalization is not complete, the evidence for the SDC hypothesis breaks down further, and when one controls for the modifying effects of exchange rate regime deduced from the game-theoretic model in Chapter 2, all evidence for the SDC hypothesis disappears entirely.

While there is little evidence that partisan differences are influenced by the modifying variables examined here, this does not necessarily mean that they do not have a direct influence on macroeconomic outcomes. There is evidence, for example, that capital-market liberalization results in greater price stability and that the loss of national policy autonomy is associated with lower growth and higher unemployment, but also lower inflation.

For the most part, the results just summarized run contrary to both of the prevailing arguments in the literature on globalization. The common wisdom is that increased competitive pressures have made the Keynesian welfare state cost-prohibitive and that rapid capital movements have made demand management impossible. Since parties of the left are thought to have pursued such policies with more enthusiasm than the right, these changes in the structural environment in which policy is made are thought to produce pressures for partisan convergence upon market-oriented policies. Most empirical studies, however, have failed to find support for this received wisdom. Garrett (1995, 1998) argues that globalization has encouraged, rather than discouraged, partisan differences; Rodrik (1997) argues that, so far, governments have been able to continue to shelter at-risk groups from the vagaries of the international economy; and Iversen (1997) argues that recent changes in social welfare provision are driven by the increased importance of the service sector and that globalization has had little effect.

Note that Garrett, Rodrik, and Iversen each explain responses to global integration in a manner that is decidedly pluralist. The international economy creates market dislocations, and those harmed or put at risk by these changes appeal to the government for some form of social insurance. And the government or the particular parties in power are only too eager to respond to these demands. While increased risk and displacement may lead harmed groups to make new or more vigorous demands, and while the government may be responsive to such demands, none of these effects follow logically. They may be equilibrium responses, but it depends on the ability of these groups to over-come collective-action barriers and on the incentives governments have to be responsive to such demands. Since an increase in international capital mobil-ity has probably changed the structural environment in such a way as to make governments more responsive to actors who are more capable of diversifica-tion (and less in need of social insurance), it is not obvious that the net effect of globalization will be an increase in the provision of social insurance.

Consistent with the studies mentioned, my results challenge the common wisdom that the recent increase in international capital mobility is leading to a withering away of the state and the end of politics. But, unlike the revision-ist literature, I find little evidence to support the notion that partisan politics continues to influence macroeconomic performance or that partisan influ-ences have actually grown. In large part, this is because I find little evidence that partisan differences were present before the increase in capital mobility.

While the evidence regarding partisan differences in macroeconomic per-formance (whether from a Hibbsian or a social democratic corporatist per-spective) is far from clear, it does not follow that the Downsian model is nec-essarily to be preferred over the Hibbsian or SDC models. Rather, if partisan differences in macroeconomic performance exist, these differences appear to be sensitive to context in ways that we do not fully understand. Further theo-rizing is certainly needed, and work that tries to endogenize the trade-off be-tween office-seeking and policy-seeking behavior is likely to be fruitful (Strøm 1990). That said, existing findings about the consequences of international cap-ital mobility that rely on the partisan approach for their depiction of domestic political processes should be treated as provisional, and future study ought to include attempts to model the effects of international capital mobility on non-partisan political behaviors related to the control of the macroeconomy.

CHAPTER 6

Elections and
Macroeconomic Outcomes

Whoever loves discipline loves knowledge, but he who hates correction
is stupid.

—Proverbs 12:1

In October [of 1960], usually a month of rising employment, the job-
less rolls increased by 452,000. All the speeches, television broadcasts,
and precinct work in the world could not counteract that hard fact.

—Richard M. Nixon (1962)

In chapters 3 and 5, I presented evidence that called into question the existence
of partisan differences both in the use of monetary and fiscal policy instruments and in macroeconomic outcomes. The scarcity of partisan differences,
furthermore, appears to be general. Before and after capital mobility, under
fixed and flexible exchange rates, under dependent and independent central
banks—there is little evidence that parties of the left implement systematically
different policies than parties of the right. Attempts to model the structural
context in which parties must implement policies failed to bring partisan differences into focus in a manner that was easily assimilated to existing bodies of
theory in comparative political economy. The empirical results in chapter 4
suggest an explanation for the absence of partisan differences. Perhaps the
rigor of electoral competition forces survival-maximizing incumbents of various political hues to behave alike. Specifically, there is evidence that when
structural conditions allow, incumbents will manipulate the most effective policy instrument they control in an expansionary manner in the period just prior
to an election. In this chapter, I will examine whether such electorally timed

manipulations of policy instruments are transmitted to macroeconomic outcomes such as unemployment and growth.

As mentioned in chapter 1, the contention that macroeconomic outcomes may be systematically tied to the electoral calendar has been challenged in the literature on both theoretical and empirical grounds. Rational expectations macroeconomic theory suggests that only unanticipated policy changes will have effects on growth and unemployment. Since the public can anticipate regularly occurring elections, any manipulation of policy instruments that is tied to the electoral calendar (such as those found in chapter 4) is not expected to have real effects. The fact that the empirical literature has failed to provide consistent support for a link between macroeconomic outcomes and the electoral calendar is consistent with this rational expectations critique of the political business cycle argument.

There are, however, reasons to remain skeptical of both the rational expectations critique and the existing empirical literature. First, the rational expectations critique assumes that voters and market actors use "all available information" to formulate their expectations of future policy. Notwithstanding pronouncements in the popular press that the 2000 U.S. presidential elections taught us that "every vote counts," the literature on the "irrationality of voting" (Fiorina 1976; Aldrich 1993; Palfrey and Rosenthal 1985) and therefore the "rational ignorance" (Downs 1960) of members of the electorate is convincing enough to suggest that voters might use crude rules of thumb consistent with retrospective economic voting to formulate their expectations. If this is true, then the concern among rational expectations critics of the political business cycle model that voters cannot be systematically fooled loses some of its prima facie appeal.

While it is plausible that voters, because they have little chance of deciding an election, have little to gain from building complex positive political economy models of candidate behavior or collecting information on individual candidates, is the same true for market actors? At first glance, the answer would be a clear no. In fact, unlike voters, market actors spend large amounts of time and money following the behavior of policymakers in an attempt to forecast future policy changes. Such behavior lends a surface plausibility to the rational expectations idea that actors will make use of all available information in formulating their expectations. But it also suggests a paradox. If, as rational expectations theorists predict, policy has no real effects, why do people spend so much time trying to predict the behavior of policymakers? The commuter train from Princeton, New Jersey, to Wall Street is filled with financiers who are attentive to every change in the facial expression of Federal Reserve Board chairman Alan Greenspan, but the economics department back at Princeton University is full of theorists who maintain that Greenspan's manipulation of the money supply has no real effects. How do these groups of very smart, hardworking people persist in such apparently contradictory behaviors in such close proximity?

One answer is that theorists maintain that it is only *unanticipated* policy that lacks real effects. If market actors were not attentive, policy would have the direct and profound effects that Keynesian models suggest. In this case, market actors could benefit from being able to predict policy interventions, and investing in the ability to do so would be prudent. If, however, enough market actors did so, policy interventions would be anticipated and would, as predicted by rational expectations models, lose their real effects—and investing in the ability to predict policy interventions would be a waste of money. The optimal rate of investment in the ability to predict policy changes, therefore, is determined by a complex interaction among market actors. If everyone else develops the ability to anticipate policy, it is cost-effective for me to remain ignorant (why spend a single dollar to learn how to predict a policy that has no effect?). But if this is true for me, it is true for every other market actor. In this case, no one invests in the ability to predict policy, so policy *does* have real effects, which means that maybe I *should* invest in the ability to predict policy! The collection of sufficient information to render policy interventions widely anticipated, therefore, is structurally similar to any other collective-action problem. And the rational expectations assumption that market actors make use of all available information is, therefore, tantamount to assuming that market actors have solved this problem and that the collective good is being optimally supplied.

Perhaps, however, while market actors may not be able to overcome this collective-action problem at all times, the temptation for incumbents to engage in expansionary policies as elections near is so great that the information threshold necessary to render interventions "anticipated" is quite modest. For macroeconomic outcomes to be tied to the electoral calendar, however, all that is required is that a mixed-strategy equilibrium exists such that incumbents play "expand" with greater probability as elections near than they do in earlier portions of their term—just as football teams trailing by large margins choose long-pass plays with higher probability as the game nears an end. In football such a strategy is, on average, effective even though it is anticipated. And just as it has the effect of increasing the number of yards gained in the fourth quarter, engaging in macroeconomic expansions may have the effect of increasing growth or decreasing unemployment even though it is, to some degree, anticipated.

The reason for skepticism about existing empirical studies of the link between macroeconomic outcomes and the electoral calendar is more clear-cut. As pointed out in chapter 1, with very few exceptions, prior cross-national studies have tested the political business cycle hypothesis in an unconditional manner. Both theoretical models in chapter 2, however, argue that the ability of survival-maximizing incumbents to engineer economic expansions just prior to elections is deeply context-dependent. Clark and Nair Reichert (1998) conducted a context-dependent test of the political business cycle and found evidence consistent with the decision-theoretic model in chapter 2. Growth in industrial output and unemployment was tied to the electoral calendar except where capital was mobile and the exchange rate was fixed or when the degree of central bank independence was high. In this chapter, I will critically reevaluate Clark and Nair's findings and compare them with a context-dependent test of the political business cycle argument based on the game-theoretic model in chapter 2.

Clark and Nair Reichert (1998) argue that any constraint on the opportunistic use of monetary policy is effectively a constraint on the use of macroeconomic policy for electoral purposes. Politicians confronting an independent central bank or a commitment to a pegged exchange rate would, they argue, be unable to use fiscal policy alone to create a preelectoral macroeconomic expansion. The decision-theoretic model in chapter 2 argues that if one constraint on monetary policy is added to another, then the resulting institutional combination will, if anything, be more constraining than would otherwise be the case.

The game-theoretic model, however, raises serious questions about both of these arguments. First, the model argues that when incumbents lose control of monetary policy for electoral purposes, they will use fiscal policy to create preelectoral macroeconomic expansions. Second, it also suggests that adding monetary constraints together can have a surprising result: when a government that confronts an independent central bank makes a commitment to a pegged exchange rate, it simultaneously enhances the effectiveness of the fiscal instruments available to incumbent politicians and reduces the bank's ability to use monetary policy to deter or offset the use of such fiscal instruments for electoral purposes. Thus, if the game-theoretic model is correct, Clark and Nair Reichert's finding that electorally induced cycles in growth and unemployment do not occur whenever the exchange rate is fixed and capital is mobile is surprising. When the exchange rate is fixed and capital is mobile, fiscal policy should be particularly effective, and monetary policy should be ineffective. Under these circumstances, survival-maximizing incumbents should be able to create preelectoral macroeconomic expansions with impunity.

Table 25 summarizes the expectations of both the decision-theoretic and game-theoretic models in chapter 2 as they relate to the existence of electoral cycles in macroeconomic performance. Note that while the game-theoretic model predicts that in the absence of central bank independence the existence of electoral cycles in macroeconomic outcomes is unaffected by either the degree of capital mobility or the choice of exchange rate regime, the decision-theoretic model predicts that electoral cycles will not occur if capital is mobile and the exchange rate is fixed. Note also that while the decision-theoretic model argues that electoral cycles will not occur whenever the degree of central bank independence is high, the game-theoretic model argues that electoral cycles under independent central banks are ruled out only when capital is mobile and the exchange rate is flexible.

In this chapter I will examine the tension between these two arguments. First, I will replicate and reexamine the findings of Clark and Nair Reichert (1998).[1] I will then test the hypotheses drawn from the game-theoretic model in chapter 2 related to the link between elections and macroeconomic performance.

A Test of the Decision-Theoretic Model

The emphasis that the integration literature places on the partisan model is probably the result of the stiff criticism received by its main competitor in the closed-economy literature—the electoralist model of the political business cycle (PBC). The existence of electoralist PBCs has remained controversial for nearly twenty years. The endurance of the debate derives from a stark contrast between the commonsense nature of the electoralist argument and the paucity of evidence supporting its key implications. PBC arguments, in their broadest formulation, assume that politicians are electoralist and can reap electoral

TABLE 25.   The Expected Effect of the Onset of an Election on Growth under Various Conditions

	No Central Bank Independence	Central Bank Independence
Fixed exchange rate and mobile capital	*Yes*	*Yes*
	No	**No**
Flexible exchange rate and mobile capital	*Yes*	*No*
	Yes	**No**
No capital mobility	*Yes*	*Yes*
	Yes	**No**

Note: Italics indicate expectations drawn from the game-theoretic model in chapter 2; bold indicates expectations drawn from the decision-theoretic model in chapter 2.

benefits by manipulating the macroeconomy with an eye toward reelection rather than long-term growth and price stabilization. PBC theorists have refined this broad argument in various ways, none of which has received unambiguous empirical support. Clark and Nair Reichert argued that prior cross-national examinations of PBC arguments were fundamentally flawed because they failed to consider the constraining influence of institutions, both domestic and international. Specifically, they argued that participation in fixed exchange rate regimes during periods of high levels of capital mobility denied policymakers the degree of national monetary policy autonomy required to manipulate macroeconomic outcomes for electoral purposes. In addition, politicians may have difficulty using macroeconomic outcomes for electoral gains if monetary policy is under the control of a relatively independent central bank. They evaluate this argument using country-specific and time-series cross-sectional tests that find evidence of context-dependent PBCs in eighteen OECD countries. In light of these tests, the absence of PBCs in several countries is comprehensible without abandoning the standard PBC model's characterization of politicians as electoralist and voters as myopic.

In what follows, I replicate their time-series cross-sectional tests, which evaluate propositions from the decision-theoretic model in chapter 2. I then conduct time-series cross-sectional tests that will allow us to evaluate implications from the game-theoretic model in chapter 2.

International or Domestic Constraints on Political Business Cycles

Although the country-specific tests in Clark and Nair Reichert 1998 are suggestive, they are also limited by relatively modest degrees of freedom. This problem is most severe in the cases where countries experienced changing institutional constraints; in some cases, data were available for only one election during the before-capital-mobility period. Clark and Nair Reichert address this problem of limited degrees of freedom by using a time-series cross-sectional research design combined with the dummy-variable interactive model used in earlier chapters. This design allows us to directly examine the effects of cross-national differences in the relevant institutional arrangements.

As a baseline, it is useful to examine the electoralist hypothesis in a time-series cross-sectional test that pays no attention to the structural conditions that are expected to encourage or discourage electoralist behavior. Standard tests of PBC arguments seek to examine whether a significant degree of covariation exists between elections and various macroeconomic outcomes. In its most general form, therefore, the PBC argument can be stated as

$$O_{it} = a + b_1 E_{it} + e_{it}, \tag{1}$$

where a is the intercept, O is a macroeconomic outcome, E is the presence of an electoral period, i indexes the country, t is the time period, and e is the error term.[2] Where data were available, I estimate two equations in each country, one using percentage change in unemployment, the other using percentage change in industrial output as the dependent variable.[3] The standard PBC hypothesis is that there is a decreasing (increasing) relationship between elections and unemployment (output).

Note that while the coefficient on the electoral variable in columns 1a and 1b in table 26 has the hypothesized sign, it is only marginally statistically significant.[4] Thus, as many prior studies have found, an institutionally naive test fails to show strong evidence of electorally motivated manipulation of the macroeconomy.

The picture changes dramatically, however, when one is attentive to the constraining effects of institutions. I begin with an examination of the effects of central bank independence on electoralist behavior and then examine the effects of a loss of national policy autonomy.

The Modifying Effects of Central Bank Independence

Clark and Nair Reichert (1998) and the decision-theoretic model in chapter 2 argue that central bank independence is sufficient to reduce the likelihood of political business cycles. To examine the modifying effect of central bank independence, I will evaluate the following model:

$$\Delta O_t = a + b_1 E_t + b_2 Cbi_t + b_3 E \cdot Cbi_t + \Sigma(b_j \Delta O_{t-j}) + e_t. \tag{2}$$

Since electorally induced cycles in outcome variables are expected to occur in the absence of central bank independence, b_1—which is a conditional coefficient for the hypothetical case where Cbi is equal to zero—is expected to be less than zero in the unemployment equation and greater than zero in the growth equation. Since central bank independence is expected to constrain the occurrence of electoral cycles in outcome variables, the coefficient on the interaction term is expected to have the opposite sign from b_1.

The results in columns 2a and 2b in table 26 are entirely consistent with these expectations. The *Election* coefficients have the expected signs and are statistically significant at conventional levels in both the unemployment and growth equations. In addition, the coefficients on the interaction terms are statistically significant and have the opposite signs as the *Election* coefficients in both equations. Note also that while the Durbin-Watson test suggests the presence of serially correlated errors, a reestimation of this model using the Prais-Winsten transformation produces strikingly similar results.[5]

The results suggest that elections have a substantial short-term impact on macroeconomic outcomes. Were central bank independence to equal zero, the occurrence of an election would be expected to decrease unemployment by almost 3 percentage points and decrease growth in industrial production by about two-thirds of a percentage point. Note that the coefficient on *Election* is about three times as large in both versions of model 2 as it is in the analogous versions of model 1; and that it meets or exceeds standard levels of significance in both models in the latter, while it was only marginally significant in the former. This suggests that central bank independence does indeed constrain the occurrence of electoral cycles in macroeconomic outcomes, and it supports the argument put forth by Clark and Nair Reichert that the absence of consistent evidence of PBCs in prior studies may be the result of a failure to control for this modifying influence.

The modifying effect of central bank independence is most clearly seen through its effect on the conditional effect of elections on growth and unem-

TABLE 26.   The Constraining Effect of Central Bank Independence on
Electoralist Behavior

	(1)		(2)	
	Unemployment (a)	Growth (b)	Unemployment (a)	Growth (b)
Election	−0.747*	0.180*	−2.731**	0.661***
	(0.522)	(0.132)	(1.285)	(0.283)
Cbi			−2.929	1.099
			(2.216)	(0.605)*
Election · Cbi			5.546**	−1.359**
			(2.968)	(0.700)
Lagged dependent variable	0.432***	−0.085***	0.431***	−0.086
	(0.043)	(0.033)	(0.043)	(0.033)**
Constant	1.291***	1.037***	2.629***	0.506
	(0.537)	(0.158)	(0.981)	(0.355)
F_{DW}	0.13	22.86	0.28	8.09
Prob. > F	0.971	0.000	0.889	0.000
Observations	1,989	1,745	1,989	1,745
Number of countries	18	16	18	16

Note: OLS estimates and standard errors are in parentheses. Country dummy variables are not reported. The term F_{DW} is the test statistic for Durbin-Watson's *m*.
*$p < .10$, **$p < .05$, ***$p < .01$. One-tailed test for variables involving *E*, two-tailed otherwise.

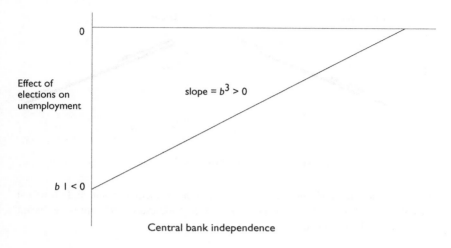

Fig. 21.   The hypothesized relationship between central bank independence and the estimated causal effect of elections on unemployment

ployment. Figure 21 displays the hypothesized relationship between central bank independence and the estimated causal effect of elections on unemployment. The vertical axis is the conditional effect of elections on growth ($b_1 + b_3Cbi$), and the horizontal axis is central bank independence. Since the hypothesis being tested asserts that unemployment should decrease during electoral periods, we expect the plot of conditional coefficients to begin appreciably below zero and to slope toward zero as central bank independence increases. The plot of conditional coefficients for the growth equation, in contrast, would begin above zero and slope downward toward zero as central bank independence increases.

Figure 22 plots the conditional coefficients from equations 2a and 2b in table 26 across the full range of logically possible values for the central bank independence measure. As expected, the conditional coefficients in the unemployment plot are appreciably below zero when central bank independence is near zero but converge toward zero as central bank independence increases. When the central bank independence measure nears the sample median, the conditional *Left* coefficients are no longer distinguishable from zero. The plot for the conditional coefficients derived from the growth equation is also consistent with the hypothesis under consideration. The conditional coefficients are positive when central bank independence is low and converge toward zero as central bank independence increases. This lends support to the claim of the

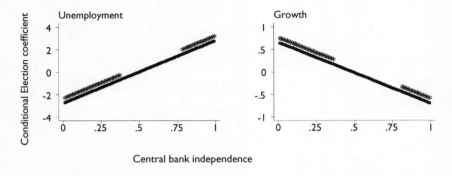

Fig. 22.   The estimated causal effect of an election on unemployment and growth at various levels of central bank independence. (*Note:* * indicates coefficient is significant at $p < .10$ level, one-tailed.)

decision-theoretic model in chapter 2 that electoral cycles in unemployment and growth do not occur in the presence of highly independent central banks.[6]

Note that in both the unemployment and growth equations, the conditional *Election* coefficients are statistically significant with the wrong sign when central bank independence is very high. This suggests that elections would induce recessions in the presence of maximally independent central banks. Since none of the world's central banks receive scores in this range, this involves making inferences about conditions beyond observed experience. Nevertheless, this result suggests that the concerns of some observers that the European Central Bank may be "too independent" (de Haan 2001) may not be unwarranted.

The Modifying Effect of Eroding Monetary Policy Autonomy

According to the decision-theoretic model in chapter 2, the erosion of national monetary policy autonomy that results from an increase in capital mobility under fixed exchange rates is also sufficient to reduce the likelihood of PBCs. Clark and Nair Reichert test this argument by constructing a variable they call "No National Policy Autonomy" (*Nonpa*), which they interact with an electoral variable in much the same way we just did to evaluate the modifying effects of central bank independence. Specifically, their model is

$$\Delta O_t = a + b_1 E_t + b_2 Nonpa_t + b_3 E \cdot Nonpa_t + \Sigma(b_j \Delta O_{t-j}) + e_t, \qquad (3)$$

where *Nonpa* is a dummy variable that equals 1 when a country lacks national policy autonomy and $E \times Nonpa$ is an interaction term that equals 1 during electoral periods in countries lacking national policy autonomy. Since according to the Mundell-Fleming model a country experiences a loss in national monetary policy autonomy when capital mobility is high and exchange rates are fixed, Clark and Nair Reichert construct the dummy variable for *Nonpa* as follows:

$$Nonpa = Fixed \cdot Capital\ Mobility. \qquad (4)$$

By substituting (4) into (3), we get

$$\Delta O_{it} = a + b_1 E_{it} + b_2 Fixed_{it} \cdot Capital\ mobility_{it}$$

$$+ b_3 E \cdot Fixed_{it} \cdot Capital\ mobility_{it} + \Sigma(b_j \Delta O_{it-j}) + e_{it}. \qquad (5)$$

Equation 5 makes it clear that Clark and Nair Reichert have violated a standard practice in the treatment of multiplicative interaction effects. It is standard practice to include all "lower-order" or constituitive terms in nonadditive models (Cleary and Kessler 1982). The fully specified interaction between E, *Capital mobility,* and *Fixed* is

$$O_{it} = a + c_1 E_{it} + c_2 Capital\ mobility_{it} + c_3 Fixed_{it}$$

$$+ c_4(Election_{it} \cdot Capital\ mobility_{it}) + c_5(Election_{it} \cdot Fixed_{it})$$

$$+ c_6(Capital\ mobility_{it} \cdot Fixed_{it})$$

$$+ c_7(Election_{it} \cdot Capital\ mobility_{it} \cdot Fixed_{it}) + c_9 Perf_{it-1}$$

$$+ \Sigma(c_k Country_{it}) + \mu_{it}. \qquad (6)$$

Equations (5) and (6) are identical when $c_2 = c_3 = c_4 = c_5 = 0$, which means that specifying the model as in (5) amounts to making the strong assumption that the coefficients c_2, c_3, c_4, and c_5 in (6) are known, with certainty, to be exactly equal to zero. The potential consequences of making such an assumption are serious, since the estimates of b_1, b_2, and b_3 are biased to the extent to which any of the coefficients c_2, c_3, c_4, and c_5 are not, in fact, equal to zero.[7]

After estimating equation (5), Clark and Nair Reichert conclude that a decline in national monetary policy autonomy prevents the occurrence of PBCs.

Furthermore, they conclude that this constraining effect also occurs when central bank independence is high. As stated earlier, these results run contrary to the game-theoretic model in chapter 2 and are in tension with the empirical results in chapter 4. For the reasons noted in the previous paragraph, however, it is possible that Clark and Nair Reichert drew conclusions about the constraining effects of these institutions from biased inferences. In the next section I determine whether this is the case by estimating (6) rather than (3).

According to the decision-theoretic model in chapter 2, macroeconomic outcomes are tied to the electoral calendar except when capital is mobile and the exchange rate is fixed. The conditional effect of elections on macroeconomic outcomes according to equation (6) is

$$\frac{\partial O_{iy}}{\partial E_{it}} = c_1 + c_4 Capital\ mobility + c_5 Fixed + c_7 Capital\ mobility \cdot Fixed. \quad (7)$$

If capital mobility constrains the survival-maximizing behavior of incumbents only when the exchange rate is fixed, we would expect to observe a link between elections and macroeconomic outcomes when neither capital mobility nor fixed exchange rates are present. Therefore, b_1 should be greater (less) than zero in the growth (unemployment) equation. In addition, the decision-theoretic model predicts that either a change to fixed exchange rates in the absence of capital mobility or an increase in capital mobility under flexible exchange rates will have no effect on the ability of incumbents to engineer preelectoral macroeconomic expansions. Since c_4 and c_5 capture the change in the estimated conditional causal effect of elections on policy when one and only one of the elements of eroding national policy autonomy occurs, the decision-theoretic model would predict that these coefficients equal zero. Since the decision-theoretic model predicts that increased capital mobility will constrain electoral cycles when the exchange rate is fixed, $c_4 + c_7$ (which captures the effect of an increase in capital mobility on the conditional effect of an election) is expected to have a different sign than c_1. Since c_4 is expected to be equal to zero, it follows that c_7 should be negative in the growth equation and positive in the unemployment equation.[8]

Estimates for equation (6) for both dependent variables are presented in table 27, and it can be seen that few, if any, of these expectations are borne out by observation. First, while the coefficient on *Election* has the hypothesized sign in both equations, the coefficients are small in magnitude (compared to the results for the case of no central bank independence) and are far from statistically significant. This indicates an absence of evidence for PBCs when capital mobility is maximally restricted and the exchange rate is flexible. Second, contrary to expectation, the coefficient on the double interaction term *Election* $\times$ *Cml* $\times$ *Fixed* (c_7) has the same sign as the coefficient on *Election*, indicating that increases in capital mobility under fixed exchange rates do not have the constraining effect on PBCs attributed to them by both the decision-theoretic model in chapter 2 and Clark and Nair Reichert.

The combined and independent modifying effects of capital mobility and fixed exchange rates on electoral cycles in macroeconomic outcomes can best be seen through an examination of conditional coefficients. Figure 23 displays the hypothesized pattern in conditional coefficients for the unemployment and growth equations. Because the exchange rate regime is not expected to infl-uence the occurrence of electoral cycles in macroeconomic outcomes when capital mobility is restricted, the plots for the fixed and flexible exchange rate

TABLE 27.   The Effect of Eroding Monetary Policy Autonomy on
Electoralist Behavior

	Unemployment (1)	Growth (2)
Election	−0.678	0.335
	(4.079)	(1.131)
Capital market liberalization (Cml)	−0.268	−0.134
	(0.480)	(0.132)
Fixed	−1.430	1.205**
	(2.004)	(0.573)
Election · Cml	−0.052	0.004
	(1.185)	(0.338)
Election · Fixed	3.940	−1.088
	(4.632)	(1.282)
Cml · Fixed	0.431	−0.078
	(0.598)	(0.171)
Election · Cml · Fixed	−1.317	0.296
	(1.390)	(0.395)
Lagged *Unemployment*	0.429***	−0.105***
	(0.043)	(0.032)
Constant	2.221	1.026**
	(1.513)	(0.448)
F_{DW}	0.02	0.09
Prob. > F	0.999	0.980
Observations	1,989	1,745
Number of countries	18	16

Note: OLS estimates and standard errors are in parentheses. Country dummy variables are not reported. The term F_{DW} is the test statistic for Durbin-Watson's m.

*$p < .01$, **$p < .05$, ***$p < .10$, one-tailed test used for coefficients involving *E*, two-tailed otherwise.

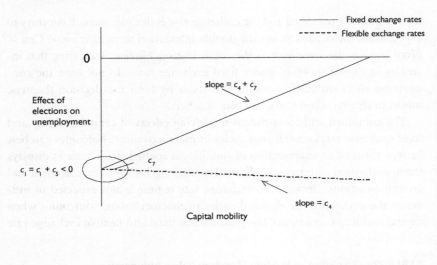

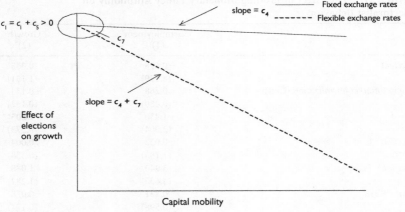

Fig. 23.   The hypothesized patterns of the conditional effect of election on macro-economic performance

cases should be near each other when capital mobility is near zero. In addition, since unemployment is expected to be tied to the electoral calendar under these circumstances, the electoral coefficients c_1 and $c_1 + c_5$ are expected to be appreciably below zero. Since an increase in capital mobility is not expected to lead to a change in the propensity of electoral cycles in unemployment to occur when the exchange rate is flexible, the slope of the plot for the flexible exchange rate case (c_4) should be close to zero. In contrast, since an increase in capital

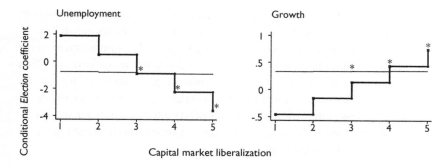

Fig. 24.   The effect of capital-market liberalization on the estimated causal effect of elections on unemployment and growth under alternative exchange rate arrangements. Solid lines denote fixed exchange rate. (*Note:* * indicates coefficient is significant at $p < .10$, one-tailed.)

mobility is expected to have a constraining effect on PBCs when the exchange rate is fixed, we expect the plot for the fixed exchange rate case to slope upward, eventually becoming indistinguishable from zero. Note that the plot for the hypothetical values for the growth equation would look like the unemployment plot rotated on its horizontal axis.

Figure 24 plots the observed, as opposed to the predicted, conditional coefficients for the unemployment and growth equations. Note first that, contrary to expectations, the conditional coefficients for the fixed and flexible exchange rate cases are further away from each other when capital mobility is low than when it is high. As expected, the slope of the plot for the flexible exchange rate case is essentially zero for both equations. But contrary to expectations, the plot for the flexible exchange rate case is always close to zero. Also contrary to expectations, the slope of the plot for the fixed exchange rate case is negative for the growth equation and positive in the unemployment equation. Consequently, capital mobility has the surprising effect of *encouraging* PBCs. The positive (negative) and statistically significant coefficients for the case where exchange rates are fixed and capital is mobile in the growth (unemployment) equations indicate that PBCs occur when the exchange rate is fixed and capital is mobile—exactly the circumstances under which the decision-theoretic model in chapter 2 and Clark and Nair Reichert suggest they should not occur.

The main expectation of the decision-theoretic model—that adding either or both constraints on monetary policy is a necessary and sufficient constraint on electoral cycles in macroeconomic outcomes— does not appear to be supported by the evidence. Electoral cycles in growth and unemployment occur when national monetary policy is absent; nor do they necessarily occur when it is absent. One reason may be that macroeconomic outcomes are not the product of the decisions of monetary policymakers alone but, rather, the product of the strategic interaction between monetary and fiscal policymakers. This strategic interaction is the focus of the game-theoretic model in chapter 2, to which I turn my attention next.

A Test of the Game-Theoretic Model

According to the game-theoretic model, the loss of national monetary policy autonomy by itself is not a determining influence on the existence of electoral cycles in outcomes. When the exchange rate is fixed, an increase in capital mobility erodes the effectiveness of monetary policy, but it enhances the effectiveness of fiscal policy. Put differently, when capital is mobile, a switch to a fixed exchange rate may not prevent electorally induced macroeconomic expansions, because survival-maximizing incumbents can switch from a focus on monetary instruments to fiscal instruments. Under these conditions, enhancing central bank independence will not help prevent the manipulation of the macroeconomy for electoral purposes, because the loss of monetary policy autonomy associated with a combination of fixed exchange rates and mobile capital will inhibit attempts on the part of independent central bankers to counteract electorally motivated fiscal expansions. Central bank independence can, however, prevent the occurrence of electoral cycles in macroeconomic outcomes when capital is mobile and the exchange rate is flexible. Since when the exchange rate is flexible an increase in capital mobility results in a decline in the effectiveness of fiscal policy, incumbents control neither macroeconomic policy instrument if the central bank is independent.

In sum, contrary to Clark and Nair Reichert and the decision-theoretic model in chapter 2, the game-theoretic model predicts that central bank independence and capital mobility have constraining effects on cycles in macroeconomic outcomes when the exchange rate is flexible, but not when it is fixed. To examine these complex conditional arguments, it is necessary to control for the modifying effects of capital mobility, exchange rate regime, and central bank independence.

Since these interactions get rather complicated, it is useful to consider the interaction of two of these variables (in this case, capital mobility and central bank independence) while holding the third factor (exchange rate regime) constant.

Expected Electoral Cycles under Fixed Exchange Rates

According to the model in chapter 2, electoral cycles in macroeconomic outcomes are expected under most conditions when the exchange rate is fixed. National income is expected to increase as elections near—both when capital is mobile and when it is not, and also when the central bank is independent (see table 25). Expansions are expected in the before-capital-mobility period, though their magnitude can be substantially reduced by central bank independence. When capital is mobile, however, cycles are expected whether or not the central bank is independent. The evidence already presented in figure 24 that, contra Clark and Nair Reichert, electoral cycles in growth and unemployment are at least as pronounced when the exchange rate is fixed as when it is flexible is relevant to this prediction. But we can also test arguments about the existence of electoral cycles under each of the institutional combinations that could occur under fixed exchange rates with a model with two modifying variables that interact with each other:

$$O_{it} = a + b_1 Election_{it} + b_2 Cbi_{it} + b_3 Cml_{it} + b_4(Election_{it} \cdot Cbi_{it})$$

$$+ b_5(Election_{it} \cdot Cml_{it}) + b_6(Election_{it} \cdot Cml_{it})$$

$$+ b_7(Election_{it} \cdot Cbi_{it} \cdot Cml_{it}) + b_9 Perf_{it-1}$$

$$+ \Sigma(b_k Country_{it}) + \mu_{it}. \qquad (8)$$

The estimated causal effect of an election under fixed exchange rate can be determined by taking the partial derivative of (8) with respect to *Election*. This yields

$$\frac{\partial O_{it}}{\partial Election} = b_1 + b_4 Cbi + b_5 Cml + b_7 Cbi \cdot Cm. \qquad (9)$$

We can then use this "conditional *Election* coefficient" to test for the existence of electoral cycles under the full range of institutional combinations that can occur under fixed exchange rates. Once again, b_1 can be used to test the electoralist argument when the other modifying variables equal zero. Since both the game-theoretic and the decision-theoretic models predict that when the exchange rate is fixed electoral cycles in macroeconomic outcomes should occur when capital is immobile and the central bank is entirely dependent, we would expect this coefficient to be positive (negative) and significant in the growth (unemployment) equation. In addition, since survival-maximizing incumbents committed to a fixed exchange rate are expected to use fiscal policy to engineer preelectoral expansions when either the central bank is independent or capital is mobile, or both, the conditional *Election* coefficient (9) is expected to be positive (negative) and significant in the growth (unemployment) equation for all possible values of the modifying variables. However, since an independent central bank can partially counteract electorally motivated fiscal expansions when capital is immobile, the magnitude of macroeconomic expansions under fixed exchange rates and immobile capital should be smaller when the central bank is independent than when it is not. Central bank independence, however, loses its constraining effect when capital becomes more mobile.

Expected Electoral Cycles under Flexible Exchange Rates

According to the model in chapter 2, national income is expected to increase during electoral periods when capital is immobile. An increase in central bank independence or an increase in capital mobility is expected to decrease the magnitude of electorally induced cycles, and an increase in both capital mobility and central bank independence is expected to inhibit electorally induced cycles in growth completely. Clark and Hallerberg (2000) (see also chap. 5) demonstrated that when the exchange rate is allowed to fluctuate, an increase in capital mobility is expected to deter electoral cycles in fiscal policy, but not monetary policy. They found evidence of monetary cycles when capital was mobile and the exchange rate was fixed, unless the central bank was independent. The game-theoretic model in chapter 2 predicts that macroeconomic outcomes may be linked to the electoral calendar when the exchange rate is flexible unless capital is mobile and the central bank is independent.

As earlier in this chapter, we can evaluate arguments about the modifying effects of central bank independence and capital mobility on electorally induced cycles in growth with the following model:

$$Growth_{it} = a + c_1 Election_{it} + c_2 Cbi_{it} + c_3 Cml_{it} + c_4(Election_{it} \cdot Cbi_{it})$$

$$+ c_5(Election_{it} \cdot Cml_{it}) + c_6(Election_{it} \cdot Cml_{it})$$

$$+ c_7(Election_{it} \cdot Cbi_{it} \cdot Cml_{it}) + c_9 Perf_{it-1}$$

$$+ \Sigma(c_k Country_{it}) + \mu_{it}. \tag{10}$$

The conditional coefficient for *Election* for the set of ideal typical contexts is strictly analogous to those in the previous example:

$$\frac{\partial Growth_{it}}{\partial Election} = c_1 + c_4 Cbi + c_5 Cml + c_7 Cbi \cdot Cm. \tag{11}$$

Once again, c_1 is the estimated causal effect of an election on macroeconomic performance when both central bank independence and capital-market liberalization equal zero, and c_4 and c_5 estimate how a change in one of the modifying variables is expected to affect the relationship between elections and macroeconomic performance when the other modifying variable equals zero. Since electoral cycles in macroeconomic outcomes are expected (hypothesis 2P) under these circumstances, we expect c_1 to be greater (less) than zero in the growth (unemployment) equation. In addition, since an increase in capital mobility or central bank independence may constrain electoral cycles, we expect c_4 and c_5 to have the opposite sign as c_1. Furthermore, since the game-theoretic model in chapter 2 predicts that electoral cycles in macroeconomic outcomes will not occur when capital is mobile *and* the central bank is independent, we expect the conditional electoral coefficient for the flexible exchange rate case to be indistinguishable from zero when capital mobility and central bank independence are both high.

Evidence of Electoral Cycles under Fixed and Flexible Exchange Rates

The preceding discussion suggests that central bank independence and capital mobility have modifying effects on the relationship between elections and macroeconomic outcomes under fixed exchange rates that are different than those under flexible exchange rates. Accordingly, I have examined the predictions of the game-theoretic model in chapter 2 under different exchange rate arrangements separately. While it is possible to divide the sample by exchange rate regime and examine these predictions separately, it is preferable to examine these differential modifying effects in the full sample using the exchange rate regime as a third modifying variable. The basic model for the case of three modifying variables can be stated as

$$O_{it} = b_1 Election_{it} + b_2 Cbi_{it} + b_3 Cml_{it} + b_4(Election_{it} \cdot Cbi_{it})$$

$$+ b_5(Election_{it} \cdot Cml_{it}) + b_6(Cbi_{it} \cdot Cml_{it})$$

$$+ b_7(Election_{it} \cdot Cbi_{it} \cdot Cml_{it}) + b_8 Fixed + \Sigma b_j Fixed \cdot (Election_{it}$$

$$+ Cbi_{it} + Cml_{it} + (Election_{it} \cdot Cbi_{it}) + (Election_{it} \cdot Cml_{it})$$

$$+ (Cbi_{it} \cdot Cml_{it}) + (Election_{it} \cdot Cbi_{it} \cdot Cml_{it})) + b_9 Perf_{it-1}$$

$$+ \Sigma(b_k Country_{it}) + \mu_{it}, \tag{12}$$

the conditional *Election* coefficient becomes

$$\frac{\partial O_{it}}{\partial Election_{it}} = b_1 Election_{it} + b_4(Cbi_{it}) + b_5(Cml_{it}) + b_7(Cbi_{it} \cdot Cml_{it})$$

$$+ b_9 Fixed + b_{12}(Fixed \cdot Cbi_{it}) + b_{13}(Fixed \cdot Cml_{it})$$

$$+ b_{15}(Fixed \cdot Cbi_{it} \cdot Cml_{it})), \tag{13}$$

and the associated conditional standard error is far more unsightly. Note, however, that when the exchange rate is flexible, the conditional coefficient reduces to

$$\frac{\partial O_{it}}{\partial Election_{it} \mid Fixed = 0} = b_1 Election_{it} + b_4(Cbi_{it}) + b_5(Cml_{it})$$

$$+ b_7(Cbi_{it} \cdot Cml_{it}), \tag{14}$$

which is identical to equation (11). Similarly, if (12) is respecified so that a variable *Flexible* (which equals 1 when the exchange rate is flexible and zero when it is fixed) replaces *Fixed*

$$O_{it} = c_1 Election_{it} + c_2 Cbi_{it} + c_3 Cml_{it} + c_4(Election_{it} \cdot Cbi_{it})$$

$$+ c_5(Election_{it} \cdot Cml_{it}) + c_6(Cbi_{it} \cdot Cml_{it})$$

$$+ c_7(Election_{it} \cdot Cbi_{it} \cdot Cml_{it}) + c_8 Fixed + \Sigma c_j Fixed \cdot (Election_{it}$$

$$+ Cbi_{it} + Cml_{it} + (Election_{it} \cdot Cbi_{it}) + (Election_{it} \cdot Cml_{it})$$

$$+ (Cbi_{it} \cdot Cml_{it}) + (Election_{it} \cdot Cbi_{it} \cdot Cml_{it})) + c_9 Perf_{it-1}$$

$$+ \Sigma(c_k Country_{it}) + \mu_{it}, \tag{15}$$

then the conditional *Election* coefficient for the fixed exchange rate case can be derived in a strictly analogous fashion, yielding

$$\frac{\partial O_{it}}{\partial Election_{it} \mid Flex = 0} = c_1 Left_{it} + c_4(Cbi_{it}) + c_5(Cml_{it})$$

$$+ c_7(Cbi_{it} \cdot Cml_{it}). \tag{16}$$

Table 28 reports the OLS results for models based on (12) and (15). There is considerably more evidence in support of context-specific electoral cycles than was found for context-specific partisan differences in macroeconomic outcomes in the preceding chapter. In addition, the evidence for context-dependent electoral cycles appears to be more consistent with the game-theoretic model than the decision-theoretic model.

Note first that the signs on all of the *Election* coefficients in table 28 are as hypothesized. Note, however, that only the *Election* coefficients for the case where exchange rates are fixed are statistically significant. This is probably due to the fact that, since flexible exchange rates were rare in the before-capital-mobility period, the standard errors on the latter are quite large.

Conditional coefficients are again useful for determining if the evidence is consistent with the game-theoretic model's predictions about the occurrence of electoral cycles in macroeconomic outcomes under other structural conditions. The conditional coefficients for the fixed exchange rate case are plotted in figure 25. Three plots are provided. The lightest line plots the conditional coefficients for the case where two capital controls are in place (*Cml* = 2). The darkest line plots the conditional coefficients for the case where no capital controls are in place (*Cml* = 0). Finally, the moderately dark line plots the conditional coefficients for an intermediate degree of capital mobility (*Cml* = 1).

The model predicts that electoral cycles in unemployment and growth will occur when the exchange rate is fixed and capital is immobile. An examination of the left-hand side of both the unemployment and the growth figures indicates that, as expected, when central bank independence is low, unemployment

TABLE 28. The Effect of Elections on Macroeconomic Performance Conditioned upon the Degree of Central Bank Independence, the Degree of Capital Mobility, and the Exchange Rate Regime

		Growth (1)	Unemployment (2)		Growth (3)	Unemployment (4)
		Regime = Flex (a)	Regime = Flex (a)		Regime = Fixed (a)	Regime = Fixed (b)
Election	b_1	2.212**	−7.969*	c_1	0.166	−7.477
		(1.306)	(5.237)		(2.466)	(9.697)
Cbi	b_2	6.461***	−24.091***	c_2	1.702	−19.480
		(2.254)	(8.618)		(3.171)	(12.692)
Cml	b_3	0.594*	−2.499*	c_3	−0.025	−3.185
		(0.318)	(1.434)		(0.537)	(2.274)
Election · Cbi	b_4	−8.635***	31.219***	c_4	0.001	14.731
		(3.217)	(12.787)		(6.396)	(22.818)
Election · Cml	b_5	−0.538*	1.514	c_5	0.265	1.597
		(0.420)	(1.755)		(0.723)	(3.168)
Cbi · Cml	b_6	−1.898***	6.303**	c_6	−0.247	5.856
		(0.632)	(2.797)		(0.964)	(4.148)
Election · Cbi · Cml	b_7	2.379***	−7.856**	c_7	−0.532	−3.384
		(0.997)	(4.111)		(1.757)	(6.928)
Regime		0.768	1.223		−0.768	−1.223
		(2.133)	(8.411)		(2.133)	(8.411)
Election · Regime		−2.047	0.492		2.047	−0.492
		(2.821)	(10.984)		(2.821)	(10.984)
Cbi · Regime		−4.759	4.611		4.759	−4.611
		(4.156)	(16.117)		(4.156)	(16.117)
Regime · Cml		−0.619	−0.686		0.619	0.686
		(0.613)	(2.666)		(0.613)	(2.666)
Election · Cbi · Regime		8.637	−16.488		−8.637	16.488
		(7.231)	(26.133)		(7.231)	(26.133)
Election · Cml · Regime		0.803	0.803		−0.803	−0.083
		(0.842)	(3.611)		(0.842)	(3.611)
Cbi · Cml · Regime		1.650	−0.447		−1.650	0.447
		(1.159)	(5.050)		(1.159)	(5.050)
Election · Cbi · Cml · Regime		−2.911*	4.472		2.911*	−4.472
		(2.026)	(8.046)		(2.026)	(8.046)
Lagged Growth		−0.110***	0.422***		−0.110***	0.422***
		(0.032)	(0.043)		(0.032)	(0.043)
Constant		−0.500	10.707**		0.268	11.931*
		(1.083)	(4.218)		(1.660)	(6.731)
F_{DW}		1.59	0.01		1.59	0.01
Prob. > F		0.17	0.999		0.17	0.999
Observations		1,745	1,989		1,745	1,989
Number of countries		16	18		16	18

Note: OLS estimates and standard errors are in parentheses. Country dummy variables are not reported. The term F_{DW} is the test statistic for Durbin-Watson's m.

*$p < .01$, **$p < .05$, ***$p < .10$, one-tailed test for variables involving E, two-tailed otherwise.

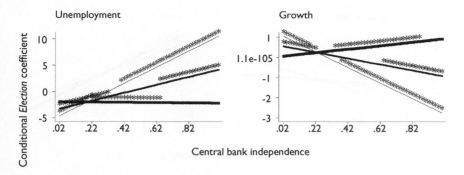

Fig. 25.   The effect of central bank independence and capital mobility on electorally in-duced cycles in growth and unemployment under fixed exchange rates. Darker lines de-note increased capital-market liberalization. (*Note:* * indicates coefficient is significant at $p < .10$, one-tailed.)

drops and growth increases in preelectoral periods when capital is relatively immobile. The constraining effect of central bank independence before capital mobility is demonstrated by the fact that the plot for conditional coefficients for the case of immobile capital converges toward zero as central bank inde-pendence increases. Note that, as predicted, when central bank independence increases, electoral cycles in growth and unemployment are dampened if and only if capital controls are present. When capital controls are removed, central bank independence has no dampening effect on the magnitude of electoral cy-cles; if anything, cycles in growth and unemployment get larger.

When the exchange rate is fixed and capital is relatively immobile, there is evidence that unemployment drops and growth increases, as long as central bank independence is limited (the lighter two lines in fig. 25). When the ex-change rate is fixed and capital is highly mobile, however, the situation is quite different. Under these circumstances, unemployment is lower and growth higher in preelectoral periods even when the exchange rate is fixed. This is con-sistent with the argument implied by the game-theoretic model in chapter 2. When capital is mobile and the exchange rate is fixed, central bank independ-ence has no teeth, because national monetary policy autonomy does not exist. In the absence of countervailing pressure from the central bank, fiscal policy can be used to produce preelectoral drops in unemployment and increases in growth. When capital mobility is limited, however, preelectoral macroeco-nomic expansions do not occur when the central bank is independent; in fact,

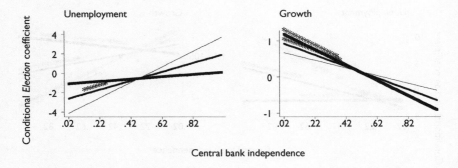

Fig. 26.   The effect of central bank independence and capital mobility on electorally induced cycles in growth and unemployment under flexible exchange rates. Darker lines denote increased capital-market liberalization. (*Note:* * indicates coefficient is significant at $p < .10$, one-tailed.)

the opposite is the case. Growth is lower and unemployment is higher in pre-electoral periods when the central bank is independent. Presumably, this is the result of restrictive policies by the independent central bank aimed at counteracting electorally motivated fiscal expansions.

When the exchange rate is flexible, the situation is quite different (fig. 26). Most broadly, it should be noted that electoral cycles in macroeconomic outcomes are now relatively rare. There is some evidence that cycles occur when central bank independence is limited. In the plot for the unemployment equation, the magnitude of the conditional coefficient converges toward zero both as capital controls are removed and when central bank independence is enhanced.[9] This suggests that, consistent with our model, each of these factors has a constraining effect when the exchange rate is allowed to fluctuate. The results for the growth equation do not entirely fit expectations. As expected, electorally induced cycles occur when central bank independence is high, but not when it is low. The removal of capital controls, however, appears to have little effect (the lines for the three levels of capital mobility are close together and nearly parallel). In fact, if capital-market liberalization in the absence of central bank independence has any effect, it is to increase the magnitude of electorally induced cycles.

While there are one or two anomalies, many of the implications of the game-theoretic model in chapter 2 are supported by the evidence, and many of these implications directly contradict those of the decision-theoretic argument and the findings of Clark and Nair Reichert. There is considerable evidence of electoral cycles in unemployment and growth when the exchange rate is fixed. Evidence that such cycles exist when central bank independence is low and capital is immobile is consistent with both models. Likewise, evidence that cycles do not occur when capital is mobile, the exchange rate is flexible, and the central bank is independent is also consistent with expectations. However, the evidence presented here that cycles occur under fixed exchange rates when capital is mobile is consistent with the game-theoretic model but not the decision-theoretic model. Similarly, and most startlingly, evidence that electorally induced cycles in outcomes occur when *both* of the constraints posited by the decision-theoretic model are present runs directly counter to that model but are entirely consistent with the game-theoretic model.

These findings suggest that fiscal policy and monetary policy can be substitutes for each other in the hands of survival-maximizing incumbents. When structural factors make it difficult for incumbents to use monetary policy to engineer preelectoral macroeconomic expansions, they will use fiscal policy to engineer such cycles. When capital is immobile, independent central banks appear to be able to counter or deter fiscal expansions in such a manner that there is no net expansionary effect on the macroeconomy. When capital is mobile and the central bank is not independent, incumbents appear to choose whichever instrument is most effective, according to the Mundell-Fleming model, to engineer preelectoral expansions. When capital is mobile and the central bank is independent, incumbents are able to use fiscal policy for electoral purposes when the exchange rate is fixed because the loss of national monetary policy autonomy weakens the ability of central bankers to oppose them. When, however, the central bank is independent and the exchange rate is flexible, an increase in capital mobility puts survival-maximizing incumbents in a tight spot. Monetary policy is effective, but it is controlled by a bank that is insulated from electoral pressures, and the loss of national fiscal policy autonomy robs them of the only other available instrument.

Conclusions

Existing models of electoralist cycles in the macroeconomy assume that elected officials can control short-term macroeconomic outcomes in politically advantageous ways. The recent changes in the international system, combined with cross-national differences in institutional arrangements, make this assumption difficult to sustain in many cases. The results presented here suggest that countries that maintain fixed exchange rates in an environment of highly mobile capital or highly independent central banks are more likely to experience electoral cycles in unemployment and growth. Thus, attention to cross-national differences in institutions reveals a link between elections and macroeconomic variables that many earlier studies missed. This finding is surprising in light of the rational expectations critique of the traditional electoralist model. Although the rational expectations approach contributes to our understanding of the strategic interaction between policymaker and voters by focusing on the way these actors formulate their beliefs, my findings suggest that one reason standard models of the political control of the economy have not received empirical support is that they ignore the institutions that structure the strategic choices of elected politicians. Domestic institutions, including the structure of the central bank, help determine which actions are possible and which strategic alternatives are desirable. Since there are substantial cross-national differences in these institutional structures, deductive models that attempt to explain the dynamics of electoral competition need to pay close attention to the way these institutions shape the institutional environment in which politicians operate. Failure to do so will lead to models with limited empirical usefulness. This study has singled out the degree of central bank independence, but other domestic institutional structures are also likely to matter. These might include the structure of party competition, the relationship between the executive and legislature, and the nature of the electoral system. Furthermore, the institutionalist approach to electoralist cycles used here can be fruitfully combined with a rational expectations approach or applied to partisan cycles as well.

Based on the evidence in this study, I also suggest that traditional PBC models can and should be extended to include insights from open-economy macroeconomics. Obviously, international factors influence the dynamics of domestic political behavior. Researchers have examined, for instance, the ways in which international economic conditions influence the effects of partisan competition on macroeconomic performance (Alt 1985; Garrett and Lange 1986). Other researchers have examined the way international economic factors influence attempts by societal groups to shape policy outcomes (Gourevitch 1986; Milner 1988; Rogowski 1989; Frieden 1991a; Garrett 1995). These insights have not made their way into formal models that attempt to explain the conditions under which politicians will manipulate the economy for electoral purposes. The evidence in this study suggests that characteristics of the international system, such as the degree of capital mobility, combine with foreign economic policy decisions, such as the commitment to a fixed exchange rate, in ways that shape the incentive structures of incumbents responsible for macroeconomic policy.

Broad statements about the effects of increased capital mobility on the political control of industrial economies and the sovereignty of nation-states should be critically viewed and carefully qualified. If these effects stem from the loss of national policy autonomy resulting from an increase in capital mobility, recognizing how these effects may be mediated by national-level policy decisions and domestic institutional arrangements is important. For example, the posited link between increased economic interdependence and macroeconomic policy convergence is, in part, mediated by national decisions (Garrett and Lange 1991, 1995). National policy autonomy, as evidenced by the existence of PBCs, is feasible in a financially integrated world—especially if national decision makers are willing to forfeit a degree of exchange rate stability. Although growing financial integration has facilitated cross-national monetary policy convergence and made the political control of the economy more difficult, it has not made convergence automatic, nor has it made political control impossible. The recent increase in the level of international capital mobility constitutes a change in the structure of the international system with historic consequences. This study suggests, however, that the consequences of this change are not the same for every state in the system.

CHAPTER 7

Conclusion

Macroeconomic policy was apparently made more in response to the outputs of the political system . . . than to the objective performance of the economy. Perhaps that is as it should be in a democracy.

—Edward R. Tufte (1978, 83)

I have offered detailed and, I hope, measured summaries of this book's empirical findings at the end of each of the empirical chapters. In this conclusion, I emphasize the broadest findings and what I see as their main implications, attempting to step out from among the trees and get a glimpse of the broader forest.

The empirical results in this book can be divided into two broad categories: those that help us decide between the veracity of the partisan and electoralist models, and those that shed light on the influence of capital mobility and central bank independence.

The Partisan and Electoralist Models of the Domestic Political Economy

A key argument of this book is that we cannot accurately gauge the effect of capital mobility and central bank independence on the politics of macroeconomic policy until we decide which model is best able to help us understand the domestic political economy of rich democracies in the late twentieth century. Consequently, a large portion of this book has been devoted to testing propositions derived from the two most prominent political models of the macroeconomy—the partisan and the electoralist models.

In contrast to many earlier studies, I find that monetary and fiscal policy and macroeconomic outcomes are tied to the electoral calendar, but the link between elections and the macroeconomy is deeply context-dependent. Elections result in monetary expansions when the central bank is not independent and when capital mobility and fixed exchange rates have not eroded national monetary policy autonomy. Elections result in fiscal expansions as long as flexible exchange rates and mobile capital have not eroded national fiscal policy autonomy. There is considerable evidence that the influence of elections on monetary and fiscal policy also filters through to macroeconomic outcomes. Elections result in reduced unemployment and increased growth when the net effect of the resulting macroeconomic policies is expansionary. Whether this is the case depends on the exchange rate regime and the degree of capital mobility and central bank independence in place.

In contrast, there is very little clear evidence—either in the expansive literature that has developed over the last twenty years or in the tests conducted here—that the ideological orientation of government influences policy and performance in the manner predicted by the partisan model of macroeconomic policy choice. This result appears to hold for a wide variety of labor-market environments, various degrees of central bank independence, and whether or not the country retains national policy autonomy.

There are two models of the underlying links between politics and macroeconomic policy that are consistent with absence of partisan effects: the Downsian median-voter model and arguments that emphasize the structural dependence of the state on capital. The median-voter approach argues that competitive pressures cause parties of all ideological stripes to implement similar policies. The evidence of electoral cycles presented here is broadly consistent with this approach. One need only add an assertion that the median voter is a retrospective, pocketbook voter.

The "structural dependence of the state on capital" argument maintains that because owners of capital control investment decisions that have broad effects on the health of the economy, and attempts to maximize returns on their assets lead them to disinvest when policy decisions threaten the existing distribution of assets, there are strict limitations on the kinds of reforms that can be initiated by elected officials (Lindbloom 1982). Indeed, because left governments may be particularly anxious to demonstrate to capital markets that they intend to "govern responsibly" (Przeworski 1985), they may be reluctant to implement any policies that differ from those of their predecessors.[1] Since capital markets stand ready to punish governments that stray too far from the markets' most preferred policies, there is little reason to expect systematic partisan differences. For example, a party of the left that makes vigorous use of macroeconomic policy instruments to redistribute income toward its constituency runs the risk of provoking an economic crisis—hardly something to be rewarded by pocketbook voters, be they partisan or Downsian. Thus, according to this perspective, it is capitalism, not globalism, that constrains the policy choices available to democratically elected governments. If the structural dependence of the state on capital is part of the explanation for the absence of partisan differences in policy, the recent increase in capital mobility (which, according to the common wisdom, increases the influence that holders of capital assets have over policy by making their exit threats more credible) can be seen as a change in degree rather than kind.

The electoralist and structural-dependence arguments are by no means mutually exclusive. In fact, they may be different sides of the same coin. If it is the case that parties have the sort of distinctive policy preferences reflecting the objective interests of distinct constituencies and that—as suggested by embryonic versions of the partisan model (Key 1949; Lipset 1960)—the constituency for "left" policies is numerically superior to the constituency for "right" policies, then the structural dependence of the state argument explains why left parties must make concessions to capital (even in majoritarian polities where they could rule without the support of bourgeois parties), and the median-voter model explains why parties of the right must accommodate the preferences of left-wing groups. Clearly, more analysis and empirical work are needed in order to better understand the logical relationship between these two arguments and to determine which elements of each are consistent with historical experience.

It is important to stress what cannot be concluded from the findings presented in this book. One cannot say that because the partisan variable was frequently not significantly different from zero, cross-national differences in the behavior of parties do not "matter." Following Garrett (1998), I used a model that included country dummy variables to control for country-specific fixed effects. Consequently, an insignificant partisan variable implied the absence of partisan differences in fiscal policy *within* countries. Since differences in spending or taxation levels—or in growth and employment—*between* countries are picked up in the country dummies, it is possible that parties could have an effect on fiscal policy that is not captured by the partisan variable in the models reported here. Thus, governments in countries that have a greater tendency to elect socialist or social democratic parties may, in the long run, choose different policies than governments in countries that have a greater tendency to elect right-wing governments—even if governments of different stripes within that country implement identical policies and compile identical performance records. But under such circumstances, it is more useful to attribute the differences in fiscal policy between countries (and the differences in propensity to elect particular parties) to differences in the preferences of the median voter than to differences in the ideological stripes of the governments in power. As a result, cross-national differences in behavior are of little help in distinguishing between the median-voter and partisan models.

Similarly, one cannot conclude from the evidence presented here that there is "one capitalism" or that it is misguided to discuss "varieties of capitalism" or emphasize the importance of national institutions. I have not examined the possibility that left governance and labor-market institutions combine to form broader policy regimes, nor have I looked at a host of other domestic institutions such as electoral systems, the structure of the party system, and executive–legislative relations, or combinations of these factors (e.g., the veto structure of domestic institutions). I have also not examined the potential effects of government budgetary institutions, the structure of domestic capital markets, or the effects of central bank independence. In sum, I have no interest in demonstrating that "politics do not matter"; I have examined a specific hypothesis about a particular way in which politics might matter and have found little evidence in support of that hypothesis.

The Effects of Central Bank Independence and Eroding National Policy Autonomy

Given the scarcity of evidence in support of the partisan hypothesis and the tendency for the globalization literature to rely, at least implicitly, on the partisan approach for its model of the domestic political economy, it should not be surprising to find conflicting results in the globalization literature that does rely (implicitly or explicitly) on that model. The common wisdom about globalization is that it represents the triumph of markets over politics—an inexorable process that strips governments of the ability to influence events. The revisionist literature maintains that this is not true; partisan differences in policies and outcomes have survived—perhaps even flourished—under the recent increase in capital mobility. Governments can still effectively intervene in market struggles on behalf of their citizens. The empirical results in the current study support and challenge elements of both of these views.

Like the revisionist approach, the findings I have presented challenge the common wisdom; the loss of national policy autonomy does not induce a partisan convergence in policies or performance. This is the case not because left governments have responded to increased demands for protection from the risks of the international economy, but because the structures of democratic capitalism have been discouraging partisan differences all along. Also contra the revisionists, the erosion of national policy autonomy and the creation of central bank independence appear to be associated with the contractionary policies traditionally associated with parties of the right (more price stability, but also more unemployment and less growth). Together, these results suggest that partisan convergence has been a characteristic of the democratic control of the macroeconomy for some time. If increased capital mobility and central bank independence have had an effect, it seems to have been in shifting—not creating—a macroeconomic consensus (McNamara 1998).

This book also departs from much of the existing literature on globalization by arguing that the domestic political effects of capital mobility will depend on both the exchange rate regime and the degree of central bank independence. Figure 27 summarizes the effects of elections on the macroeconomy under various combinations of the contextual factors considered in this book according to the evidence presented in chapter 6 (table 28 and figs. 25 and 26).

Note first that none of the contextual factors has an unconditional modifying effect on the relationship between the macroeconomy and the electoral calendar. Central bank independence, for example, inhibits electoral cycles in growth and employment when capital is immobile (cells a and e). But when capital is mobile, the political consequence of central bank independence depends on the exchange rate. If the exchange rate is fixed (cell b), the absence of national monetary policy autonomy means that independent central bankers are unable to prevent the use of fiscal policy for electoral purposes. If the exchange rate is allowed to fluctuate (cell f), the resulting decline in national fiscal policy autonomy means that incumbents cannot use fiscal policy to override an independent central banker's veto of a preelectoral monetary expansion. As a consequence, the macroeconomy will not be tied to the electoral calendar when capital is mobile, the exchange rate is flexible, and the central bank is independent.

The domestic political effect of increased capital mobility is also conditioned by the choice of exchange rate regime and the degree of central bank independence. Unless the central bank is independent, an increase in capital mobility is not expected to have profound effects on the political control of the economy. When the exchange rate is fixed, an increase in capital mobility under a dependent central bank (a move from cell c to cell d) means that survival-maximizing incumbents must abandon the use of monetary policy for electoral purposes and embrace fiscal policy as their instrument of choice. In contrast, when the exchange rate is flexible, an increase in capital mobility under a dependent central bank (a move from cell g to cell h) means that incumbents must use

	Exchange rate is:				
	Fixed			**Flexible**	
	Capital is:			Capital is:	
	Immobile	*Mobile*		*Immobile*	*Mobile*
Independent	(a) Contradiction in growth and employment	(b) Fiscal-induced expansion in growth and employment	*Independent*	(e) Offsetting fiscal and monetary policies	(f) Offsetting fiscal and monetary policies
Central bank is:					
Dependent	(c) Expansion in growth and employment	(d) Fiscal-induced expansion in employment	*Dependent*	(g) Offsetting fiscal and monetary policies	(h) Monetary-induced expansion in growth

Fig. 27.   The context-dependent effect of elections

monetary policy if they wish to engineer a preelectoral expansion in growth and employment. Note that the absence of an electorally induced change in growth and employment (in cell g) is an anomaly. When the central bank is independent, then the effect of an increase in capital mobility depends crucially on the choice of the exchange rate regime. Contra Clark and Nair Reichert (1998), when the central bank is independent, capital mobility constrains the manipulation of the macroeconomy for electoral purposes if the exchange is flexible (cell f), but not if it is fixed (cell b).

Finally, in an era of capital mobility, pegging the exchange rate does not "depoliticize" macroeconomic policy. In fact, if the central bank is independent, pegging the exchange rate is a prerequisite if incumbents are going to use the economy for electoral purposes. In the absence of central bank independence, the decision to peg or not to peg amounts to a decision on the part of incumbents about *how*, not *whether*, to manipulate the macroeconomy for electoral purposes.

Normative Implications

Having found a world that is more complicated than both the common wisdom and the revisionist response would have us think, it is not trivial to assess the normative implications of increased capital mobility and the growing propensity to entrust monetary policy to an independent central bank. If one accepts the common wisdom that globalization represents a universal threat to governmental control of the economy, and if one views market forces as expanding human freedom by spurring innovation—and views government as a part of the problem rather than the solution—one might welcome the forces of globalization as oppressed people might welcome an invading army. If, however, one views market forces as a threat to human freedom, as the fomenter of privation and injustice—and views government as the last, best hope that the disadvantaged can also experience human freedom—one is likely to be more troubled by the empirical claims connected to the common wisdom. Though we may disagree strenuously on the precise mix of government and market, most of us at this point in history recognize that neither of these forces is an unmitigated evil, nor is either an unqualified good. Thus, even if we were to accept the empirical claims of the common wisdom, a normative assessment of the effects of capital mobility would have to pay close attention to the potential trade-offs between market efficiency and government regulation. Nevertheless, those inclined to see the good in markets and the bad in government are likely to be more enthusiastic about globalization than those that see markets as fundamentally destructive forces.

In the more complicated world implied by the findings in this book, there are a number of competing normative concerns vying for attention. First, in contrast to the claims of many of their adherents, there is little evidence to be found in this book that structural factors such as central bank independence, capital-market liberalization, or fixed exchange rates are technologies that costlessly generate economic benefits. Central bank independence, for example, does appear to encourage price stability, but this typically comes at the expense of growth and employment. Because it is an inherently distributional question, whether the benefit of price stability is "worth" the cost is a political question that cannot be resolved analytically. Since the loss of policy autonomy appears to have similar effects, much the same can be said about capital-market integration and fixed exchange rates.

Second, and as a consequence, the fact that central bank independence and declining national policy autonomy remove effective control from the hands of apparently self-interested politicians does not guarantee the implementation of socially optimal policies. In most of the literature on "opportunistic" political business cycles, the electorally timed manipulations of the macroeconomy are implicitly treated as "bads"—they result in a benefit for survival-maximizing incumbents at the expense of the public good. While I have not devoted sufficient attention to normative questions to demonstrate that this view is inappropriate, I believe that the results in this book do call this common assumption into question. Macroeconomic policy made with an eye toward the polls may be more inflationary than policy made by policymakers who are freed from such concerns by institutional constraints. But these policies also tend to produce more growth and less unemployment. Encouraging policymakers to be responsive to public opinion may not be as destructive to public welfare as some economists have led us to believe. In fact, as Edward Tufte said, "Perhaps that is as it should be in a democracy" (1978, 83).

Finally, in the absence of compelling empirical evidence that central bank independence or globalization can provide a free lunch—in the form of lower inflation than is obtainable under other structural conditions with no cost in terms of growth, employment, or equity—attempts to influence the structure in which macroeconomic policy is made will remain a political, rather than a technocratic, question. In fact, since changing governments appears to have little effect on macroeconomic outcomes, it is likely that larger structural choices, such as the degree of central bank independence, the nature of exchange rate commitments, and the optimal degree of financial integration, will become the locus of political contestation.

Appendix A
Derivation of Proposition 1

The reaction functions in proposition 1 in chapter 2 follow directly from the actor's loss functions and the Phillips curve mechanism. The government's problem is to choose g so as to minimize its loss function, which, if we substitute in the Phillips curve process (equation (4) in chap. 2) that determines y and the right-hand side of (2) for the government's ideal point for output and assume (without loss of generality) that $\pi^* = 0$, becomes

$$L_i = (y^n + \mu(\pi - \pi^e) + \phi g - k^{gov} y^n)^2 + a\pi^2. \tag{A.1}$$

To find the minimum, we take the partial derivative with respect to g:

$$\frac{\partial L}{\partial g} = 2\phi(y^n + \mu(\pi - \pi^e) + \phi g - k^{gov} y^n), \tag{A.2}$$

which when set equal to zero and solved for g becomes

$$g = \frac{1}{\phi}\left[y^n(k^{gov} - 1) + \mu(\pi - \pi^e) \right] \tag{A.3}$$

as proposed.

An analogous process can be used to determine the central bank's optimal response. Here the problem is to find the level of inflation that minimizes its loss function. Once again, substituting the Phillips curve process (equation (4)) and the right-hand side of (3) for the bank's ideal point for output and assuming (without loss of generality) that $\pi^* = 0$, the bank's loss function is

$$L_{cb} = (y^n + \mu(\pi - \pi^e) + \phi g - k^{cb} y^n) + \alpha \pi^2. \tag{A.4}$$

Differentiating with respect to π yields

$$\frac{\partial L}{\partial \pi} = 2\mu(y^n + \mu(\pi - \pi^e) + \phi g - k^{cb} y^n) + \alpha \pi, \tag{A.5}$$

which when set to zero and solved for π becomes

$$\pi = \frac{1}{\mu + \frac{\alpha}{\mu}} \left[\mu \pi^e + y^n(k^{cb} - 1) - \phi g \right] \tag{A.6}$$

as proposed.

Since the central banker observes the government's choice before setting monetary policy, the equilibrium policies in table 2 were deduced in the following manner. Because the government anticipates central banker's response to be (A.6), this is substituted for π in the government's loss function (A.1). Differentiating with respect to, and solving for g, yields the equilibrium fiscal policies in table 2. These are then substituted into the central banker's loss function to derive equilibrium monetary policies.

Notes

CHAPTER 1

1. Simmons 1994 and Helleiner 1994 are excellent introductions to these earlier periods.

2. I have chosen to use the word *electoralist* rather than *opportunistic* (Alesina, Cohen, and Roubini 1992) to describe such behavior because the former term is more descriptive and less normatively loaded. The term *opportunism* has a technical rather than a normative meaning in the principal-agent/game-theory literature, but this technical meaning is not obviously well served in the case of Nordhaus-type electoralist tendencies. In the technical sense, *opportunism* means ex post behavior on the part of the agent that frustrates goal attainment on the part of the principal. In the current context, the incumbent could be viewed as the agent and the electorate as the principal, in which case an agent that manipulates the macroeconomy for electoral purposes is engaging in precisely the type of behavior that the principal is likely to reward.

3. Central bank independence and international capital mobility do not have identical effects on the control of macroeconomic policy instruments, but because there is considerable overlap, they can, under some conditions, be seen as alternative means to similar ends. It is for this reason that I attempt to examine their joint effects in this volume.

4. Lewis-Beck (1988) refers to voters as "myopic" under the same assumption.

5. Nordhaus's model also has implications for the dynamic behavior of inflation rates with respect to elections, but these implications are unclear. Nordhaus predicts an increase prior to the elections, but as Alesina and Roubini point out, "given time lags between the effects of aggregate demand policies on output and inflation, one can build a model in which inflation increases after, rather than before the election" (1992, 665 n. 3; see also Lindbeck 1976).

6. For a good, nontechnical review of the early PBC literature, see Alt and Chrystal 1982.

7. For my present purposes, what is important is that convergence is not complete

and that the dimension along which parties are differentiated is related to macroeconomic performance.

8. Butler and Stokes (1974, 369) argue that in Britain, cabinet "dissolutions are more easily timed to coincide with [economic] expansion than the other way around."

9. Lewis-Beck (1988) also argues that the inability of elected officials to steer the economy may explain the lack of evidence for PBCs; he does not, however, entertain the possibility that control of the economy may vary systematically across cases.

10. This metaphor is a twist on Greider's depiction (1987) of the monetary policy process in the United States as a "car with two drivers." See also Maxfield 1994.

CHAPTER 2

1. The founding works in this approach are Fleming 1962 and Mundell 1963. For a comprehensive, nontechnical introduction, see Dornbusch and Fischer 1987. Frieden 1991b and Cohen 1993 are two important extensions of the framework into political economy. The standard Mundell-Fleming model has been criticized for lacking adequate microfoundations (Dornbusch 1976). Attempts to construct a model of policy interdependence with adequate microfoundations (Dornbusch 1976; Obstfeld and Rogoff 1996; Corsetti and Pesenti 1997) have produced positive conclusions broadly consistent with the standard model. At any rate, the standard model is clearly what has guided policy for the last thirty years. See Ghironi and Giavazzi 1998 for a model of interdependence that emphasizes the size of the economy.

2. Dooley (1996) suggests in his literature review of capital controls that they be removed in some cases to make fiscal policy more effective in stabilization programs.

3. See Oatley 1999 for a discussion of how eroding monetary and fiscal policy autonomy is expected to influence partisan differences; and Clark and Hallerberg 2000 for a discussion of the influence of such erosion on electoral cycles.

4. There is no reason to believe that W will fall between L and R. This assumption is for analytical convenience here; but the conclusions drawn from this example hold for all values of W.

5. This section draws directly from Clark and Hallerberg 2000.

6. This possibility creates the opportunity for conflicts between governments and even the most independent of central banks. See Berger and Thum 1997 for an analysis of such conflicts; and Berger and Schneider 1998 for evidence that such conflicts occur in Germany.

7. The same may be true of ministers of finance, who generally have greater concern for the overall health of the economy than do other ministers (Hallerberg and von Hagen 1998).

8. Two ways of capturing cross-actor differences can be found in the literature. Actors may differ in their ideal points for inflation and/or output ($\pi^{*i} \neq \pi^{*-i}$ and $y^{*i} \neq$

y^{*-i}) (Svensson 1995), or they may differ in the importance they place on inflation sta-bilization relative to hitting output targets ($\alpha^i \neq \alpha^{-i}$) (Rogoff 1985; Lohmann 1992). I adopt the former approach.

9. If one is uncomfortable with deriving explanatory power through arbitrary as-sumptions about changing preferences—and Stigler and Becker (1977) provide good reasons why one would be—the current setup can be motivated by the assumption that the government is engaged in strategic behavior; it is acting "as if" it were minimizing a loss function where $k > 1$ in preelectoral periods in order to maximize its utility in the game it is playing with voters.

10. Note that this is the flip side of the logic employed by Alan Blinder (1998), who recommends that politicians instruct the central bank to act "as if" their ideal point were the natural rate of growth.

11. For simplicity, I assume that either central banks are dependent or they are not.

12. This is merely a shorthand way of saying it manipulates the money supply and/or short-term interest rates in an attempt to effect changes in inflation.

13. These stark conclusions are drawn from a version of the Mundell-Fleming model in which prices are held constant, capital is fully mobile, and the short-term ef-fects of policy are ignored. More measured and realistic conclusions are produced by re-laxing these strong assumptions. Nevertheless, the strong conclusions are adopted as a starting point.

14. Specifically, fiscal expansions are smaller under independent central banks as long as $\alpha > \mu^2$. Consider the case where $\mu = .50$ (which is halfway between ineffective monetary policy under fixed exchange rates and mobile capital and hypereffective mon-etary policy under flexible exchange rates and mobile capital). Central bank independ-ence results in smaller fiscal expansions as long as policymakers place at least one-quar-ter the weight on hitting their inflation target as on hitting their growth target (i.e., $\alpha > .25$). As α rises above the point where policymakers place twice as much weight on hit-ting their inflation target, the effect of central bank independence on fiscal expansions converges toward one-half.

15. This somewhat artificial resolution of the "assignment problem" is an artifact of the model and should not be taken literally. If, for example, the government found that the transmission mechanism in monetary policy was more effective than that in fiscal policy, we would expect politically induced expansions in monetary policy.

16. How constraining is a switch to central bank independence when capital is im-mobile? Recall that the parameters μ and ϕ have been set up so that when capital is im-mobile, they are both equal to about one-half. Thus, the key factor in determining the constraining effect of central bank independence would be the parameter α, which is the common weight that both fiscal and monetary policymakers place on hitting their in-flation goal relative to the weight they place on hitting their growth goal. Not surpris-ingly, the effectiveness of this constraint on politically induced changes in growth is re-lated to the emphasis that policymakers place on price stabilization. As price stabilization increases in importance relative to meeting output goals, the magnitude of politically

induced increases in growth shrinks. When α is close to zero, central bank independence does not reduce the size of politically induced expansions very much when capital is immobile, but as α increases to about 2 or 3 (indicating that policymakers are two or three times more concerned with meeting inflation targets than growth targets), then

$$\frac{\mu(\mu + \alpha)}{\mu^2 + \alpha} \Rightarrow .50,$$

which means that the size of politically induced expansions in income would be cut about in half.

17. The size of this increase will be

$$1 - \frac{\mu(\mu + \alpha)}{\mu^2 + \alpha},$$

that is, about one-half.

18. Recall that this indeterminancy with respect to monetary policy when capital is immobile and the central bank is not independent is due to the arbitrary way in which the model solves the "assignment problem."

19. Interestingly, this is just the institutional combination that the International Monetary Fund (IMF) encourages developing countries to adopt. I am indebted to Shanker Satyanath for this insight.

20. This issue is explored further in Clark 2002.

21. I thank two anonymous reviewers for their comments on this issue.

22. This section is drawn from Clark and Nair Reichert 1998.

23. On the timing and significance of the increase in capital mobility, see Kurzer 1993; Frieden 1991b; Webb 1991, 1995; Andrews 1994; and Cohen 1993.

24. Webb cites a 1973 Bundesbank report stating that recent experience had "made it abundantly clear that even stronger administrative action against capital flows from foreign countries . . . does not suffice when speculative expectations run particularly high" (1991, 336 n. 80). Similarly, Cohen argues that "restrictions merely invite more and more sophisticated forms of evasion, as governments from Europe to South Asia to Latin America have learned to their regret" (1993, 147).

25. Savings and investment data were drawn from OECD, *National Account Statistics,* various years.

26. See Frankel 1991 for a discussion of alternative measures of capital mobility.

27. Other studies that examine savings–investment coefficients have chosen to report particular periods rather than moving periods across time. Feldstein and Horioka, for example, report coefficients for five-year periods ending in 1964, 1969, and 1974, none of which is significantly different from 1 (Feldstein and Horioka 1980). Penati and Dooley (1984) report coefficients for a fifteen-year period ending in 1974 and a five-year period ending in 1979 that are also not significantly different from 1.

28. In his attempt to calculate a savings–investment coefficient for the United States, Frankel uses ten-year averages to remove some of the cyclical variation, leaving

him with only twelve observations in a data set that runs from 1870 to 1987. To address this problem, he also specifies a model using cyclically adjusted annual savings and investment rates. This option is less promising for work aimed at cross-national comparisons, since the cyclical adjustment is based on the Bureau of Economic Analysis's "middle expansion trend" of the U.S. economy. See also Hallerberg and Basinger 1998; Baxter and Crucini 1993; Frankel 1991; and Obstfeld 1995.

29. New Zealand is not included due to missing data. Individual country indexes are constructed by summing across the restrictions on (1) the capital account, (2) bilateral payments with IMF members, (3) bilateral payments with nonmembers, and (4) foreign deposits. Data are from IMF, *Exchange Arrangements and Exchange Restrictions*, various years.

30. The bivariate correlation between these indicators is $R^2 = 0.91$.

31. Simmons argues that "to capture arbitrage conditions, rates on similar financial instruments (e.g., treasury bills of similar maturity) must be collected for precisely the same point in time (e.g., the last trading day of the year)" (1996, 5).

32. Austria, Finland, Ireland, New Zealand, and Norway also maintained pegged exchange rates outside the snake or EMS for a substantial part of the post–Bretton Woods era.

33. This finding for advanced industrialized nations is corroborated by Alesina and Summers 1993.

34. See Maxfield 1997, chap. 4, for a discussion of recent changes in the degree of central banks' independence. The Maastricht Treaty required all member nations' banks to achieve a significant degree of independence prior to the completion of monetary union, and changes are also taking place in Japan.

35. Cukierman, Webb, and Neyapti (1992) report roughly decade-long averages. These averages were assigned to their respective individual quarterly observations used in the current study and then averaged to yield a single score that could be compared to the measures generated by other scholars. Note that little within-country variance exists across the Cukierman, Webb, and Neyapti measure. Only seven of the nineteen countries in the sample exhibited any change in their approximately decade-long averages (interestingly, with the exception of Spain, all of these changes occurred between the 1960–71 period and the 1972–79 period, that is, during a period of dramatic changes in the international environment, including the first oil shock, the decline of Bretton Woods, and, as I have argued, a large increase in capital mobility).

CHAPTER 3

1. The foundational works include Hibbs 1977; and Tufte 1978.

2. This is not to say that the partisan model has not been subjected to rigorous analysis. See, for example, Wittman 1983; Calvert 1985; and, with respect to macroeconomic

policy, Chappell and Keech 1986; Alesina 1988a; and Alesina and Rosenthal 1995. Much of the literature on the partisan sources of macroeconomic policy, however, is only loosely connected with this formal literature.

3. See also Hotelling 1929; and Black 1958.

4. Some of these are discussed in chapter 1.

5. See Alt and Chrystal 1982 for a critical review of the early macroeconomics and politics literature, including Hibbs's classic article.

6. In fact, as Cameron (1978) points out, Downs himself conjectured that in "democratic society, the division of resources between the public and private sectors is roughly determined by the desires of the electorate" (1960, 541). These cross-national differences also encourage differences in political institutions that aggregate these preferences (Rogowski 1987).

7. Because Garrett does not evaluate the unconditional relationship between partisanship and tax policy, the results of his studies will be addressed below.

8. There are a number of influential statements of this argument, including Miliband 1969; Block 1977; and Lindbloom 1977, 1982. See Przeworski and Wallerstein (1988) for a precise statement of the argument.

9. Because shifting alliances made measurement of his main variable of interest (electoral competition) difficult, Comiskey excluded France, Belgium, Denmark, and the Netherlands from his study.

10. It is possible that partisanship "matters" in certain strategic situations but not others. For example, Beck and Katz find a negative but insignificant coefficient on the *Left Government* variable, but since *Left Government* enters into a multiplicative interaction with *Center Opposition*, this merely means that there is no evidence of an association between left governance and welfare effort *when Center Opposition equals zero*. First, it is not clear whether this condition occurs in the sample. Second, since the *Center Opposition* × *Left Government* interaction term is statistically significant and negative, it is possible that *Left Government* is significantly and negatively related to welfare effort over a broad (and potentially more representative) range of values for the modifying variable. A similar argument could be made about the *Center Government* and *Right Government* variables, which are also insignificant when the *Left Opposition* variable equals zero and the *Left Opposition* × *Center Government* and *Left Opposition* × *Right Government* interaction terms are statistically significant. Clearly, the implications of the Hicks and Swank (1992) and Beck and Katz (1995) tests of the partisan hypothesis will be indeterminate until their results are reestimated and conditional coefficients and standard errors are calculated for the variables of interest.

11. Initially, Blais, Blake, and Dion (1993) reported that this was the case only when a majority government was in power, but a reanalysis of their data led to the removal of this condition (Blais, Blake, and Dion 1996).

12. It should be noted that Ross's study does not approach de Haan and Sturm's in terms of degree of econometric sophistication. Particularly worrisome is her decision to

pool together budget cuts across eight different spending categories without any attempt to determine the presence of, or control for, heteroskedasticity.

13. While these results are provocative, the absence of control variables and tests for statistical significance renders them provisional.

14. De Haan and Sturm (1994b) also found no evidence of partisan effects on debt during the 1980s.

15. Clark and Hallerberg (2000) point out that increased use of fiscal instruments in the face of eroding fiscal policy autonomy may simply reflect the need to move instruments further in order to hit existing policy targets; but there is no reason to believe that this should differentially affect left and right governments.

16. This result was challenged (Jackman 1989) and was the subject of a number of refinement papers culminating in Alvarez, Garrett, and Lange 1991.

17. This interaction, if it exists, is likely to be ordinal in nature. That is, Hicks, Swank, and Ambuhl seem to be arguing that the degree of labor-market encompassment affects the magnitude, not the nature, of left governance's effect on spending. In contrast, the degree of labor-market encompassment is typically thought to affect the nature of relationship between left governance and macroeconomic outcomes.

18. At any rate, Beck and Katz's reanalysis (1995) revealed the left corporatist coefficient to be, at best, only marginally significant in the statistical sense.

19. His failure to include a term for the organizational power of labor, however (as opposed to its interaction with socialist control of government), makes the interpretation of his results difficult.

20. Indeed, this was the same view that John Maynard Keynes and Harry Dexter White enshrined in the Bretton Woods institutions. See Helleiner 1994 for an excellent historical analysis of this period.

21. Without endorsing it, Huber and Stephens (1998) do an excellent job of describing the common wisdom regarding the effects of the internationalization of capital markets.

22. To see why, consider the following. By rearranging terms, it is easy to see that when $\gamma_1 = -\gamma_2$, $\gamma_1 + \gamma_2 = 0$. The expected change in spending resulting from a change in P_1 is found by differentiating equation (1) with respect to P_1. This yields $\delta G/\delta P_1 = g_1 + g_2$, which, as stated at the outset, equals zero under the proposed condition.

23. Note the pluralist nature of this argument. Internationalization causes grievances; these grievances are translated into demands for policies, to which the state responds automatically. Little attention is given to the way in which internationalization affects the structural conditions that can be expected to affect both the propensity of grieved actors to make policy demands and the government's responsiveness to such demands (Hirschman 1971; Olson 1965).

24. In Garrett's words, the compensation hypothesis maintains that "the positive relationship between left-labor power and expansionary and interventionist economic policies will *increase* with greater trade and capital mobility—as the political incentives

to compensate for market dislocations grow (leading to positive coefficients on the internationalization left-labor power terms for spending, deficits, and capital taxation). In this case, the compensation hypothesis would also suggest that interest rates would be even lower under leftist governments at high levels of international than in more closed economies (hence, negative coefficients for the interaction terms in the interest rate equations). In contrast, the efficiency hypothesis implies that the positive relationships between left-labor power and expansionary and interventionist policies will *weaken* with greater internationalization—as the macroeconomic costs of compensation increase (subject to the qualification of new growth theory with respect to government spending)" (1995, 671–72).

25. Among the differences are that Garrett 1998 does not include Australia; and Garrett 1995 uses instrumental variables to control for autocorrelation, while 1998 uses a simple lagged dependent variable and panel-corrected standard errors.

26. The data used are from a data set that Garrett was kind enough to share.

27. These control variables are *Gdp growth, Unemployment,* and *Old age population* in all equations but the one used for interest rates. The controls in the interest-rate equation are *Inflation, US interest rates,* and *Central bank independence.*

28. The Durbin-Watson m-test regresses the errors (e_{it}) against lagged errors (e_{it-1}, e_{it-2}, e_{it-3}, e_{it-4}) and the other predictor variables in the model and uses an F-statistic to test the significance of the lagged errors. Rejection of the null hypothesis (H_0: $e_{it-1} = e_{it-2} = e_{it-3} = e_{it-4} = 0$) implies that the lagged dependent variable was not a sufficient control for serial correlation (Greene 1990, 428; Kmenta 1986, 333). The decision to include four lagged error terms to test for autocorrelation was made after examining the autocorrelation and partial autocorrelation functions for the dependent variables examined here.

29. I am grateful to Rob Franzese for a helpful discussion on this matter.

30. Because the intercept is suppressed, a high level of statistical significance on the country dummies is not necessarily a sign of country-specific differences in policy not captured by the model. This is because the t-test generated by standard software packages tests the null hypothesis that the coefficient equals zero. When nearly all the country dummies have the same sign and are significant, we know that the intercept would be different from zero (were the intercept and $k - 1$ country dummies used). To test whether there are country-specific differences in the current model, one would compare the country dummy coefficients to each other (or, perhaps, their mean) in light of their respective standard errors.

31. There is some evidence of a relationship between *Left-labor power* and subsidies to industry, but *Left-labor power* appears to be associated with a *decrease* in spending on subsidies to industry.

32. While Garrett's capital-control measure can theoretically take on any of five values, less than 7 percent of the sample has a *Cml* value of less than 2 (i.e., very few countries used more than two capital controls at any time). Thus, we can restrict our attention to the cases where *Cml* > 1 and still make inferences about the vast majority of

observed experience. Recall that a *Cml* score of 2 indicates that two capital controls are in place, a *Cml* score of 3 indicates that one capital control is in place, and a *Cml* score of 4 indicates that all capital controls have been removed.

33. The proclivity of policymakers (Downsian, Hibbsian, or Keynesian) to use fiscal instruments when exchange rates are fixed but not when they are flexible is reinforced by the fact that monetary policy is expected to be ineffective in the former case and effective in the latter.

34. This does not necessarily imply capital flight when left governments are elected; the threat of such exit may be enough to encourage left governments to mimic the policies of their right-wing opponents.

35. By *paradigm*, I mean the set of policies that is likely to produce the kind of macroeconomic outcomes that will be rewarded by voters. A change in the paradigm may be a shift in beliefs about appropriate policies, or it could be changes in material conditions that make some policies more effective than others.

CHAPTER 4

This chapter was written with Mark Hallerberg and is a revised version of Clark and Hallerberg 2000.

1. See chap. 2, n. 1.

2. The decision-theoretic model has the same predictions as the game-theoretic one when capital is mobile; but when capital is immobile, the decision-theoretic model predicts monetary contractions before elections, whereas the decision-theoretic one does not.

3. Clark and Nair Reichert based their codings of exchange rate restrictions on Coffey 1984; IMF, *International Financial Statistics*, various years; and OECD 1985. Their dummy variable for central bank independence equals 1 when the Cukierman, Webb, and Neyapti score for legal independence is above the median. See Cukierman, Webb, and Neyapti 1992 for an extensive discussion of the construction of this measure.

4. The large F-score indicates that the null hypothesis—that the coefficients on the lagged error terms in the autocorrelation equation are simultaneously zero—is unlikely to be true.

5. See Friedrich 1982; and Jaccard, Turrisi, and Wan 1990 for a useful introduction to the conditional interpretation of multiplicative interaction models.

6. Prais-Winsten estimates were calculated using the panel-corrected standard errors routine in Stata and specifying that there is first-order autocorrelation within the panels. Following Beck and Katz (1996), the coefficient of the AR(1) process is held to be common across panels. This parameter (ρ) is reported whenever the Prais-Winsten method is used.

7. Alesina and Roubini (1997) also find evidence of electorally induced monetary

expansions in their sample of eighteen OECD countries, but they assume that the occurrence of monetary cycles is uniform within their sample. Our evidence suggests that their results inappropriately pool cases where monetary cycles occur with those where they do not. Note that while we do not conduct country-specific tests here, this result is in tension with evidence of an electoral monetary cycle in the United States (Grier 1989) and consistent with studies that find a lack of evidence for such a cycle (Beck 1987). For more on the U.S. case, see contributions to Mayer 1990.

8. Recall that the Mundell-Fleming model predicts that the effectiveness of fiscal policy on output increases under fixed exchange rates when capital is mobile.

9. Quarterly data on expenditures and tax collections can have a seasonal element both within and across countries that is difficult to control for even with sophisticated econometric techniques.

10. There is some controversy on whether to include growth in GDP as an independent variable, because real GDP appears in the denominator on the left-hand side of the equation (see also Borrelli and Royed 1995). We are interested in the value added to preexisting work and not in this controversy per se, so we follow the practice of Roubini and Sachs by not including growth as a control variable.

11. These expectations are only valid for industrialized countries. Tavli and Végh (1997) find that the sign on economic growth is reversed in Latin American countries. They hypothesize that governments can justify painful cuts in expenditures or increases in taxes to their constituencies only when economic conditions worsen.

12. Hallerberg and von Hagen 1998 refer to a strong finance minister as a "delegation" approach and to negotiated targets as a "contract" approach. See Clark and Hallerberg 2000 for a test similar to the ones reported here that controls for the modifying effects of fiscal institutions.

13. In particular, Franzese codes elections as being relevant to economic policy, which can include presidential elections in Finland, France, and the United States, as well as elections to the upper house. He then codes the variable as divided among those separate elections, so that, for example, a French presidential election is a .5 and a French parliamentary election another .5.

14. The large standard error or the election coefficient in column 3 is the result of the fact that there are very few observations of a maximally closed ($Cml = 0$) economies in the observed sample.

15. We want to be clear about one important difference between the EMU case and the more general cases we have examined. When countries control both fiscal and monetary policy, a fiscal expansion under fixed exchange rates leads to a reinforcing monetary expansion to maintain the exchange rate. When the central bank is in Frankfurt, however, states face a "fixed" exchange rate, but they do not anticipate a similar expansion of the money supply. The effect of the fiscal expansion may therefore be less pronounced in EMU countries than in other countries that still have their own central banks controlling the money supply. We thank Fabio Ghironi for thoughtful comments on this issue.

16. Eichengreen and Wyplosz (1997) provide a good discussion of the different rationales for the Stability and Growth Pact.

17. The text of the agreement appears in Committee on Economic and Monetary Affairs and Industrial Policy 1997.

18. Personal interviews, conducted by Mark Hallerberg, with two members of Directorate General II, June and July 1997.

19. One additional tool that could be used to restrict governmental abuses will also be absent under EMU. We have assumed that the decisions to pursue capital mobility or fixed exchange rates are exogenous. One could argue, of course, that when banks are independent and governments are especially fiscally irresponsible, the bank may decide to stop defending the currency and simply let it float, putting the country in the scenario of flexible exchange rate and capital mobility that is advantageous to the bank. Under EMU, however, this is extremely unlikely.

20. The ultimate form that these institutions should take is still open to discussion. Strach (1998) finds that numerical restrictions on the size of the deficit do restrict its actual size. Von Hagen (1998) notes, however, that such numerical restrictions can merely encourage politicians to be more creative with their accounting, and he suggests more centralized procedures to ensure that someone monitors the actors.

CHAPTER 5

1. See also Cameron 1978; Lange and Garrett 1985; Garrett and Lange 1986; Hicks 1988; Hicks and Patterson 1989; and Alvarez, Garrett, and Lange 1991; for critiques, see Jackman 1989; and Beck et al. 1993. Beck et al. find that when the results of Alvarez, Garrett, and Lange 1991 are reanalyzed using ordinary least squares with panel-corrected standard errors rather than feasible generalized least squares, only the findings related to growth remain unchanged. But they do not calculate conditional coefficients nor conditional standard errors, so it remains to be seen whether Alvarez, Garrett, and Lange's findings require broad revision.

2. Calmfors and Driffill (1988) explain the effects of labor-market institutions on wage restraint; and Alvarez, Garrett, and Lange (1991, 542–44) show how such dynamics interact with the partisan orientation of government.

3. A one-tailed test is appropriate because the SDC hypothesis, while conditional, is directional: when labor-market institutions are weak and decentralized, we should observe a positive association between left governance and unemployment, but when labor-market institutions are encompassing, we should observe a negative association between left government and unemployment.

4. Another anomaly in the inflation equation is worth mentioning. The positive and significant coefficient for the labor-market encompassment variable suggests that when left governance is zero, encompassing labor unions produce more inflation than

weak and decentralized unions. By itself, this observation could be assimilated by the SDC hypothesis—indeed, it would support the idea that left participation in government is the linchpin of the tripartite bargaining underlying neocorporatist wage restraint. Note, however, that the coefficient on the interaction term is very small compared to the coefficient on *Lmi*—so much so that the conditional coefficient for *Lmi* would not be negative even if the government were composed entirely of members of leftist parties. Thus, there is no evidence that labor-market encompassment is associated with increased price stability. In fact, the evidence seems to suggest that it is associated with inflation. (In a model without interaction effects [not reported], there is evidence of a linear *positive* relationship between labor-market encompassment and inflation.)

5. Coefficients and standard errors for the dummy variables for the countries, which are not reported, are also identical.

6. To make this and the following graphs easier to read, I did not plot the conditional *Left* coefficients for the case where three or four capital controls are in effect (*Cml* = 0, *Cml* = 1). Little is lost, since only a small percentage of the sample falls into this category (less than 7%); virtually every dot on that line would have been an extrapolation to unobserved conditions.

7. One could, of course, look at these results from a slightly different perspective. Perhaps it is labor-market institutions that are the key in explaining variation in inflation rates, with the ideological composition of government serving as a modifying variable. With a bit of algebra, the results in column 3 of table 19 can be interpreted this way. Such an exercise produces results that suggest that when capital markets are moderately open (one or zero capital controls), an increase in labor-market encompassment leads to increased inflation when right parties are in power but has no statistically significant effect when left parties are in power.

8. Similarly, Beck et al. (1993) find that only the inferences drawn from Alvarez, Garrett, and Lange's growth equation survive after the panel-corrected standard errors estimation technique is used.

9. Unexpectedly, this relationship is affected very little by the degree of central bank independence.

10. This may be because of partisan differences in growth targets or because of partisan differences in the weights assigned to growth as opposed to price stabilization.

11. This result is consistent with Alesina, Cohen, and Roubini 1992, who found support for their "rational partisan model" but little support for the Hibbsian partisan model.

CHAPTER 6

1. The following section draws heavily upon Clark and Nair Reichert 1998.

2. The exact model employed varies across studies in the literature, because different macroeconomic outcomes are used for the dependent variable (unemployment,

growth, and inflation are the most common), and different techniques are used to control for serial autocorrelation and heteroskedasticity.

3. Quarterly data from the OECD Main Economic Indicators data set were used. With one exception (New Zealand), percentage change in the seasonally adjusted number of unemployed was used to measure unemployment. Data for New Zealand are not seasonally adjusted. Growth in output was measured by seasonally adjusted total industrial production, except for Canada (where data were not seasonally adjusted) and Australia (where seasonally adjusted real gross product volume was used). These indicators were the most comparable and widely available indicators. Use of the unemployment rate rather than number of unemployed would control for demographic changes, but a seasonally adjusted version of this indicator was not available for several countries. Other studies have used change in real GDP, but seasonally adjusted quarterly data were unavailable for several countries. Both dependent variables were multiplied by 100 to ease interpretation of coefficients. Elections were coded as the three quarters preceding and the quarter containing a general election. Sources for electoral data are Mackie and Rose 1982; and *Europa World Year Book,* various years.

4. While the Durbin-Watson test for serial correlation suggests that autocorrelation may be present, I reestimated model 1b using Prais-Winsten regression and found that the coefficient of autocorrelation was small ($r = 0.085$), and the estimated electoral coefficient and its standard error were nearly identical to those produced by OLS.

5. The coefficients for the electoral and interaction variables in the Prais-Winsten regression model were (0.684) and (-1.41), respectively. The associated standard errors were 0.299 and 0.739, suggesting that serial correlation in the OLS model led to an underestimation of the standard error of only 5 percent, which was not enough to lead to inferential errors.

6. This finding is not, strictly speaking, inconsistent with the predictions of the game-theoretic model in chapter 2—which predicts that electoral cycles will occur when central bank independence is high, except when capital is mobile and the exchange rate is flexible. The conditional coefficients in figure 22 are the weighted average of various combinations of exchange rate regimes and degree of capital mobility. The interaction between open-economy arrangements and central bank independence as they pertain to the game-theoretic model will be examined later in this chapter.

7. See Cleary and Kessler 1982 for a clear statement as to why this is the case.

8. More precisely, the model's prediction is that b_4*Capital mobility* $+ b_7$*Capital mobility* $\times$ *Fixed* is less (greater) than zero in the growth (unemployment) equation. This captures the idea that an increase in capital mobility will have a constraining effect when the exchange rate is fixed, but since the model also predicts that b_4*Capital mobility* will be close to zero, it follows that b_7 would be less than zero.

9. Note that none of the conditional coefficients for the cases of low capital mobility and flexible exchange rates are statistically significant. The conditional coefficients are very large, probably because this institutional combination is historically rare; as a result, the estimates are based on a small number of observations.

CHAPTER 7

1. The results from Alesina and Perotti 1995 and Ross 1997 discussed in chapter 3 suggest that left governments may act more like right governments than right governments do. Swank (1992) provides evidence for several propositions derived from the structural-dependence argument.

References

Aldrich, John H. 1993. Rational Choice and Turnout. *American Journal of Political Science* 37 (1): 246–78.

Alesina, Alberto. 1987. Macroeconomic Policy in a Two-Party System as a Repeated Game. *Quarterly Journal of Economics* 102:651–78.

———. 1988a. Credibility and Policy Convergence in a Two-Party System with Rational Voters. *American Economic Review* 78, no. 4: 796–805.

———. 1988b. Macroeconomics and Politics. *Macroeconomics Annual, 1988,* 13–52.

———. 1989. Politics and Business Cycles in Industrial Democracies. *Economic Policy* 8:55–87.

Alesina, Alberto, Gerald D. Cohen, and Nouriel Roubini. 1992. Macroeconomic Policy and Elections in OECD Democracies. In *Political Economy, Growth, and Business Cycles,* edited by Alex Cukierman, Zvi Hercowitz, and Leonardo Leiderman. Cambridge: MIT Press.

———. 1993. Electoral Business Cycle in Industrial Democracies. *European Journal of Political Economy* 9:1–23.

Alesina, Alberto, and Roberto Perotti. 1995. Fiscal Expansions and Adjustments in OECD Countries. *Economic Policy* (October): 207–18.

Alesina, Alberto, and Howard Rosenthal. 1995. *Partisan Politics, Divided Government, and the Economy.* New York: Cambridge University Press.

Alesina, Alberto, and Nouriel Roubini. 1992. Political Cycles in OECD Economies. *Review of Economic Studies* 59:663–88.

Alesina, Alberto, and Nouriel Roubini, with Gerald Cohen. 1997. *Political Cycles and the Macroeconomy.* Cambridge: MIT Press.

Alesina, Alberto, and Lawrence H. Summers. 1993. Central Bank Independence and Macroeconomic Performance: Some Comparative Evidence. *Journal of Money, Credit, and Banking* 25:151–62.

Alt, James E. 1985. Political Parties, World Demand, and Unemployment: Domestic and International Sources of Economic Activity. *American Political Science Review* 79: 1016–40.

Alt, James E., and K. Alec Chrystal. 1982. *Political Economics*. Berkeley: University of California Press.

Alvarez, R. Michael, Geoffrey Garrett, and Peter Lange. 1991. Government Partisanship, Labor Organization, and Macroeconomic Performance. *American Political Science Review* 85:539–56.

Andrews, David M. 1994. Capital Mobility and State Autonomy: Toward a Structural Theory of International Monetary Relations. *International Studies Quarterly* 38 (June): 193–218.

Bade, Robin, and Michael Parkin. 1982. Central Bank Laws and Monetary Policy. Manuscript, University of Western Ontario, Department of Economics, London, Ontario.

Baxter, Marianne, and Mario J. Crucini. 1993. Explaining Savings-Investment Correlations. *American Economic Review* 83, no. 3: 416–36.

Beck, Nathaniel. 1987. Elections and the Fed: Is There a Political Monetary Cycle? *American Journal of Political Science* 31 (February): 194–216.

Beck, Nathaniel, and Jonathan N. Katz. 1995. What to Do (and not to do) with Time-Series—Cross-Section Data in Comparative Politics. *American Political Science Review* 89:634–48.

———. 1996. Nuisance vs. Substance: Specifying and Estimating Time-Series-Cross-Section Models. *Political Analysis* 6:1–36.

Beck, Nathaniel, Jonathan N. Katz, R. Michael Alvarez, Geoffrey Garrett, and Peter Lange. 1993. Governments Partisanship, Labor Organization, and Macroeconomic Performance: A Corrigendum. *American Political Science Review* 87:945–48.

Beer, Samuel H., and Adam B. Ulam, eds. 1958. *Patterns of Government: The Major Political Systems of Europe*. New York: Random House.

Berger, Helge, and Friedrich Schneider. 1998. The Bundesbank's Reaction to Policy Conflicts: Evidence and Implications. Typescript, University of Munich.

Berger, Helge, and Marcel Thum. 1997. Central Bank vs. Government: Strategic Information Policy and Its Consequences. Typescript, University of Munich.

Bernhard, William, and David Leblang. 1999. Democratic Institutions and Exchange Rate Commitments. *International Organization* 53 (1): 71–97.

Black, Duncan. 1958. *Theory of Committees and Elections*. Cambridge: Cambridge University Press.

Blais, A., D. Blake, and S. Dion. 1993. Do Parties Make a Difference? Parties and the Size of Government in Liberal Democracies. *American Journal of Political Science* 37, no. 1: 40–62.

———. 1996. Do Parties Make a Difference? A Reappraisal. *American Journal of Political Science* 40, no. 2: 514–20.

Blanchard, Olivier. 1990. Suggestions for a New Set of Fiscal Indicators. OECD Working Paper, no. 79, April.

Blinder, Alan S. 1998. *Central Banking in Theory and Practice*. Cambridge: MIT Press.

Block, Fred. 1977. The Ruling Class Does Not Rule: Note on the Marxist Theory of the State. *Socialist Revolution* 33:6–28.

Boix, Carles. 1995. Partisan Governments and Macroeconomic Policies in OECD Countries, 1964–93. *World Politics* 53:38–73.

———. 1998. *Political Parties, Growth, and Equality: Conservative and Social Democratic Economic Strategies in the World Economy.* New York: Cambridge University Press.

———. 2000. Partisan Governments, the International Economy, and Macroeconomic Policies in Advanced Nations, 1960–93. *World Politics* 53, no. 1: 38–73.

Borrelli, Stephen A., and Terry J. Royed. 1995. Government "Strength" and Budget Deficits in Advanced Democracies. *European Journal of Political Research* 28 (September): 225–60.

Branson, William H., and Willem H. Buiter. 1983. Monetary and Fiscal Policy with Flexible Exchange Rates. In *Economic Interdependence and Flexible Exchange Rates,* edited by Jagdeep S. Bhandari and Bluford H. Putnam, 251–85. Cambridge: MIT Press.

Bruno, Michael, and Jeffrey Sachs. 1985. *Economics of Worldwide Stagflation.* Cambridge: Harvard University Press.

Burdekin, Richard C. K., and Leroy O. Laney. 1988. Fiscal Policymaking and the Central Bank Institutional Constraint. *Kyklos* 41 (4): 647–62.

Butler, David, and Donald Stokes. 1974. *Political Change in Britain.* 2d ed. New York: St. Martin's Press.

Calmfors, Lars, and John Driffill. 1988. Bargaining Structure, Corporatism, and Macroeconomic Performance. *Economic Policy* 3:13–61.

Calvert, Randall. 1985. Robustness of the Multidimensional Voting Model: Candidates' Motivations, Uncertainty, and Convergence. *American Journal of Political Science* 29:69–95.

Cameron, David R. 1978. The Expansion of the Public Economy: A Comparative Analysis. *American Political Science Review* 72:1243–61.

Cargill, Thomas F., and Michael M. Hutchison. 1991. Political Business Cycles with Endogenous Election Timing: Evidence from Japan. *Review of Economics and Statistics* 73:733–39.

Castles, Francis G. 1982. The Impact of Parties on Public Expenditure. In *The Impact of Parties,* edited by Francis G. Castle, 21–96. Berkeley: Sage Publications.

Castles, Francis G., and R. D. McKinley. 1979. Does Politics Matter? An Analysis of the Public Welfare Commitment in Advanced Democratic States. *European Journal of Political Research* 7:169–86.

Chappell, Henry W. Jr., and William R. Keech. 1986. Policy Motivation and Party Differences in a Dynamic Spatial Model of Party Competition. *American Political Science Review* 80, no. 3: 881–99.

Clark, William Roberts. 2002. Partisan and Electoral Motivations and the Choice of Monetary Institutions Under Fully Mobile Capital. *International Organization* 56 (4): 725–49.

Clark, William R., and Mark Hallerberg. 2000. Mobile Capital, Domestic Institutions, and Electorally-Induced Monetary and Fiscal Policy. *American Political Science Review* 94, no. 2: 323–46.

Clark, William Roberts, Mark Hallerberg, and Won Ik Kim. 2000. Partisan Effects on Fiscal and Monetary Policy in the Open Economy: A Reappraisal. New York University. Manuscript.

Clark, William R., and Usha Nair Reichert. 1998. International and Domestic Constraints on Political Business Cycles in OECD Economies. *International Organization* 52:87–120.

Cleary, Paul D., and Ronald C. Kessler. 1982. The Estimation and Interpretation of Modifier Effects. *Journal of Health and Social Behavior* 23 (June): 159–69.

Coffey, Peter. 1984. *The European Monetary System: Past, Present, and Future.* Hingham, MA: Kluwer Academic.

Cohen, Benjamin J. 1993. The Triad and the Unholy Trinity: Lessons for the Pacific Region. In *Pacific Economic Relations in the 1990s: Cooperation or Conflict?* edited by Richard Higgot, Richard Leaver, and John Ravenhill, 133–58. Boulder: Lynne Rienner.

Comiskey, M. 1993. Electoral Competition and the Growth of Public Spending in Thirteen Industrial Democracies, 1950 to 1983. *Comparative Political Studies* 26, no. 3: 350–74.

Corsetti, Giancarlo, and Paolo Pesenti. 1997. Welfare and Macroeconomic Interdependence. National Bureau of Economic Research working paper 6307.

Cukierman, Alex, Pantelis Kalaitzidakis, Lawrence H. Summers, and Steven B. Webb. 1993. Central Bank Independence, Growth, Investment, and Real Rates. *Carnegie-Rochester Conference Series on Public Policy* 39:95–140.

Cukierman, Alex, and Allan Meltzer. 1986. A Positive Theory of Discretionary Policy, the Cost of a Democratic Government, and the Benefit of a Constitution. *Economic Inquiry* 24:367–88.

Cukierman, Alex, Steven B. Webb, and Bilin Neyapti. 1992. Measuring the Independence of Central Banks and Its Effect on Policy Outcomes. *World Bank Economic Review* 4:353–98.

Cusack, T. R. 1997. Partisan Politics and Public Finance: Changes in Public Spending in the Industrialized Democracies, 1955–1989. *Public Choice* 91, nos. 3–4: 375–95.

De Haan, Jakob. 2001. Accountability and Transparency in EMU. Paper presented to the European Community Studies Association meeting, Madison, Wisconsin.

De Haan, Jakob, and Jan-Egbert Sturm. 1994a. The Case for Central Bank Independence. In *The Theory of Inflation,* edited by Michael Parkin, 627–49. Aldershot: Edward Elgar.

———. 1994b. Political and Institutional Determinants of Fiscal Policy in the European Community. *Public Choice* 80, nos. 1–2:157–72.

———. 1997. Political and Economic Determinants of OECD Budget Deficits and Government Expenditures: A Reinvestigation. *European Journal of Political Economy* 13 (December): 739–50.

Dooley, Michael. 1996. A Survey of Literature on Controls over International Capital Transactions. *IMF Staff Papers* 43 (September): 639–87.

Dornbusch, Rudiger. 1976. Expectations and Exchange Rate Dynamics. *Journal of Political Economy* 84:1161–76.

Dornbusch, Rudiger, and Stanley Fischer. 1987. *Macroeconomics*. New York: McGraw-Hill.

Downs, Anthony. 1957. *An Economic Theory of Democracy*. New York: Harper and Row.

———. 1960. Why the Government Budget Is Too Small in a Democracy. *World Politics* 12:541–63.

Edin, Per-Anders, and Henry Ohlsson. 1991. Political Determinants of Budget Deficits: Coalition Effects Versus Minority Effects. *European Economic Review* 35 (December): 1597–1603.

Eichengreen, Barry, and Jürgen von Hagen. 1996. Fiscal Restrictions and Monetary Union: Rationales, Repercussions, Reforms. *Empirica: Journal of Applied Economics and Economic Policy* 23, no. 1: 3–23.

Eichengreen, Barry, and Charles Wyplosz. 1997. The Stability Pact: More than a Minor Nuisance? University of California at Berkeley. Working Paper.

Eijffinger, Sylvester C., and Jakob de Haan. 1996. The Political Economy of Central-Bank Independence. Special Papers in International Economics 19, Princeton University.

Europa World Year Book. Various years. London: Europa Publications.

Feldstein, Martin, and Charles Horioka. 1980. Domestic Saving and International Capital Mobility. *Economic Journal* 90:314–29.

Fiorina, Morris P. 1976. Voting Decisions: Instrumental and Expressive Aspects. *Journal of Politics* 38(2): 390–413.

Fleming, J. M. 1962. Domestic Financial Policies under Fixed and Floating Exchange Rates. *IMF Staff Papers* 9:369–80.

Frankel, Jeffrey A. 1991. Quantifying International Capital Mobility in the 1980s. In *National Saving and Economic Performance*, edited by Douglas Bernheim and John Shover, 227–70. Chicago: University of Chicago Press.

Franzese, Robert J. 1996. The Political Economy of Public Debt: An Empirical Examination of the OECD Post-war Experience. Paper presented at the annual meeting of the Midwest Political Science Association, Chicago.

Frieden, Jeffry A. 1991a. *Debt, Development, and Democracy: Modern Political Economy and Latin America, 1965–1985*. Princeton: Princeton University Press.

———. 1991b. Invested Interests: The Politics of National Economic Policies in a World of Global Finance. *International Organization* 45:425–51.

Friedrich, Robert J. 1982. In Defense of Multiplicative Terms in Multiple Regression Equations. *American Journal of Political Science* 26:797–833.

Garrett, Geoffrey. 1995. Capital Mobility, Trade, and the Domestic Politics of Economic Policy. *International Organization* 49:657–87.

———. 1998. *Partisan Politics in the Global Economy*. New York: Cambridge University Press.

Garrett, Geoffrey, and Peter Lange. 1986. Performance in a Hostile World: Economic Growth in Capitalist Democracies, 1974–1982. *World Politics* 38:517–47.

———. 1991. Political Responses to Interdependence: What's "Left" for the Left? *International Organization* 45:539–64.

———. 1995. Internationalization, Institutions, and Political Change. *International Organization* 49:627–55.

Ghironi, Fabio, and Fancesco Giavazzi. 1998. Currency Areas, International Monetary Regimes, and the Employment-Inflation Tradeoff. *Journal of International Economics* 45 (August): 259–96.

Golden, Miriam A. 1993. The Dynamics of Trade Unionism and National Economic Performance. *American Political Science Review* 87 (2): 439–54.

Gourevitch, Peter. 1986. *Politics in Hard Times.* Ithaca: Cornell University Press.

Gowa, Joanne. 1983. *Closing the Gold Window: Domestic Politics and the End of Bretton Woods.* Ithaca: Cornell University Press.

Greene, William H. 1990. *Econometric Analysis.* 2d ed. Englewood Cliffs, NJ: Prentice-Hall.

Greider, William. 1987. *Secrets of the Temple.* New York: Simon and Schuster.

Grier, Kevin B. 1987. Presidential Elections and Federal Reserve Policy: An Empirical Test. *Southern Economic Journal* 54:475–86.

———. 1989. On the Existence of a Political Monetary Cycle. *American Journal of Political Science* 33 (May): 376–89.

Grilli, Vittorio, Donato Masciandaro, and Guido Tabellini. 1991. Political and Monetary Institutions and Public Financial Policies in the Industrial Countries. *Economic Policy* 13 (October): 341–92.

Hahm, S. D. 1996. The Political Economy of Deficit Spending: A Cross Comparison of Industrialized Democracies, 1955–90. *Environment and Planning, C: Government and Policy* 14, no. 2: 227–50.

Hahm, S. D., M. S. Kamlet, and D. C. Mowery. 1996. The Political Economy of Deficit Spending in Nine Industrialized Parliamentary Democracies: The Role of Fiscal Institutions. *Comparative Political Studies* 29, no. 1: 52–77.

Hall, Peter A., and Robert J. Franzese Jr. 1998. Mixed Signals: Central Bank Independence, Coordinated Wage-Bargaining, and European Monetary Union. *International Organization* 52:505–35.

Hallerberg, Mark, and Scott Basinger. 1998. Internationalization and Changes in Tax Policy in OECD Countries: The Importance of Domestic Veto Players. *Comparative Political Studies* 31 (June): 321–53.

Hallerberg, Mark, and William Roberts Clark. 1997. How Should Political Scientists Measure Capital Mobility? Paper presented at the 93rd Annual Meeting of the American Political Science Association, August, Washington, DC.

Hallerberg, Mark, and Jürgen von Hagen. 1998. Electoral Institutions and the Budget Process. In *Democracy, Decentralisation, and Deficits in Latin America,* edited by Kiichiro Fukasaku and Ricardo Hausmann, 65–94. Paris: Organisation for Economic Cooperation and Development.

———. 1999. Electoral Institutions, Cabinet Negotiations, and Budget Deficits within the European Union. In *Fiscal Institutions and Fiscal Performance*, edited by James Poterba and Jürgen von Hagen, 209–32. Chicago: University of Chicago Press.

Helleiner, Eric. 1994. *States and the Emergence of Global Finance*. Ithaca: Cornell University Press.

Henning, C. Randall. 1994. *Currencies and Politics in the United States, Germany, and Japan*. Washington, DC: Institute for International Economics.

Hibbs, Douglas A. 1977. Political Parties and Macroeconomic Policy. *American Political Science Review* 71:1467–87.

———. 1978. On the Political Economy of Long-Run Trends in Strike Activity. *British Journal of Political Science* 8 (2): 153–75.

———. 1987. *The Political Economy of Industrial Democracies*. Cambridge: Harvard University Press.

Hicks, Alexander. 1988. Social Democratic Corporatism and Economic Growth. *Journal of Politics* 50:677–704.

Hicks, A., and J. Misra. 1993. Political Resources and the Growth of Welfare in Affluent Capitalist Democracies, 1960–1982. *American Journal of Sociology* 99, no. 3: 668–710.

Hicks, A., and W. D. Patterson. 1989. On the Robustness of the Left Corporatist Model of Economic Growth. *Journal of Politics* 51, no. 3: 662–75.

Hicks, A., and D. H. Swank. 1984. Governmental Redistribution in Rich Capitalist Democracies. *Policy Studies Journal* 13, no. 2: 265–86.

———. 1992. Politics, Institutions, and Welfare Spending in Industrialized Democracies, 1960–82. *American Political Science Review* 86, no. 3: 658–74.

Hicks, A., D. H. Swank, and M. Ambuhl. 1989. Welfare Expansion Revisited: Policy Routines and Their Mediation by Party, Class, and Crisis, 1957–1982. *European Journal of Political Research* 17, no. 4: 401–30.

Hirschman, Albert O. 1971. *Exit, Voice, and Loyalty*. Cambridge: Harvard University Press.

Hotelling, H. 1929. Stability in Competition. *Economic Journal* 39:41–57.

Huber, E., C. Ragin, and J. D. Stephens. 1993. Social-Democracy, Christian Democracy, Constitutional Structure, and the Welfare-State. *American Journal of Sociology* 99, no. 3: 711–49.

Huber, Evelyne, and John D. Stephens. 1998. Internationalization and the Social Democratic Model. *Comparative Political Science* 31, no. 3: 353–97.

International Monetary Fund (IMF). Various years. *Exchange Arrangements and Exchange Restrictions*. Washington, DC: International Monetary Fund.

———. Various years. *International Financial Statistics*. Washington, DC: International Monetary Fund.

Iversen, Torben. 1997. The Dynamics of Welfare State Expansion: Trade Openness,

De-industrialization, and Partisan Politics. Paper presented at Future of the Welfare State Workshop, Center for European Studies, Harvard University, December 5–7.

———. 1998. Wage Bargaining, Central Bank Independence, and the Real Effects of Money. *International Organization* 52:469–504.

Jaccard, James, Robert Turrisi, and Choi K. Wan. 1990. *Interaction Effects in Multiple Regression*. Berkeley: Sage Publications.

Jackman, Robert. 1989. The Politics of Growth, Once Again. *Journal of Politics* 51:646–61.

Katzenstein, Peter J. 1985. Small States in World Markets. Ithaca: Cornell University Press.

Keech, William R. 1995. *Economic Politics: The Costs of Democracy*. New York: Cambridge University Press.

Key, V. O. 1949. *Southern Politics in State and Nation*. New York: Knopf.

King, Gary, Robert O. Keohane, and Sidney Verba. 1994. *Designing Social Inquiry*. Princeton: Princeton University Press.

Kmenta, Jan. 1986. *Elements of Econometrics*. 2d ed. New York: Macmillan.

Kurzer, Paulette. 1993. *Business and Banking: Political Change and Economic Integration in Western Europe*. Ithaca: Cornell University Press.

Lange, Peter, and Geoffrey Garrett. 1985. The Politics of Growth: Strategic Interaction and Economic Performance in the Advanced Industrial Democracies, 1974–1980. *Journal of Politics* 47:792–827.

Lewis-Beck, Michael S. 1988. *Economics and Elections*. Ann Arbor: University of Michigan Press.

Lindbeck, A. 1976. Stabilization Policies in Open Economies with Endogenous Politicians. *American Economic Review Papers and Proceedings* 66:1–19.

Lindbloom, Charles. 1977. *Politics and Markets*. New York: Basic Books.

———. 1982. The Market as Prison. *Journal of Politics* 44:324–36.

Lipset, Seymour Martin. 1960. *Political Man: The Social Bases of Politics*. New York: Doubleday.

Lohmann, Susanne. 1992. Optimal Commitment in Monetary Policy: Credibility versus Flexibility. *American Economic Review* 82 (March): 273–86.

Mackie, Thomas T., and Richard Rose. 1982. *The International Almanac of Electoral History*. 2d ed. New York: Facts on File.

MacRae, Duncan. 1977. A Political Model of the Business Cycle. *Journal of Political Economy* 95:239–63.

Maxfield, Sylvia. 1994. Financial Incentives and Central Bank Authority in Industrializing Countries. *World Politics* 46:556–88.

———. 1997. *Gatekeepers of Growth: The International Political Economy of Central Banking in Developing Countries*. Princeton: Princeton University Press.

Mayer, Thomas, ed. 1990. *The Politics of American Monetary Policy*. Cambridge: Cambridge University Press.

McCallum, B. 1978. The Political Business Cycle: An Empirical Test. *Southern Economic Journal* 44:1–19.

McNamara, Kathleen R. 1998. *The Currency of Ideas: Monetary Politics in the European Union.* Ithaca: Cornell University Press.

Miliband, Ralph. 1969. *The State in Capitalist Society.* New York: Basic Books.

Milner, Helen. 1988. *Resisting Protectionism.* Princeton: Princeton University Press.

Mundell, Robert A. 1963. Capital Mobility and Stabilization Policy under Fixed and Flexible Exchange Rates. *Canadian Journal of Economic and Political Science* 29:475–85.

Nolling, Wilhelm. 1993. *Monetary Policy in Europe after Maastricht.* New York: St. Martin's Press.

Nordhaus, William D. 1975. The Political Business Cycle. *Review of Economic Studies* 42:169–90.

———. 1989. Alternative Approaches to the Political Business Cycle. *Brookings Papers on Economic Activity* 2:1–68.

Oatley, Thomas. 1999. How Constraining Is Capital Mobility? The Partisan Hypothesis in an Open Economy. *American Journal of Political Science* 43 (October): 1003–27.

Obstfeld, Maurice. 1995. International Capital Mobility in the 1990s. In *Understanding Interdependence: The Macroeconomics of the Open Economy,* edited by Peter B. Kenen, 201–61. Princeton: Princeton University Press.

Obstfeld, Maurice, and Kenneth Rogoff. 1996. *Foundations of International Macroeconomics.* Cambridge: MIT Press.

Odell, John S. 1982. *U.S. International Monetary Policy: Markets, Power, and Ideas as Sources of Change.* Princeton: Princeton University Press.

OECD. 1985. *Exchange Rate Management and the Conduct of Monetary Policy.* Paris: OECD.

———. Various years. *National Account Statistics.* Paris: OECD.

Olson, Mancur. 1965. *The Logic of Collective Action.* Cambridge: Harvard University Press.

Palfrey, T. R. 1984. Spatial Equilibrium with Entry. *Review of Economics Studies* 51:139–56.

Palfrey, T. R., and H. Rosenthal. 1985. Voter Participation and Strategic Uncertainty. *American Political Science Review* 79 (1): 62–78.

Palmer, Harvey D., and Guy D. Whitten. 1995. Economic Conditions and Endogenous Election Dates. Paper presented at the 91st Annual Meeting of the American Political Science Association, August 31–September 3, Chicago, Illinois.

Pampel, F. C., and J. B. Williamson. 1988. Welfare Spending in Advanced Industrial Democracies, 1950–1980. *American Journal of Sociology* 93, no. 6: 1424–56.

Penati, Alessandro, and Michael Dooley. 1984. Current Account Imbalances and Capital Formation in Industrial Countries, 1949–81. *IMF Staff Papers* 31:1–24.

Persson, T., and G. Tabellini. 1990. *Macroeconomic Policy, Credibility, and Politics.* London: Harwood Academic Publishers.

Pindyck, Robert S., and Daniel L. Rubinfeld. 1991. *Econometric Models and Economic Forecasts.* 3d ed. New York: McGraw-Hill.

Pollard, Patricia S. 1993. Central Bank Independence and Economic Performance. Federal Reserve Bank of St. Louis. *Review* 75 (July/August): 21–36.

Poterba, James M., and Kim S. Rueben. 1999. State Fiscal Institutions and the U.S. Municipal Bond Market. In *Fiscal Institutions and Fiscal Performance*, edited by James Poterba and Jürgen von Hagen, 181–207. Chicago: University of Chicago Press.

Przeworski, Adam. 1985. *Capitalism and Social Democracy.* Cambridge: Cambridge University Press.

Przeworski, Adam, and Michael Wallerstein. 1988. The Structural Dependence of the State on Capital. *American Political Science Review* 82, no. 1: 11–29.

Putnam, Robert D., and Nicholas Bayne. 1984. *Hanging Together: The Seven-Power Summits.* Cambridge: Harvard University Press.

Rice, Tom W. 1986. The Determinants of Western European Government Growth, 1950–1980. *Comparative Political Studies* 19:233–59.

Rodrik, Dani. 1997. *Has Globalization Gone Too Far?* Washington, DC: Institute for International Economics.

Rogoff, K., and A. Sibert. 1988. Equilibrium Political Business Cycles. *Review of Economic Studies* 55:1–16.

Rogoff, Kenneth. 1985. The Optimal Degree of Commitment to an Intermediate Monetary Target. *Quarterly Journal of Economics* 100 (November): 1169–89.

Rogowski, R. 1989. *Commerce and Coalitions.* Princeton: Princeton University Press.

Rogowski, Ronald. 1987. Trade and the Variety of Democratic Institutions. *International Organization* 41:202–23.

Rose, Andrew K. 1994. Exchange Rate Volatility, Monetary Policy, and Capital Mobility: Empirical Evidence on the Holy Trinity. Center for Economic Policy Research discussion paper 929, Center for Economic Policy Research, London.

Ross, F. 1997. Cutting Public Expenditures in Advanced Industrial Democracies: The Importance of Avoiding Blame. *Governance: An International Journal of Policy and Administration* 10, no. 2: 175–200.

Roubini, Nouriel, and Jeffrey D. Sachs. 1989a. Government Spending and Budget Deficits in the Industrial Countries. *Economic Policy* 8:100–132.

———. 1989b. Political and Economic Determinants of Budget Deficits in the Industrial Democracies. *European Economic Review* 33 (May): 903–33.

Simmons, Beth. 1994. *Who Adjusts?* Princeton: Princeton University Press.

———. 1996. Capital Mobility and National Politics: The Capital Constraint and Fiscal Policy, 1967–1990. Paper presented at the 37th Annual Conference of the International Studies Association, April 16–20, San Diego, California.

Simmons, Beth, and William Roberts Clark. 1997. Capital Mobility and Partisan Economic Policy Choice: Conditional Effects of International Economic Integration on Fiscal Policy in the OECD. Paper presented at the annual meeting.of the American Political Science Association.

Smith, Alastair. 1996. Endogenous Election Timing in Majoritarian Parliamentary Systems. *Economics and Politics* 8:85–110.

Stephens, John D. 1979. *The Transition from Capitalism to Socialism.* London: MacMillan.

Stigler, George J., and Gary S. Becker. 1977. De Gustibus Non Est Disputandum. *American Economic Review* 67 (March): 76–90.

Strach, Rolf. 1998. Budget Processes and Fiscal Discipline: Evidence from the U.S. States. University of Bonn. Typescript.

Strøm, Kaare. 1990. A Behavioral Theory of Competitive Political Parties. *American Journal of Political Science* 34:565–98.

Svensson, Lars E. O. 1995. Optimal Inflation Targets, Conservative Central Banks, and Linear Inflation Contracts. National Bureau of Economic Research working paper 5251.

Swank, D. H. 1988. The Political-Economy of Government Domestic Expenditure in the Affluent Democracies, 1960–80. *American Journal of Political Science* 32, no. 4: 1120–50.

———. 1992. Politics and the Structural Dependence of the State in Democratic Capitalist Nations. *American Political Science Review* 86, no. 1: 38–54.

Tavli, Ernesto, and Carlos Végh. 1997. Can Optimal Fiscal Policy Be Procyclical? *Inter-American Development Bank.* Typescript.

Terrones, Marco E. 1989. Macroeconomic Policy Cycles under Alternative Electoral Structures. Department of Economics research report 8905, University of Western Ontario.

Tufte, Edward R. 1978. *The Political Control of the Economy.* Princeton: Princeton University Press.

Von Hagen, Jürgen. 1998. Budgeting Institutions for Aggregate Fiscal Discipline. Zentrum für Europäisch Integrations Forrschung Working Paper. B-98-01.

Way, Christopher. 2000. Central Banks, Partisan Politics, and Macroeconomic Outcomes. *Comparative Political Studies* 33, no. 2: 196–224.

Webb, Michael C. 1991. International Economic Structures, Government Interests, and International Coordination of Macroeconomic Adjustment Policies. *International Organization* 45:309–42.

———. 1995. *The Political Economy of Policy Coordination: International Adjustment since 1945.* Ithaca: Cornell University Press.

Wildavsky, Aaron. 1974. *The Politics of the Budgetary Process.* 2d ed. Boston: Little, Brown.

Wittman, Donald. 1983. Candidate Motivation: A Synthesis of Alternative Theories. *American Political Science Review* 77:42–57.

Index

Aldrich, John, 142
Alesina, Alberto, 7, 8, 9, 11, 37, 42, 49, 89, 94
Alt, James E., 7, 166
Alvarez, R. Michael, 106, 107, 110
Ambuhl, Martin, 50, 51
Andrews, David M., 31, 88
Australia, 36
Autocorrelation, 58, 90, 148

Bade, Robin, 37
Bank of England, 1, 19, 103
Basinger, Scott, 53
Bayne, Nicholas, 35
Beck, Nathaniel, 47, 57, 81, 90
Beer, Samuel, 82
Belgium, 35, 36
Bernhard, William, 30
Blair, Tony, 1, 41, 119
Blais, André, 47
Blake, Donald E., 47
Blanchard, Oliver, 48
Boix, Carles, 49, 51, 67
Branson, William H., 22
Bretton Woods system, 32, 33, 34, 35, 49, 76, 86
Brown, Gordon, 103
Bruno, Michael, 117
Budget cuts, 48

Budget deficits, 7, 45, 67, 71, 80, 95
Buiter, Willem H., 22
Bundesbank, 1, 20
Burdekin, Richard C. K., 86

California, 102
Calvert, Randall, 7
Cameron, David, 45, 50, 51, 64
Canada, 35
Capital controls, 32, 33, 35
Capital mobility, 1, 13, 14, 22, 52
    cause of increase in, 31
    effect on centralized bargaining, 53
    effect on electoral control of the economy, 18, 22
    effect on electoral cycles
        in fiscal policy, 86, 99
        in monetary policy, 86
        in outcomes, 144–45, 150–56
            under fixed exchange rates, 157–58, 161–64
            under flexible exchange rates, 158–59, 164–65
    effect on fiscal policy, 17, 22
    effect on monetary policy effectiveness, 16, 17, 22
    effect on partisan control of the economy, 17, 18, 22, 105
    measurement of, 31–35, 37–38, 88

Cargill, Thomas F., 8, 10
Castles, Francis G., 46, 47, 52
Central bank independence (CBI), 2, 13,
    14–16, 19, 25
  choice of level, 30, 103
    left government and, 119
  effect on electoral cycles, 15, 25, 29
    in outcomes, 144–45, 147–50
      under fixed exchange rates,
        157–58, 161–64
      under flexible exchange rates,
        158–59, 164–65
  effect on partisan cycles, 15, 25, 29
    in fiscal and monetary policy, 56–83,
      105
  measurement of, 89
  monetary policy, 93
Chappell, Henry W., 8
Clark, William R., 19, 22, 27, 31, 39, 49, 51,
    54, 73, 86, 87, 88, 90, 99, 103, 122, 126,
    144, 146, 148, 151, 152, 153, 156, 157, 174
Cleary, Paul D., 151
Clinton, Bill, 71
Coffey, Peter, 36, 37
Cohen, Benjamin J., 35
Cohen, Gerald D., 7, 8
Collective action, 140, 143
Comiskey, Michael, 47
Common pool resource problem, 101
Compensation hypothesis, 53, 56, 65, 67,
    72, 79, 122, 124, 125
Conservative Party (UK), 43, 82, 105
Context-dependent electoral cycles, 13,
    87, 88
Convergence hypothesis, 1, 2, 7, 41, 42, 56,
    62, 65, 67, 71, 72, 74, 79, 85, 122, 123,
    124, 125, 139, 167, 172
Council of Ministers (European Union),
    101
Covered interest-rate parties, 34
Cukierman, Alex, 6, 37, 89
Cusack, Thomas R., 42, 53, 54, 55

Debt servicing costs, 95
de Haan, Jakob, 48, 86, 94, 95, 96, 150
Demand management, 44, 53
Democracy, 169, 171
Democratic Party (U.S.), 41, 43, 85
Denmark, 35, 36
Deutschemark, 119
Dion, Stéphane, 47
Dornbusch, Rudiger, 22
Downs, Anthony, 3, 42, 142
Downsian approach, 7, 42, 48, 55, 111, 170

Early elections, 9
Economic and Monetary Union (EMU),
    100–102, 103
Edin, Per Anders, 96
Eichengreen, Barry, 102
Eijffinger, Sylvester C., 86
Elections, effect on money supply
  when high CBI, fixed, 92
  when high CBI, flexible, 92
  when low CBI, fixed, 93
  when low CBI, flexible, 92, 93
Election year, measurement of, 94, 97
Electoral cycles
  context dependent, 10
  in budget deficits, 7
  in fiscal policy, 94–100, 103
  in inflation, 6
  in macroeconomic outcomes, 26–28,
    159
  in monetary policy, 7, 25, 26, 89–94, 103
  in unemployment, 6
Electoral model, 3, 4, 10, 13, 141, 169–72
Endogenous elections, 8, 10
Euro, 101
European Central Bank, 150
European Commission, 101
European Community, 95
European exchange rate crisis, 95
European Exchange Rate System, 35, 36
European integration, 48

European Monetary System (EMS), 36, 49, 95
European Union, 87, 95, 99, 100–102
Exchange Rate Mechanism. *See* European Monetary System
Exchange Rate Mechanism II, 103
Exchange rate regime, 14, 17, 22, 29
    choice of, 30, 103
        left government and, 119
    classification of, 35, 36, 88
    effect on electoral cycles
        in outcomes, 144–45, 150–56
        in fiscal policy, 97, 99, 100
    effect on partisan differences in fiscal and monetary policy, 73–82
    fixed, 17, 22, 29, 75
        expected electoral cycles under, 157–58
    flexible, 17, 22, 29
        expected electoral cycles under, 158–59

Falsificationism, 141
Federal Reserve, 20, 142
Feldstein, Martin, 33
Feldstein-Horioka coefficients, 32, 35
Finance ministers, 1, 20, 103
Financial innovation, 31
Financial integration, 1, 4
Financial market, deregulation of, 31
Finland, 36
Fiorina, Morris P., 142
Fiscal policy
    definition, 20
    effectiveness, 14, 49
    institutions
        antideficit rules, 102
        negotiated targets, 96
        strong finance minister, 96
Fixed effects, 89, 107, 171
Football, 143
France, 6, 35, 36, 41

Frankel, Jeffrey A., 33, 34
Franzese, Robert J., 86, 94, 97, 107, 126
Frieden, Jeffry A., 88, 166
Friedrich, Robert J., 62

Garrett, Geoffrey, 4, 11, 34, 42, 45, 50, 53, 54, 56, 57, 62, 64, 67, 71, 76, 79, 80, 82, 83, 106, 107, 110, 112, 139, 166, 167, 171
Globalization, 1, 4, 14, 41
Golden, Miriam A., 117
Gold standard, 35
Gourevitch, Peter, 166
Gowa, Joanne, 32
Greene, William H., 58
Greenspan, Alan, 143
Grier, Kevin B., 7
Grilli, Vittorio, 37, 86
Growth (output), 3, 110

Hahm, Sung Deuk, 49
Hall, Peter A., 107, 126
Hallerberg, Mark, 19, 22, 31, 39, 49, 53, 54, 73, 87, 88, 90, 94, 96, 99, 102
Heller, Walter, 85
Henning, C. Randall, 35
Hibbs, Douglas A., 3, 7, 9, 43, 45, 50
Hibbsian variant. *See under* Partisan model
Hicks, Alexander, 46, 47, 50, 51
Horioka, Charles, 33
Huber, Evelyne, 45, 48, 53, 73
Hutchison, Michael M., 8, 10
Hypothesis 1F, 25, 94
Hypothesis 1M, 26
Hypothesis 1P, 28, 129, 136
Hypothesis 2F, 25, 94, 97
Hypothesis 2M, 26, 92, 93
Hypothesis 2P, 28, 129, 136

Inflation
    natural rate of, 21

Inflation (*continued*)
  price stability, 3, 7
  target of central bank, 25
Inflationary expectations, 8
Interaction effects, 62, 81, 107, 120, 149, 151
Interest rates, 16, 17, 32, 33, 67, 71, 80, 102
  premium paid by left governments, 71, 80
Interwar period, 50
Ireland, 35, 36
Italy, 6, 35, 36
Iversen, Torben, 4, 48, 58, 126, 139

Jaccard, James, 62
Johnson, Lyndon B., 85

Kamlet, Mark S., 49
Katz, Jonathan N., 47, 57, 81, 90
Katzenstein, Peter, 52, 64, 106
Keech, William R., 8, 11, 86
Kessler, Ronald C., 151
Key, V. O., 171
Keynesian consensus, 53, 82, 83
Kim, Won-Ik, 55
Kmenta, Jan, 58
Kohl, Helmut, 1
Kurzer, Paulette, 88

Labor-market institutions, 50–52, 57, 105, 106, 107, 109, 110, 111
Labor unions, 48, 50, 51
Labour Party (UK), 1, 43
Lafontaine, Oskar, 1
Lagged dependent variable, 89, 107
Laney, Leroy O., 86
Lange, Peter, 50, 67, 106, 107, 110, 166, 167
Leblang, David, 30
Lewis-Beck, Michael, 6
Lindbloom, Charles, 170
Lipset, Seymour M., 171
Luxembourg, 35, 36

MacRae, Duncan, 6, 86
Macroeconomic policy, democratic control, 3
Masciandaro, Donato, 37, 86
McCallum, Bennett T., 6
McKinley, R. D., 46
McNamara, Kathleen R., 88, 173
Median voter, 3, 7, 13, 43, 170, 171, 172
Meltzer, Allan, 6
Milner, Helen, 166
Misra, Joya, 47
Mitterrand, François, 41
Monetary policy, 17
  definition, 17, 19
  effectiveness, 14, 80
Money supply, 7, 16, 89
Moral hazard, 101
Mowery, David C., 49
Mundell, Robert A., 22
Mundell-Fleming model, 16–18, 22, 23, 31, 49, 73, 86, 87, 102, 119, 122, 151, 165

Nair Reichert, Usha, 19, 27, 39, 86, 88, 104, 122, 126, 144, 146, 148, 151, 152, 153, 156, 157, 174
Netherlands, 35, 36
New Zealand, 36
Neyapti, Bilin, 37, 89
Nixon, Richard M., 35
"Nixon in China" metaphor, 48
Nordhaus, William D., 3, 6, 7, 8, 9, 86
Norges Bank, 19
Normative implication, 5
Norway, 19, 35

Oatley, Thomas, 42, 55, 73
Odell, John S., 32
Ohlsson, Henry, 96
Orange County, CA, 102
Organization for Economic Cooperation and Development (OECD), 6, 7, 14, 87

Palfrey, Thomas R., 7, 142
Palmer, Harvey D., 8
Pampel, Fred C., 47, 51
Panel-corrected standard errors, 90
Parkin, Michael, 37
Partisan cycles
    in fiscal policy, 8
    in macroeconomic outcomes, 26–28,
        105
    in monetary policy, 8, 25, 26, 85
    in unemployment, 7, 43
Partisan differences
    in budget deficits and public debt,
        48–50, 85
    in revenue collection, 45, 46, 66
    in spending and welfare effort, 46–48,
        51
    in taxation of capital, 45, 46, 49, 59
    in taxation of income, 46, 49, 59
Partisan model, 3, 4, 10, 13, 42, 171
    Hibbsian variant, 43, 49, 106, 140
        and macroeconomic outcomes,
            128–37
            under fixed exchange rates, 129–31
            under flexible exchange rates,
                131–33
            modifying effect of CBI, 136–37
            modifying effect of exchange rate
                regime, 133–37
    in the open economy, 44, 52–56, 56–81
    rejection of, 82, 141, 169–72
    social democratic corporatist variant,
        44, 140
        and fiscal and monetary policy,
            50–52, 56–81
        and growth, 115, 118, 127
        and inflation, 115, 117, 123, 126
        and macroeconomic outcomes,
            107–28
            in the open economy, 111–26
            modifying effect of capital mobil-
                ity, 112–19

modifying effect of CBI, 126–28
modifying effect of exchange rate
    regime, 119–26
and unemployment, 114, 115, 117, 123,
    126
Perotti, Roberto, 48, 49
Persson, Torsten, 6, 9
Phillips curve, 21, 43
Pindyck, Robert S., 58
Pluralism, 139
Political parties
    ideological mobility, 111
    left, 7, 41, 45
        credibility problem facing, 119
        number of, in government, and effect
            on fiscal discipline, 95, 96
    right, 7, 41
Pollard, Patricia S., 86
Poterba, James M., 102
Pound sterling, 119
Poverty, 105
Prais-Winsten regression, 91, 93, 148
Presidential elections (U.S.), 6
Princeton University, 143
Przeworski, Adam, 1, 2, 170
Public debt, 45, 95
Putnam, Robert D., 35

Ragin, Charles, 45, 48
Rational electoral cycles, 6, 142
Rational expectations, 5, 10, 142–43, 166
Rational partisan model, 8
Reagan, Ronald, 71
Redistribution of wealth, 44
Republican Party (U.S.), 41, 43
Revenues, 44
Rice, Tom W., 47
Rodrik, Dani, 4, 53, 139
Rogoff, Kenneth, 6, 9
Rogowski, Ronald, 166
Rose, Andrew K., 34
Rosenthal, Howard, 7, 9, 11, 42, 142

Ross, Fiona, 49
Roubini, Nouriel, 7, 8, 11, 48, 51, 89, 94, 95, 96
Rubinfeld, Daniel L., 58
Rueben, Kim S., 102

Sachs, Jeffrey D., 41, 48, 95, 96, 117
Savings-investment coefficients. *See* Feldstein-Horioka coefficients
Schroeder, Gerhard, 1, 41
Sibert, Anne C., 6, 9
Simmons, Beth, 34, 51, 54
Smith, Alastair, 10
Snake, the. *See* European Exchange Rate System
Social democratic corporatism, 56, 105. *See also* Partisan model, social democratic corporatist variant
Social Democratic Party (Germany), 1
Social insurance, 140
Socialist Party (France), 119
Social welfare programs, 44
Stability and Growth Pact, 101
Stephens, John D., 45, 46, 48, 53, 73
Strikes, 50
Strøm, Kaare, 140
Structural dependence of the state on capital, 49, 71, 72, 170
Sturm, Jan-Egbert, 48, 86, 95, 96
Substitution of policy instruments, 86, 103, 156, 165, 173
Summers, Lawrence H., 37
Swank, Duane H., 46, 50, 51
Sweden, 36

Tabellini, Guido, 6, 9, 37, 86
Taxation, 45

on capital or profits, 45
on income, 44
Terrones, Marco E., 10
Tories. *See* Conservative Party
Trade openness, 52, 57, 71, 72
Treaty of Maastricht, 101
Tripartite bargaining, 50
Tufte, Edward R., 3, 7, 86, 169, 176
Turrisi, Robert, 62

Ulam, Adam B., 82
Unemployment, 7, 95, 141
United Kingdom, 1, 6, 7, 19, 35, 36, 41, 43, 82, 97, 103
United States, 6, 7, 19, 43, 102

Varieties of capitalism, 172
von Hagen, Jürgen, 49, 94, 96, 102
Voters
    adaptive/retrospective, 5, 6, 7, 8, 170
    pocketbook, 6, 170, 171
    rational, 5, 10

Wage
    contracts, 8
    indexation, 51
    restraint, 50, 106, 110
Wallace, George, 41
Wan, Choi K., 62
Way, Christopher, 107
Webb, Michael C., 31, 32, 35, 88
Webb, Steven B., 37, 89
West Germany, 1, 6, 19, 35, 36, 41
Whitten, Guy, 10
Wildavsky, Aaron, 45
Williamson, John B., 47, 51
Wilson, Harold, 41, 119

Printed and bound by CPI Group (UK) Ltd, Croydon, CR0 4YY

16/04/2025

14658542-0002